Insiders' Guide®

to the

Four Corners

Help Us Keep This Guide Up to Date

Every effort has been made by the author and editors to make this guide as accurate and useful as possible. However, many things can change after a guide is published—establishments close, phone numbers change, hiking trails are rerouted, facilities come under new management, etc.

We would love to hear from you concerning your experiences with this guide and how you feel it could be improved and be kept up to date. While we may not be able to respond to all comments and suggestions, we'll take them to heart and we'll also make certain to share them with the author. Please send your comments and suggestions to the following address:

The Globe Pequot Press
Reader Response/Editorial Department
P.O. Box 480
Guilford, CT 06437

Or you may e-mail us at: editorial@globe-pequot.com

Thanks for your input, and happy travels!

Insiders' Guide® Series

Insiders' Guide®
to the
Four Corners

By Dorothy Nobis

Guilford, Connecticut
An imprint of The Globe Pequot Press

Front cover photo by Chip Henderson/Index Stock Imagery
Back cover photos (from left) by Elizabeth Atteberg, Robert Royem, Kristen Hartzell, Elizabeth Atteberg, National Park Service
Maps by Trapper Badovinac

ISBN 1-57380-148-8

Manufactured in the United States of America
First Edition/First Printing

Contents

Directory of Maps

FOUR CORNERS—OVERVIEW

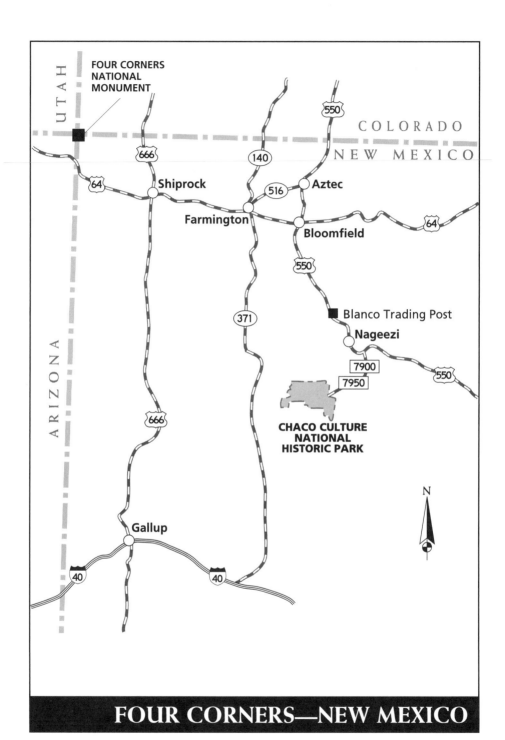

FOUR CORNERS—NEW MEXICO

FOUR CORNERS—COLORADO

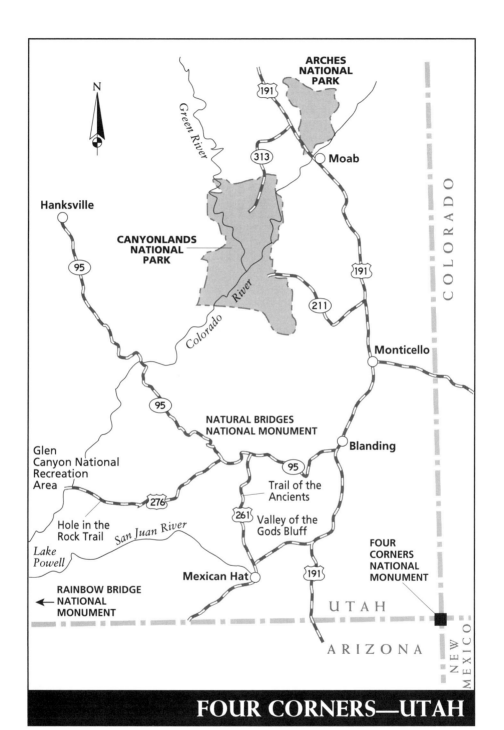

FOUR CORNERS—UTAH

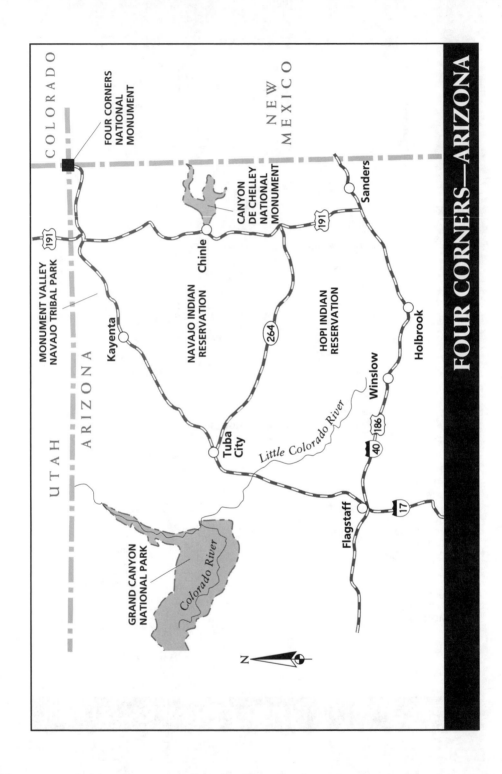

FOUR CORNERS—ARIZONA

Acknowledgments

I would not have been so lucky to have the opportunity to write this book were it not for friend, conspirator, and fellow journalist Bill Papich, who recommended me to the publisher. While not sure what I was getting into, this book has been a source of delight, hard work, and sheer pleasure. I was confident I knew all there was to know about the beautiful Four Corners, but learned so much more about this area once I started writing the book. My research led me down paths I had not considered taking before, and brought me friends I might never have been fortunate enough to meet. I thank Bill for his confidence in my ability to do the book and for his friendship, and for being the very unique personality he is.

I was equally fortunate to have an editor who provided guidance, support, and comfort when deadlines were imminent and creative juices did not flow. Anne Felstet is a writer's dream come true and her friendship is my most treasured reward for this book. I wish her well in her new endeavors, as she prepares to sail new waters. Without her great sense of humor, professionalism, incredible knowledge, and her commitment to this book, I would have lost my sanity long before the book was finished.

I am grateful to my husband, Phil, for his understanding when I felt the need to work all hours of the day and night to capture the beauty of the Four Corners and put it into words. He has always supported my efforts and has encouraged me to do what makes me happy, and that is to write. I have driven him nuts with my ideas, made him crazy with my enthusiasm for my work, and pushed him near the edge with my need to create. But through it all, he has taken great pride in my accomplishments and survived the writing of this book with grace, good humor, and lots of love. I thank him for being my partner in life and for loving me, even when I'm my least lovable—when I'm on deadline!

I would also like to thank my two very best friends for their constant support, encouragement, and understanding. Liz Attebery, who is not only a gifted writer, but also an accomplished photographer, received my frequent long distance phone calls, looking for advice and asking for help and was always there. Connie Dinning has lunch with me every Wednesday, and has encouraged my writing and has inspired me by always believing in me. Few people are as fortunate as I in having friends like Liz and Connie and the gift of their friendship is something I will cherish forever. Without them and their constant support and encouragement, I would never have attempted this book.

Twenty years ago, the editor of my hometown newspaper encouraged me to do what I'd long wanted to do—and that was to write. Miles F. Porter IV believed in my ability to put my thoughts into words and into newsprint. Without his unwavering confidence in my abilities during those early days, and his continued support over the years, I would not be writing these words now. He was my editor, my mentor, and more importantly, my friend, and I will never be able to thank him enough for all he's done for me.

My brother, Hugh Humphreys, was the writer in our family and is talented beyond words. His career took a different path, however, and the lives he has touched are better for it. He has always taken great pride in my writing and no matter how bad a story is, he claims it's the best he's ever read! He is the ultimate big brother, one of my biggest fans and I am incredibly lucky to be related to him! My sister, Marianne Cherry, has also encouraged my writing and has always been there when all I needed was to laugh and to vent to someone who understood me. She is more than a sister, she is a friend.

My children have been supportive of my writing and I appreciate all the times they were content to have pizza and take-out while I was working late or fighting a deadline. To Todd, Tim, Jon, Jeremy and Jennifer, I offer my love and my thanks for your understanding. And to Jeremy, who has unconditional love and total devotion to his crazy ole "Ma," I give my deepest appreciation and everlasting love for believing I'm the best mother, the best writer, and the best friend he has!

I would be remiss not to thank Bob, the cat, for his constant companionship and love as I toiled over copy. He understood when I forgot the tuna I promised and he was forced to eat regular dry cat food. He didn't mind when I made him move from his spot in the middle of my half of the bed, when I had to get up in the middle of the night to change a paragraph or add a new one. He loved having me home and he loved creating new "copy" when I left the computer for a few minutes! Bob is a book to be written and I have promised my friend Liz, I will do a Bob book as soon as this book is completed. Bob thinks I owe him that!

And lastly, I thank my late mother, Lorena Humphreys, who raised me to believe in myself, to think for myself, and to care for others. She lived by the Golden Rule and encouraged all of her children to do the same. "Wealth," she used to say, "is not measured by what's in your bank account, but by what's in your heart." I am fortunate in that I am very wealthy. I have my family, my friends, my cat, my work, and my memories of a mother who put others before herself. She would be proud of this book and I dedicate it to her.

How to Use This Book

From the majesty of the snow-topped mountains of Colorado to the quiet solitude of Arizona's deserts, the Four Corners is a wonderful tourist attraction. But many of those who visit, fall in love with the area and the people, and find themselves a home.

I am one of those who visited, only to find once I arrived that I could not leave. There is a inherent wealth in the states that comprise the Four Corners, and after some 20 years, I am still discovering treasures in the land, the people, and the spirit that make this area of our country a wonderful place to live—and to visit. For it is here that you will find the culture and the traditions of four great Indian tribes—the Navajos, the Southern Utes, the Utes, and the Hopis. These strong and proud people create not just some of the most beautiful art found in America, but are committed to preserving their heritage for generations to come. In this book, you'll be introduced to these Native Americans, and will discover where to find the best arts and crafts and where to go for festivals and special events that celebrate the Indian history. You'll also learn of some of the hardships that remain for these people, and what is being done to eliminate them.

Ask people just how much area the Four Corners encompasses and you'll receive many different answers. For those of us who live in the area, it's more than just a few hundred miles in four of the most beautiful states in the Union. It goes south in New Mexico to include Chaco Canyon, south in Arizona to Lake Powell, northwest into Utah to include the Glen Canyon National Recreation Area, and north into Colorado to include Pagosa Springs and the Wolf Creek Ski Area. This book will be divided into sections that will make it easier for you to use it. Each state will be covered separately, and will include chapters on where to stay during your visit, some of the best places to eat and shop, where to take the kids for family fun, where to go for recreation, area attractions, and what fine arts are available. Each of these chapters also includes a Close-up of an interesting person, event, or business located in the area. In addition, each Indian tribe will be represented in separate sections. The history and traditions of our Native Americans, and their attempts to keep that history and tradition alive in the 21st century, will be shared. You'll discover where to go for the great art these people are famous for, where to stay during your visit to the reservation, and how each tribe cares for the health and education of its people.

For those who are looking to relocate to the Four Corners, a section is provided that will include real estate, educational opportunities, healthcare, spiritual guidance, and opportunities for retirees.

A separate section will introduce you to the media of the Four Corners—what the newspapers are, which television stations offer local news, which radio station provides your favorite music, and the magazines that the locals turn to for relaxation and learning.

There are many national and state parks and Indian dwellings that are scattered throughout the Four Corners. In the chapter Four Corners Attractions you'll learn all about how to find them, and what to expect when you arrive.

As you read through this book, remember that I have highlighted only some of the features of this great area. As a guest of the Four Corners, you will have the opportunity to visit with shopkeepers, hotel, motel and campground owners, and service people in our restaurants, who will likely have their own favorite spots you might want to visit. Each state in the Four Corners is unique, and I encourage you, as you travel through the area, to ask questions, take time to explore, and keep film in your camera. The sights and scenes you'll discover in the Four Corners will provide memories you'll want to share with your family and friends.

Your journey through the Four Corners will take you through northwestern New Mexico, northeastern Arizona, southeastern Utah, and southwestern Colorado. You'll begin your travels in New Mexico, where you'll discover a growing retail community and a population which makes family a priority and supports events that bring families together. Such attractions include the Connie Mack World Series of Baseball, the largest county fair in the state, soccer fields, and a golf course that delights duffers of all ages. Arizona is home to Monument Valley Navajo Tribal Park, scene of many Hollywood movies. Arizona and Utah are home to the Glen Canyon National Recreation Area, which offers boating, fishing, water sports and some of the most beautiful and awe-inspiring landscape found anywhere. As you travel to Utah, you'll find an environment that encourages hiking, biking, and four-wheeling. You'll be captivated by the beauty of the natural wonders that will take your breath away. Finally, you'll find yourself in the high country of Colorado, where winter sports share space with deer and elk, and where fishing isn't just a sport; it's an art. You'll discover Indian ruins that will take you back thousands of years, and give you a glimpse of a people struggling to survive.

As you travel through the Four Corners, you'll visit trading posts on the Indian reservations, and talk to those who create the beautiful works of art the Native Americans produce. And you'll learn a little about their cultures, traditions, and native ways of life.

If the beauty of the landscape in the Four Corners isn't enough to win your heart, the recreational opportunities just might. Whether you enjoy mountain biking, motorcycling, hiking, fishing, water sports or winter sports, you'll find them all in great abundance. I'll tell you where to go for world renowned trout fishing and off-the-beaten-path fly fishing streams, and where you can go for a sleigh ride in the winter that will create beautiful memories for years to come. You'll discover the mountain trails bicyclists enjoy for professional gains as well as for simple pleasure. Great snow skiing is available in the Four Corners, with ski season beginning in late fall and continuing through late spring. If you like taking risks in a four-wheel-drive vehicle, you'll find events and roads that will challenge even the most ardent off-road enthusiast. And if your idea of a perfect day is lying on a boat, enjoying the sunshine and the water, there are places to go that will give you that perfect day.

But if you're looking for peace and tranquility, the Four Corners can provide that, too. There are winding mountain roads that will take you to places not frequented by the masses, where you can enjoy the quiet of a summer day alongside the wildlife that is also glad to call the Four Corners home.

And if it's shopping you're interested in, the Four Corners has much to offer—from the hand-woven works of the Native Americans to major department stores. You'll find shop owners who have lived here forever and take pride in the goods they sell, and in the artists who create them. You'll discover dream catchers, antiques, woodcarvings, jewelry, and rugs that should be hung, not walked on, because of their great beauty.

For those who just might think that, because the Four Corners is hundreds of miles away from major metropolitan areas, there is a lack of fine arts, you'll be pleasantly surprised. Broadway shows, great symphonies, music of every definition, outdoor theater, and music superstars who enjoy performing in this area provide constant entertainment.

As you travel through the pages of the *Insiders' Guide® to the Four Corners*, I hope you'll be encouraged to pack your bags and visit. Life isn't quite as hectic in this part of the country, and the people tend to be as mellow as the lifestyle. There is much to see and to do here, but there is also the attitude that to truly appreciate all the Four Corners has to offer, you must pause, for an hour or a day, and reflect in the beauty and the serenity of the area. And while you're here, introduce yourself to us. For not only do we want to share with you our scenery and our lifestyle, we want to make you our friend.

Area Overview and History

It is a thrill for youngsters to stand at the only point in the United States where four states come together. In a square that includes a small portion of New Mexico, Arizona, Utah, and Colorado, youngsters find they can put one hand and one foot in each state, and "visit" four states in a matter of seconds.

The Four Corners National Monument was originally surveyed and established by United States government surveyors and astronomers in 1868 with the survey of Colorado's southern boundary. In 1878, surveys of New Mexico's west boundary and Utah's east boundary were completed and, in 1901, the northern boundary of Arizona was done. A small marker was erected in 1912, where the boundaries of the four states intersected. In 1992, the monument was refurbished, with a bronze disk embedded in granite.

The Four Corners National Monument is located 40 miles southwest of Cortez, Colorado, on U.S. Highway 160. The area surrounding the monument is Indian land, which includes 25,000 square miles of portions of New Mexico, Utah and Arizona. Artisans and craftspeople from the Navajo and Ute reservations are represented at the monument, where they sell their works of art.

The visitor center at the monument is open year-round. Picnic tables and restrooms are available, but there is no water available at the park. Services and accommodations within 30 miles of the monument are limited to small restaurants, grocery stores, and gas stations. Plans for a larger visitor center are in the works, to replace the small center now available.

The colored concrete that shows four states joined together by a single pivot symbolizes far more than a tourist attraction. The flags of the states of the Four Corners fly alongside the flags of the Native American tribes, whose history, traditions, and struggles help create the beauty and deepen the soul of this unique area. To visit the Four Corners and not feel the spirits of Americans—all Americans—is to miss something far more than the incredible scenery of the area. The tribes represented in the Four Corners—the Navajos, Utes, Southern Utes and the Hopis—continue to struggle, even as we enter the 21st century, to bring paved roads, electricity, telephone service, and quality healthcare to their people. In addition, the tribal nation officials are concerned about their young people, many who choose to leave their homes on the reservations and, in doing so, leave their native traditions and legacies behind as well. Alcoholism is a disease and another concern that plagues the Native Americans and one that healthcare professionals and tribal leaders fight to control.

It's not just the struggle for survival of today's Native American that the visitor to the Four Corners will find. Chaco Canyon, Aztec Ruins, Mesa Verde, Salmon Ruins, and Hovenweep are preserved dwellings of Indians who lived and roamed the Four Corners thousands of years ago. To discover these great remains and to walk the ground where the Anasazi worked, played, and prayed can be a spiritual experience you won't soon forget.

Each of the states in the Four Corners has area attractions that are highlights of any visit. In New Mexico, you'll take rugged, weather beaten roads to the Angel Peak Recreation Area, which is 19 miles southeast of Bloomfield, and to Chaco Culture National

Four Corners National Monument. PHOTO: DOROTHY NOBIS

Historical Park, which is 54 miles south of Bloomfield. Paved roads will take you to Aztec Ruins National Monument, one mile from Aztec; to Salmon Ruins Heritage Park, two miles west of Bloomfield; and to Navajo Lake State Park, 25 miles northeast of Bloomfield.

Mesa Verde National Park, nine miles east of Cortez, is a highlight of many visitors' trip to Colorado and the Four Corners. Hovenweep National Monument is 40 miles west of Cortez; and the Durango & Silverton Narrow Gauge Railroad will take you back in time and through some of the most breathtaking natural beauty anywhere.

In Utah, you'll be amazed at the wonders of Mother Nature when you visit Arches National Park, five miles north of Moab, where the world's largest concentration of natural stone arches stands as a monument to the passing of time. Canyonlands National Park, 35 miles southwest of Moab, is a haven for hikers, bikers, rafters, and four-wheelers. The Natural Bridges National Monument, 42 miles west of Blanding, contains three sandstone bridges; and the Rainbow Bridge National Monument, found southwest of Lake Powell, is one of the seven natural wonders of the world and one of the largest known natural bridges. Seen only by boat or a full-day hike, the Rainbow Bridge attracts thousands of visitors each year.

The Canyon de Chelly National Monument in Arizona, three miles east of Chinle, offers visitors the opportunity to see ruins of Anasazi cliff dwellings. The Navajo National Monument, 30 miles southwest of Kayenta, offers cliff dwellings of Hopi ancestors, who lived in the canyon seven centuries ago; and Monument Valley Navajo Tribal Park displays the natural beauty that has made it popular with movie makers. Monument Valley is 23 miles north of Kayenta. The Grand Canyon National Park is a popular destination for visitors from throughout the world. The Colorado River has carved deep canyons over billions of years, and fishing, boating, and water sport enthusiasts take great pleasure in exploring the canyons. The Grand Canyon National Park is located 80 miles west of Flagstaff and the drive to the park is almost as spectacular as the park itself.

While most visitors to the Four Corners enjoy the popular attractions, there are those who come to our area to find quiet solitude, and to participate in activities that are often done alone, or in small groups. Those people are never disappointed. For here, where the ancient ruins of the Native Americans meet the technology of a modern world, the best of all worlds is found. Anglers find countless streams, lakes, and rivers to wet their lines and catch everything from salmon to crappie. The Quality Waters of the San Juan River, 30 miles east of Farmington, attracts top anglers from all over the world. The Quality Waters is specially regulated, with catch-and-release enforced in part of the area, and lures and limits enforced in other areas of the popular fishing "hole." Other, more out-of-the-way, fishing areas abound in the Four Corners, where wildlife competes with the fishing for a visitor's attention.

Bicycling, river rafting, hiking, and four-wheeling are enjoyed by Insiders of the Four Corners and by visitors alike. As with fishing and water sports, these activities may be enjoyed in quiet solitude, or by participating in the many scheduled events and tours that attract thousands of people each year.

For those who measure the quality of life of an area by the food it offers, they, too, will enjoy the cuisine of the Four Corners. While Mexican food is considered by many Insiders to be the fifth food group, great restaurants abound. The atmosphere of the Four Corners is decidedly casual—Insiders know that "formal dress" means a clean western shirt, jeans, and polished cowboy boots. Ties are optional almost everywhere in the Four Corners, where "casual Friday" is enjoyed five days a week.

There are too many attractions, too many quaint little shops, too many out-of-the-way trading posts, and too many wonderful restaurants to include them all in this guide. I'll highlight but some of them and urge each visitor to spend some time with the locals of the area to discover more about this wonderful part of the world that brings four states together—not simply sharing a common point, but sharing some of the very best America has to offer.

Getting Here, Getting Around

Air
Vehicle Rental
Bus Lines

Since the Four Corners is hundreds of miles away from major airports, getting here won't be as simple as getting on an airplane and landing at your destination. All you need is proper planning, and the realization that getting here will be part of your fun. Be prepared to deal with commuter airlines, smaller airports, few if any taxis, and limited bus transportation.

However you get here, the locals look forward to your arrival. We feel the Four Corners is a beautiful, unique area, where history meets modern technology and life is good. We are proud and protective of our natural resources and our communities, and ask only that you respect the traditions of the Native Americans while you're here and that you enjoy the scenery, and leave with wonderful memories and all of your trash.

Air

If you plan to come by air, your best bet is to fly into the Albuquerque International Sunport. The Sunport's terminal was expanded in the late 1980s and includes 574,000 square feet of space, with 23 gates on three concourses. A four-gate extension of Concourse "A" was completed in 1996.

The Sunport shares its runways with Kirtland Air Force Base, which provides aircraft rescue and firefighting services for the airport. It is not unusual to see military planes parked alongside the runways, and youngsters, especially, will enjoy seeing the huge planes.

Southwest Airlines is the Sunport's largest carrier, handling some 49 percent of its 1999 passengers. Eight additional major commercial carriers serve the Sunport, as well as several commuter airlines. It will be one of those commuter planes that will fly you into Farmington, where your visit to the Four Corners will begin.

The Sunport offers nonstop service to 28 cities, including Amarillo, Atlanta, Chicago, Cincinnati, Dallas, Denver, El Paso, Houston, Kansas City, Las Vegas, Los Angeles, Lubbock, Midland/Odessa, Minneapolis, Newark, Oakland, Orlando, Phoenix, St. Louis, Salt Lake City, San Diego, Seattle, Tampa, and Tucson.

Facilities for those with disabilities include elevators in the parking structure and between each of the terminal's three levels, wheelchairs, Braille signage, wheelchair-accessible restrooms and drinking fountains, and telecommunications devices for the deaf (TDD).

All major car rental agencies are available at the Sunport, and shuttles take passengers to all local hotels. Bus service is sporadic, but taxi cabs are in abundance for the trip to your motel.

If you find you must wait at the Sunport for a rental car or for a connecting flight to Farmington, the wait will be enjoyable. The Albuquerque International Sunport Art Collection is displayed throughout the terminal, and includes work by New Mexico, Native American, and Hispanic artists. If you're hungry while waiting for your ride, I suggest you try Garduno's Chile Packing Company and Cantina. Garduno's offers the best of New Mexican cuisine, and makes some of the best margaritas you'll enjoy anywhere.

The Sunport also offers a bakery and coffee shop, a deli, ice cream, pizza, other Mexican restaurants; and for those who enjoy beer, the Route 66 Microbrewery offers ten beers on-tap, including three from local breweries and 20 varieties of bottled beers.

Gift shops offer up everything from chewing gum to the most beautiful jewelry and works of art from area artists.

Flying out of the Sunport into Farmington is about a 45-minute flight. Understand this flight will be on a small commuter airplane, and the flight may not be smooth. If you tend toward squeamishness, plan on taking something to soothe your tummy. Many of the commuter planes do not have bathrooms, so make sure you go before you go.

Your plane will land at the Four Corners Regional Airport in Farmington, which is a small airport that is also the pilot training area for Mesa Airlines. You won't find long lines at the Farmington airport, and you won't find many amenities. You won't have to go far or wait long for your luggage, either, though, since the baggage claim is in the same room you will walk through on your arrival. If you're hungry, you'll find what the Insiders consider the best Mexican restaurant in the area, Señor Peppers. Señor Peppers has been spotlighted in many national cuisine magazines and it continues to offer great food and reasonable prices. There is a restaurant and a separate lounge, both of which offer views of the landing strip.

The Four Corners Regional Airport in Farmington has two car rental agencies, Budget and National. There is no citywide bus service in Farmington, but again, most of the motels offer shuttle services to their guests.

You may decide you want to fly into Denver International Airport (DIA), then take a commuter plane into Durango to begin your tour of the Four Corners. DIA covers 53 square miles, twice the size of Manhattan Island, New York, and larger than the city boundary of Boston, Miami, or San Francisco. With 1,200 flight or baggage information display monitors, you won't have difficulty knowing where you need to be, but getting there may be a problem. An average number of 104,000 passengers arrive and depart from DIA on a daily basis, traveling an average of 1,371 flights each day.

Most major national and international airlines fly into and out of DIA and several commuter airlines service smaller airports, such as the Durango La Plata County Airport. A variety of shops and restaurants are available for passengers, including a food court and a casual dining establishment. All of the usual amenities are available at DIA, including an interfaith chapel and Islamic prayer hall. A collection of Native American art and photographs, gargoyles, fossils discovered during the construction of the airport, and other displays are there for passenger and visitor enjoyment.

All major car rental agencies are represented at DIA, if you have a long layover and wish to tour the area. Bus service is also available; check at the ticket counter for rates and routes.

The flight to Durango from DIA will be about one hour. Again, this flight will be on a small commuter airplane, so be prepared for a rougher flight than you enjoyed on the big jet that took you into DIA. The Durango La Plata Airport is ten miles from Durango, and has limited car rental services at its airport and no bus service. The airport is small, but a snack bar and gift shop are on the premises.

Phoenix Sky Harbor International Airport also has commuter service into Farmington and Durango. Plan on about a two-hour flight on the commuter. Salt Lake City has no direct flight into Farmington or Durango, but does have a regular flight into Albuquerque, where you can fly into Farmington on a commuter flight.

Sky Harbor has all the major car rental agencies available. Bus service to the surrounding area is also available; check at the ticket counter for rates and routes.

The Gallup Municipal Airport has two car rental agencies, with shuttles to your favorite hotel.

Flagstaff Pulliam Airport, located two miles south of town on I–17, offers daily flights to and from Phoenix Sky Harbor International Airport. Flagstaff's airport is small, but does have shuttles to major hotels. There is limited bus service available; check at the information center for routes and rates. Southeastern Utah has no major airport, so it's easiest to fly into one of the airports in the other three states and rent a car for the trip to this portion of the Four Corners

Vehicle Rental

When you arrive at your destination and arrange for a rental vehicle, remember that many of the roads on the Indian reservations are dirt, and a four-wheel-drive vehicle is recommended.

If you'd rather rent a car, major car rental agencies are provided at the Sunport in Albuquerque as well as Flagstaff Pulliam Airport. Prices vary from state to state, depending on the type of vehicle you rent and the distance you plan to travel. There is usually no additional cost to use the rental car to travel from state to state, but it's always best to check with your agent when you rent your vehicle. Rental cars are most easily obtained at the airport.

If you decide to rent a vehicle in Albuquerque, the fastest and easiest route to Farmington is via U.S. Highway 550. The trip is 150 miles, and there aren't many places to stop and rest along the way. The community of Cuba is about halfway, and most Insiders plan their trips to Albuquerque to include a lunch or dinner stop at El Bruno's, another top-notch Mexican restaurant. Cuba is also a good place for restroom and stretching-your-legs breaks before you continue the drive to the Four Corners. U.S. Highway 550 has been a deadly stretch of road for years, but the New Mexico Transportation and Highway Department has worked hard to widen the road and make it safer for travelers. Nevertheless, it's a good idea to remain alert and watch for animals who like to stroll across the highway, and for drivers who either like to go way below the speed limit, which ranges between 55 and 65 mph, and those drivers who ignore the speedometer and the speed limit and roar along at high speeds. In addition, New Mexicans are notorious for going the speed limit or slower in the left lane, which for most folks is the passing lane. It does no good to cuss or curse these drivers, simply to pass on the right.

You'll continue on U.S. Highway 550 to Bloomfield. At the intersection of U.S. Highways 550 and 64, you can either turn left to go into Farmington, where most of the hotels and motels are, or you can stay in Bloomfield, which has two motels. Or you may decide to continue north and go to Aztec, an historic community that has several motels. Whichever community you decide to stay in, you'll find nice folks who will be

Insiders' Tip

Many of the roads to area attractions in the Four Corners are two lanes, and care should always be taken when driving them. There are countless side roads with heavy oil field traffic, and many roads that lead back into settlements with several homes. Please obey the speed limits and watch for vehicles coming onto the major roads from the side roads.

more than happy to offer advice and guidance for your tour of the Four Corners. The towns in the tri-city area—Aztec, Bloomfield and Farmington—are less than 12 miles from each other.

Your trip to Flagstaff from Phoenix will be a beautiful drive, with good roads and friendly, courteous drivers. It's easy to get distracted with the scenery, however, so it's a good idea to take turns driving if you have companions, so everyone has the opportunity to view the magnificent vistas and wildlife you'll encounter. You'll marvel at the abundance of cactus near Phoenix, and you'll be equally awed by the forests as you enter Flagstaff. No matter how often Four Corners' residents make the drive between Flagstaff and Phoenix, they look forward to the drive, which should take about two hours.

If you fly into Durango, you'll discover the airport out in the middle of nowhere—at least it may seem that way. It's actually only a few miles from downtown Durango, but the highway is only two lanes, and people do tend to get in a hurry, so drive carefully. There is also an abundance of deer along the road into Durango, so please watch for them, especially near dawn and dusk.

Bus Lines

Greyhound and Texas, New Mexico & Oklahoma Coaches (TNM&O) have major routes through the Four Corners. Flagstaff and Farmington have limited bus schedules. Routes and rates will vary. Bus travel in the Four Corners is relatively good, but bus stops may not be accessible to the places you choose to visit.

Four Corners Attractions

New Mexico
Colorado
Utah
Arizona

While the Four Corners has many wonderful places for visitors to see and things for them to do, there are several that you won't want to miss. Those attractions are highlighted here, which should be especially helpful if you're short on time. You'll find more on these great places in the state chapters.

New Mexico

Aztec Ruins National Monument
Ruins Rd., Aztec
(505) 334–6174

Aztec Ruins National Monument is located on Ruins Road, about 0.75 mile north of New Mexico Highway 516, just outside of Aztec. Aztec Ruins includes several multi-story buildings called "great houses," small residential pueblos, tri-wall kivas, great kivas, road segments, and earthworks, all in an area just two miles long and one mile wide. Aztec Ruins, built and used over a 200-year period beginning in the late 1000s, is one of the largest ancestral Pueblo communities in the Animas River valley. Early builders were influenced by Chaco Canyon. By the 1200s, the people who used the area showed a strong cultural relationship to the people in the Mesa Verde region.

The West Ruin, the excavated great house that visitors may tour, had at least 400 interconnected rooms built around an open plaza. Its stone walls rise to more than 30 feet and several rooms contain the original wood materials placed in its roofs by the builders.

A 0.25-mile self-guided trail winds through the West Ruin and passes through several rooms with intact original roofs, as well as the reconstructed Great Kiva, a round semi-subterranean room used for important events. Park rangers will talk you through the tour. Rangers are nice, knowledgeable people who will answer your questions and who take great pride in these ruins.

The Aztec Ruins Visitor Center features exhibits and a 25-minute video, *Hisatsinom—The Ancient Ones*, which is shown several times a day and is worth

Aztec Ruins National Monument.
PHOTO: ELIZABETH ATTEBERY

viewing. You may also purchase books, postcards, slides, posters, and videos of the ruins.

It will take you about 1.5 hours to see the exhibits and the video, and to walk the paved trail. The monument is open from 8 A.M. to 6 P.M. Memorial Day through Labor Day, and from 8 A.M. to 5 P.M. the rest of the year. It is closed Thanksgiving Day, Christmas Day and New Year's Day.

Aztec Ruins surrounds you with the awesome power of the ancient Pueblo people who were the first people to settle in the New Mexico area. A visit to the Four Corners would not be complete without this slice of history that has endured thousands of centuries.

Salmon Ruins and Heritage Park
San Juan County Archaeological Research
Center and Library
6131 U.S. Hwy. 64, Bloomfield
(505) 632–2013
www.more2it.com/salmon

Salmon Ruins and Heritage Park is located just outside of Bloomfield. The Primary occupation (initial builders and occupants of the site) were colonists from or had close ties to the people of Chaco Canyon. Primary occupation inhabitants abandoned the site about A.D. 1130. It was reoccupied during the end of the 12th century, A.D. 1185, and was termed the Secondary occupation. Based on research, it was determined the Secondary occupation of the Salmon Pueblo were from or had close ties to the inhabitants of the Mesa Verde area.

Salmon Ruins is named for George Salmon, who homesteaded the property in the late 1800s. His family protected the ruins from vandals and treasure seekers for more than 90 years, and the family home and outbuildings remain standing near the ruins.

The Ruins is also home to the San Juan County Archaeological Research Center and Library, also known as the Salmon Ruins Museum. Archaeological digging continues to this day under the careful supervision of Salmon Ruins directors and volunteer board. The museum includes exhibits of prehistoric Anasazi pottery and Navajo and Spanish culture items. The library offers a wonderful place to research some of the early settlers of the area, as well as the oil and gas activity of the San Juan Basin.

The Heritage Park at the Ruins opened in 1990 and showcases a series of exhibits displaying traditional habitations of numerous native groups of the Four Corners. During the summer months the park offers demonstrations and tours. Children, especially, enjoy the activities provided.

Insiders know that the gift shop at Salmon Ruins provides the perfect place to find an unusual gift for family and friends. Books, beautiful Indian jewelry, and Indian arts and crafts are available, and the prices attached to them will pleasantly surprise you!

Chaco Culture National Historic Park
Visitor Center
54 miles south of Bloomfield
(505) 786–7014

Chaco Culture National Historic Park preserves one of America's richest and most fascinating cultural and historical areas. Chaco Canyon, a major center of ancestral Pueblo culture between A.D. 850 and A.D. 1250, was a center of ceremony, trade, and culture for the prehistoric Four Corners area. Chaco is noted for its public and ceremonial buildings and its distinctive architecture—an ancient urban center that continues to amaze visitors.

Because of the remoteness of Chaco, the recommended access route is from the north, via New Mexico Highway 44/550. Turn off the highway at County Road 7900, three miles southeast of Nageezi and about 50 minutes west of Cuba. The route includes five miles of paved road and 16 miles of dirt road. The roads are generally maintained, but rain and snow can make them impassable, so please call ahead for road conditions before you begin your trip back to the area.

Chaco Culture National Historic Park. PHOTO: NATIONAL PARK SERVICE

There are no services available at Chaco—no food, gas, lodging or auto repair—so plan ahead. Bring a picnic lunch and plenty of water, and make sure your gas tank is full! Camping is available at Gallo Campground, one mile east of the visitor center. There are 47 sites with picnic tables and fire grates. All sites are on a first-come, first-served basis; and during the tourist season (April through October), the sites fill up quickly. If you plan to camp, bring your own firewood, as gathering wood is not permitted.

Chacoan cultural sites are part of the sacred homelands of the Pueblo Indian peoples of New Mexico, the Hopi Indians of Arizona, and the Navajo Indians of the Southwest. The sites are very fragile and irreplaceable, so please take extra care not to damage or destroy them. The Indian tribes that the sites represent continue to live in the Four Corners, and visitors are asked to respect the culture Chaco stands for. Stay on designated trails and obey the signs. Do not stand, walk, or climb on the walls of the ruins—they are fragile and could crumble beneath you, taking away a wonderful part of our nation's history.

Artifacts, plants, animals, and rocks are protected in all national parks, so don't remove any of them as souvenirs. If you are caught, you will definitely pay the price in strictly enforced fines.

You will want to begin your tour of Chaco at the visitor center, where the staff will help you plan your time. The center has a museum, theater, and bookstore, and offers daily tours. The center is open from 8 A.M. to 6 P.M. Memorial Day through Labor Day, and from 8 A.M. to 5 P.M. the remainder of the year. The center is closed on Christmas Day, Martin Luther King Jr.'s Birthday, and President's Day, but the park remains open.

There are six major Chacoan cultural sites, which may be viewed by driving the nine-mile paved loop drive. Park and walk the short, self-guided trails to the sites. It's best to plan to spend 45 minutes to an hour at each site. Four backcountry trails lead from the canyon to more remote cultural sites. Backcountry trails require a free permit, which may be obtained at the visitor center or from a park ranger. All trails and Chacoan cultural sites are closed from sunset to sunrise.

Aztec UFO Symposium

While the city of Aztec prides itself on being the home of 5,600 people and "six ole soreheads," it isn't the soreheads who bring an ever-increasing number of people to the town each spring.

The visitors aren't the little people who, legend has it, landed near Aztec in 1948, one year after the Roswell UFO crash, in a flying saucer-shaped object, but those who attend the annual UFO Symposium. They have a great interest in the information surrounding the legend.

According to Frank Scully, a newspaper columnist, a flying saucer landed about 12 miles northeast of Aztec, killing the 14 humanoids on board, who ranged in height from 36 to 48 inches tall. According to Scully, the saucer survived the crash and its landing on Earth was covered up by the government. Scully included his information about the UFO in a book, *Flying Saucers*, published in 1950.

While Scully's story was met with skepticism by many, there are those today who are convinced the flying saucer did land near this historic little town in northwestern New Mexico.

Leanne Hathcock was one of the skeptics of the alleged UFO landing. However, hired as the librarian for the Aztec Public Library in 1997, Hathcock began researching the landing.

"I'm not a 'Trekkie,' and I don't watch the [popular television series] *The X Files*, but I found two books on UFO's in the library when I started, and I found it pretty interesting," Hathcock admitted. "I'd heard about the one [landing] out here, and I decided I wanted to find out more."

As her interest piqued, Hathcock saw an opportunity to raise some much-needed money for the city's library, and to have a lot of fun. "I knew a lot of people are interested in UFO's," Hathcock explained, "and I was interested in the town's lore, which included this wonderful legend of the landing of a flying saucer."

In 1998, Hathcock and a dedicated group of volunteers from the Aztec Friends of the Library had the first UFO Symposium. "We had a small group," Hathcock remembered. "But then we started getting calls from all over the world. People were really interested in it."

From the first group of about 50 people, the symposium attracted 250 people its second year. "That year, we had Edgar Mitchell, the sixth man to walk on the moon and who had three Congressional Medals of Honor, come to speak," Hathcock said. "He said they [UFO's] do exist and he had seen the files."

Joe Firmage, who had gone public about his alien visitation in *Newsweek* and *Time*, was also a guest speaker. "I couldn't believe these important people wanted to come to this small town to speak," Hathcock said, shaking her head in continued disbelief. "Every year, we have people who are willing to come here to speak, and do not expect to be paid for it."

Hathcock said she gets requests from researchers who continue to seek information about UFO's, but refuse to attend the huge Roswell UFO event because of the ever-increasing circus they believe it has become. "They say Roswell is a media circus, and they want to come here because they believe we're very serious about what we're doing," Hathcock explained. "They think we're doing pretty good stuff."

"Pretty good stuff" indeed. Today, the symposium includes a kick-off banquet, mountain bike competition, an art and writing contest, a play production, vendor gallery, stargaze, and tours to the site. As the word of the symposium reaches far beyond the Four Corners, the symposium attracts more media attention and more interest from around the world. "In 2000, we had people from 12 different states, with a lot of people coming from Alaska, Minnesota, and California, as well as the Four Corners," Hathcock said proudly. "Our web site has generated interest from all over the world, from as far away as South Africa."

While Hathcock doesn't admit to being convinced little men landed near Aztec in a flying saucer, she does say she's impressed with the number of people who do. "I'm not sure it's just a figment of someone's imagination," Hathcock said. "We have a man who we refer to only as Mr. X, who's one of our biggest supporters. He's got a government job and has a security clearance, so he can't reveal his name. But he really believes in UFO's and in what we're doing here."

While the legend continues to grow, and interest in the Aztec UFO Symposium increases, the city's six ole soreheads may find themselves in an ever-increasing minority. For the hundreds of people who descend on the city each March, searching for information, answers, and a belief that flying saucers and aliens from other worlds do exist, it may be difficult to not smile and enjoy the festivities for those six people.

Besides, you never know where the next visitor calls home. He may arrive in Aztec by SUV, truck, or auto—or in an odd-shaped aircraft no one may recognize!

Information: Aztec UFO Symposium, 201 W. Chaco, Aztec, New Mexico 87410; (505) 334–7658; www.aztecufo.com; aztecpl@cyberport.com.

The summers at Chaco can be very warm, so make sure you have plenty of water for the tour of the ruins. There is very little shade available, so it may be wise to wear a hat.

Chaco is an incredible visit to the past. It is amazing to look at the ruins, the tiny rooms, and the huge ceremonial rooms and realize that long before telephones, television, shopping malls, and SUVs, the area was inhabited by people who planned and built beautiful structures without the benefit of architects and contractors. Chaco is a beautiful spot and sure to be a favorite memory of your trip to the Four Corners.

Colorado

Hovenweep National Monument
On Colorado/Utah border
(435) 459–4344
www.nps.gov/hove

Those who have a special interest in archaeology won't want to miss a visit to Hovenweep National Monument, located just an hour west of Cortez. The ride through either McElmo Canyon or via Pleasant View will make for an enjoyable day trip. Hovenweep is off the beaten path, and if you opt to arrive by way of Pleasant View, you'll find a dirt road that, if the weather is rainy, may be impassable. Make sure you call the ranger station before you set out if rain is in the forecast. Six ancestral Pueblo sites are located at Hovenweep, all erected around A.D. 1200. The sites are characterized by their unique square, oval, circular, and D-shaped towers. The Square Tower is easy to get to; getting to the others, however, requires driving along bumpy roads and doing some hiking. A four-wheel-drive

Mesa Verde National Park. PHOTO: ARA MARK MESA VERDE COMPANY

vehicle should be your choice for driving to Hovenweep, and hiking shoes, not sandals, should be your footwear. There are no services at Hovenweep, and no water is available. However, the beauty of the area and the serenity that surrounds it makes spending a day here one of the best days of your vacation to the Four Corners.

Mesa Verde National Park
P.O. Box 8, Mesa Verde National Park
(970) 529–4313
www.nps.gov/meve

For many people, the highlight of their trip to the Four Corners is Mesa Verde National Park, and for good reasons. The cliff dwellings and artifacts of ancestral Puebloans have earned the park international designation as a place to see. Almost 100 years ago, two brothers-in-law were tracking lost cattle when they decided to rest on a mesa bordering a small branch canyon. They walked to the cliff's edge and, looking across the canyon, discovered a long, deep opening in the face of the cliff. There, outlined against the dark shadows of the cave, were traces of a most spectacular cliff dwelling. Later, the two learned what they had seen is the largest of the abandoned 700-year-old cliff dwellings in the western United States. Fourteen centuries of history are meticulously cared for at Mesa Verde National Park. Mesa Verde offers an opportunity to see and experience the life of the ancestral Puebloans. Spectacular cliff dwellings and many mesa-top villages were built between A.D. 450 and 1300. There are endless options for visitors to enjoy the park—you may take a walk, drive, or participate in a bus tour of the park. You may hike and climb ladders in and out of these famous cliff dwellings, or simply stroll through less rigorous, but equally beautiful, self-guided tours. Services at Mesa Verde are many—you'll find food, gasoline, and lodging available from early spring to late fall. Morefield Campground, four miles into the park, is open from late April through mid-October and offers single and multiple campsites. Mesa Verde National Park is open year round, but schedules vary with the season, so call for information before you make your plans to visit the Four Corners. Insiders know it will take two days to see everything at Mesa Verde, and you will want to see everything. Please remember, however, that Mesa Verde's cultural heritage depends on visitors' help in caring for this wonderful park. Do not disturb, remove, or mar archaeological sites, structures, rock art, or other antiquities. Federal and state laws prohibit disturbance of cultural resources on public lands and law enforcement officers are committed to upholding those laws.

Utah

Natural Bridges National Monument
47 miles southwest of Blanding
(435) 692–1234

Natural Bridges National Monument is out of the way and pretty remote, so many visitors to the Four Corners opt to pass it up in favor of one of the many other area attractions. While Insiders understand time is important when trying to cover all of the Four Corners during a vacation, we realize that often, it is the jewel less polished that shines the most brightly. So it is with Natural Bridges National Monument.

Insiders encourage you to spend some time in the visitor center, located near the entrance of the park, before embarking on your tour of the park. By doing so, you will better understand the area and it will most certainly increase your appreciation of it.

There are only three bridges here, but Indian cliff dwellings, pictographs, and white sandstone canyons are scattered throughout the area, making your trip through Natural Bridges National Monument a treasure search. The Photovoltaic Array, one of the largest solar power generators in the world, stands as a testimonial to modern civilization amongst the historical elements of the park. Of the three bridges, the last of them is likely the most spectacular and the easiest to hike to. It is the oldest bridge in the park, and rock falls have reduced the thickness of the bridge to just nine feet, which may limit its lifetime. Walking on this bridge, or any of the others, is prohibited.

Hiking is popular in the park, and several trails offer varying degrees of difficulty and challenge. Short, often used trails lead from the loop road to the bridges, while a slightly more difficult, eight-mile path connects all three.

There are 13 campsites available on a first-come, first-served basis in the park. There is a 21-foot combined length limit for RV's and vehicles with trailers. All sites have a fire grill, tent pad, and picnic table. Water is available at the visitor center. Firewood gathering is prohibited, so remember to bring your own. Pets are allowed in the campground, but must be kept on a leash no longer than six feet. Pets are not allowed on designated trails or in the backcountry. The campground has no designated site for wheelchairs, but it has several sites and one restroom that is wheelchair accessible.

Mountain biking through the park should be done only on paved roads. Natural Bridges National Monument is worth the travel and time it takes to get there.

Insiders' Tip
The weather in the Four Corners will range from very warm to cool, especially during the spring and summer months. It's always wise to take along a jacket, a hat, and sunscreen when you leave your home base for day trips. Water isn't always accessible in remote areas of the Four Corners, where much of the beauty of the area is located, so you're encouraged to take along enough water for the day.

Druid Arch, Needles District, Canyonlands National Park. PHOTO: NATIONAL PARK SERVICE

With helpful rangers anxious to answer any question and offer assistance, and because of the lack of crowds in this attraction, you may find you'll want to linger here, soaking up the beauty and the blissful isolation.

Canyonlands National Park Visitor Center Island in the Sky District and Needles District
2282 S. West Resource Blvd., Moab
(435) 259–7164

Visitor centers are open from 8 A.M. to 4:30 P.M. daily, with extended hours during the spring and fall. Centers are closed on some federal holidays. Centers offer exhibits and sell books, maps and other publications.

Canyonlands National Park is 527 square miles of some of the most beautiful country you will ever see. Mesas, buttes, arches, and spires enhance the beauty of southeastern Utah's Colorado Plateau. The park is divided into four districts by the Green and Colorado Rivers—the Island in the Sky, the Maze, the Needles, and the winding course of the two rivers. While the four districts are not directly

linked by any roads, each district is unique and offers much to explore. The Island in the Sky is the easiest to get to. The drive is paved and you will see incredible views from the many overlooks provided. If you feel like getting off that paved road, the Island in the Sky offers miles of hiking trails and four-wheel-drive roads. If you're looking for a backcountry experience, the Needles District may be the one you'll want to start with, and you'll see the best views if you hike or take a four-wheel-drive road. The Maze is a totally backcountry district and you'll need to plan a lot more time and have an experienced four-wheel driver to enjoy this part of the park. Backcountry permits are required for overnight use and are limited in number. Reservations are suggested if you plan to spend the night and enjoy the beauty of the dusk and the dawn.

If you plan to camp in Canyonlands, be aware that the campgrounds are primitive, but extremely popular, and are usually full each night from mid-March to Memorial Day. While backcountry permits and group campsites may be reserved in advance, all developed campgrounds are first come, first served. Developed campgrounds are found in the Needles and Island in the Sky districts. Campsites have picnic tables, fire pits, and restroom facilities close by. There are no showers.

If you love to hike, you'll love Canyonlands! There are many great hiking trails in the park, whether you're looking for a short walk or a week-long backpacking trip. You won't find much water, however, so make sure you have enough for the length of hike you plan. No pets are allowed on hiking trails.

Mountain bikers are also welcome in Canyonlands. Its 100-mile White Rim Road at the Island of the Sky is a popular ride. Mountain bikes must remain on established roads and they are not allowed on hiking trails. If you plan to spend the night in the backcountry, make sure you have a permit and use designated campsites.

Canyonlands National Park is a unique gem in the treasure chest of the Four Corners. The ever-changing landscape Canyonlands provides is incredible and it's easy to imagine the pioneers of hundreds of years ago traveling across this beautiful country, wondering if they had found Utopia right here in southeastern Utah.

Arizona

Canyon de Chelly National Monument
Chinle
(520) 674–5500
www.nps.gov/cach

Canyon de Chelly National Monument is located close to Arizona Highway 63, at the community of Chinle. It is 95 miles from Gallup, New Mexico, via U.S. Highway 666/191 and Arizona Highway 264. These incredible canyons provided shelter for prehistoric Pueblo Indians for a thousand years and were considered an ancestral stronghold for the Navajo Indians. Steep walled canyons and ruins of prehistoric Indian dwellings are highlights of Canyon de Chelly, but for many, it is the beauty of the area that is most memorable. There are more than 7,000 archaeological sites in Canyon de Chelly, which attract archaeologists from around the world. At the bottom of the canyon, Navajos still live and work the fields during the summer months.

The best and easiest way to see the ruins and the canyons is to drive along the two scenic routes, the South Rim, which is 36 miles round trip, and the North Rim Drive, which is 34 miles round trip. The South Rim, with the most popular overlooks, boasts access roads to eight overlook points. Junction Overlook offers views of First Ruin and Junction Ruin.

If you want to travel into the canyon, you may only do so on foot and in the company of a park ranger or guide. The only exception is the White House Trail, a 2.5-mile, round-trip walk that leads to the best known Anasazi ruin in the canyon. The trail is named after a long wall in the upper ruin that is covered with white plaster. The trail begins at the White House Overlook, six miles from the park headquarters and visitor center. The village was home to some 100 Anasazi between 1060 and 1275. You'll travel 500 feet down, with the trail crossing the river. Plan on about two hours for this trip.

A guided tour, offered by nearby Thunderbird Lodge, is the best way to see the other ruins in the canyon. The lodge is inside the monument and is near the visitor center. It uses vehicles that can cross the sandy terrain, which contains some quicksand, and the mud, which inevitably follows rain and flash floods. You can use your own four-wheel-drive vehicle, and hire a Navajo guide through the Park Service. If you'd rather, you can take a horseback trip into the canyon. Check at the visitor center.

Other attractions you'll want to see while at Canyon de Chelly include Spider Rock, an 800-foot sandstone spire that rises from the floor of the canyon at the junction of Canyon de Chelly and Monument Valley; Antelope House, named for the drawings of antelope by a Navajo artist 150 years ago; and Mummy Cave, one of the most spectacular dwellings in the park, which was occupied from A.D. 300 to 1300.

The monument provides a few picnic sites and Cottonwood Campground is located near the headquarters. The campground features fireplaces, drinking water and restrooms. Any other needs you may have should be available in nearby Chinle.

The hogan on the south side of the visitor center is designed just like the ones Navajos have lived in for centuries. Step inside and find a museum with regional books and cultural demonstrations, local artist exhibits, and ranger-staffed information desk. Restrooms are also available at the visitor center, which is open from 8 A.M. to 5 P.M. daily October to April, and from 8 A.M. to 6 P.M. May to September.

As you marvel at the ruins and gaze at the canyons, please remember that Canyon de Chelly remains home to some Navajo families. As such, you're asked to respect the traditions, culture, and history of the Navajo. Do not enter a hogan or take photographs of the Navajo without asking their permission first.

Canyon de Chelly will be a highlight of your trip to the Four Corners. The canyons, the ruins, the stone formations, and the people who continue to live there are sure to make an impression that you'll carry with you for some time.

**Monument Valley Navaho Tribal Park
East of U.S. Hwy. 163, about 24 miles
north of Kayenta
(801) 737–3287
www.navajonationparks.org**

You may never have visited Monument Valley, but chances are excellent that you've seen it. One of the most photographed areas in the country, Monument Valley has been featured in countless movies and television commercials. The automobile industry likes using the top of Right Mitten for TV ads. Noted

Hollywood director John Ford first used Monument Valley in a movie when he directed *Stagecoach*, starring John Wayne. Other notable movies shot in Monument Valley include *She Wore a Yellow Ribbon* in 1949; *How the West Was Won* in 1962; *Back to the Future I and II* in 1983 and 1991; and *Forrest Gump* in 1993.

Monument Valley may epitomize the Wild West to many, but for those of us who live in the Four Corners, it is more than a great spot to shoot movies and television commercials, it is a place where the beauty of the area seeps deep into the soul. Great formations rise from a flat, sandy desert like hands reaching to the gods. A canvas of color created by the rising and setting of the sun offers different shades and incredible shadows. Monument Valley lies entirely within the Navajo Indian Reservation on the Arizona/Utah border. The state line passes through many of the landmarks, giving residents of both states bragging rights. There is but one main road, U.S. Highway 163, which links Kayenta with U.S. Highway 191 in Utah. The most photographed image of Monument Valley can be seen from the stretch of road that approaches the border of the two states from the north. And while visitors can see a lot of the valley from that road, much of the beauty is hidden behind cliffs.

The view from the visitor center is wonderful, but the valley can be best seen from Valley Drive, a 17-mile dirt road that winds from the visitor center among great towering cliffs and mesas, including the beautiful Totem Pole. Unfortunately, the road isn't a very good one, and four-wheel-drive vehicles are recommended. There are Navajo guides and four-wheel-drive rental outfitters who will gladly take visitors on the tour. You also have the option of touring the valley on horseback.

Youngsters will especially enjoy Monument Valley because of the great rock formations that resemble animals or other images. Kids will get a kick out of the Right Mitten; the Three Sisters, which resemble three nuns dressed in habits; the

Monument Valley. PHOTO: ELIZABETH ATTEBERY

Hub, which not only looks like the center of a wagon wheel but is also the geographic center of Monument Valley; and the Totem Pole, a 400-foot high rock formation that looks like a replica of a totem pole. Once you've actually visited Monument Valley, it will be easily recognizable in movies and commercials, but only those who know firsthand how incredibly beautiful the valley is can truly appreciate the magic that surrounds it.

The visitor center provides assistance from 7 A.M. to 8 P.M. May through September, and from 8 A.M. to 5 P.M. October through April.

Glen Canyon National Recreation Area/Lake Powell
691 Scenic View Dr., Page
(520) 608–6404
www.nps.gov/glca

It was the early 1950s when the Bureau of Reclamation proposed building a dam on the Colorado River at Glen Canyon's southern end. The area was relatively unrecognized, although those who had passed through Glen Canyon were aware of the majestic beauty it offered. Construction of the dam began in 1956 and was completed in 1962. The lake behind the dam, Lake Powell, did not completely fill until 1980. Today, Glen Canyon Dam provides electricity for millions of people, as well as water for irrigation. The water depth drops more than 500 feet at the dam and its crest spans 1,560 feet, rising more than 700 feet above bedrock. There are five rivers that feed into Lake Powell—the Green River from Wyoming, the Colorado River from Colorado, the San Juan River from New Mexico, the Escalante River from Utah, and the Dirty Devil River from Utah. It is the second largest man-made lake in the United States, with 1,960 miles of shoreline and 96 different canyons to explore. Lake Powell provides relaxation and recreation for thousands of people who come from all over the world to bask in the sunshine and beauty of the area. The Glen Canyon National Recreation Area stretches for hundreds of miles and offers boating, fishing, swimming, backcountry hiking, and four-wheel-drive enthusiasts plenty of space to enjoy their sport.

Most visitors begin their tour of Glen Canyon and Lake Powell at Page, which is two miles from the dam and the visitor center. Page is a friendly community and offers stores, motels, restaurants, churches and a hospital. While many people opt to stay in Page, Wahweap Marina, 5.5 miles from the visitor center, includes Wahweap Lodge

(520) 645-2433, which is on the shores of the lake and is a pleasant place to stay. In addition, housekeeping units are available at Hite Marina, Hall's Crossing, and Bullfrog Resort and Marina. The units include separate bedrooms, two bathrooms with tub and shower combination, a full kitchen with dishes and utensils for eight people, a microwave, linens, television, and a picnic table and grill. The housekeeping units are comfortable and offer more privacy than the lodge. For those who plan to stay more than a couple of days exploring Lake Powell, a housekeeping unit may be more economical, as well as a lot of fun. For information on housekeeping units, call the visitor center.

Many people opt to take advantage of all Lake Powell's offerings by renting a houseboat and cruising the lake. Houseboats vary in size (from 36 feet to 59 feet), amenities (swim slides to sound systems), and cost (about $1,100 to about $3,000 for three days). All houseboats come with everything you need for your Lake Powell cruise, including life jackets, toilet tissue, and a corkscrew! Be forewarned, however, that reservations must be made well in advance, and flexibility in your vacation plans will help you get the boat you want. Reservations should be made at least one year in advance, and even then, you may expect scheduling challenges. Once you've confirmed your rental, a deposit must be made to secure the houseboat. If you cancel or change your reservation, a portion or all of your deposit may be retained by the rental company. Deposits run from $350 to $600, depending on which houseboat you select. For more information on renting houseboats, call (800) 530-3406. Those who have rented houseboats are enthusiastic about the experience and fun they have on the boats and return again and again for their vacation on beautiful Lake Powell.

Fishing is a popular attraction at Lake Powell and residents of the Four Corners frequently make the trip to catch stripers, largemouth and smallmouth bass, and crappie. Some anglers fish walleye, channel catfish, and bluegill sunfish from the waters of Lake Powell. The Colorado squawfish, humpback and bonytail chub, and razorback sucker are endangered species that are also fished from the waters. However, if you catch them, you must release them alive immediately. The penalties for keeping endangered fish are stiff and law enforcement officers enforce those laws vigorously. You must have a valid Utah and/or Arizona fishing license to fish Lake Powell. Licenses may be purchased at all the marinas. Check at the marina before packing your tackle box and fishing pole and heading out. Record-sized fish have been caught at Lake Powell and anglers are always hoping to top those records. Records range from a 5-pound smallmouth bass to a 48-pound striped bass.

Hiking is also popular at Glen Canyon National Recreation Area and the staff at the visitor center will be happy to direct you to the best places to hike and the challenges they offer.

Almost everyone who spends time at Lake Powell visits the Rainbow Bridge National Monument, which is about 50 miles by water from Wahweap, Bullfrog, or Hall's Crossing. This beautiful natural bridge is one of the most photographed bridges in the world. Please stay on the approved paths, however, because Rainbow Bridge remains a scared ground to the Native Americans. (See the Attractions section in the Utah chapter for more information about Rainbow Bridge.)

There is so much to see and do at Lake Powell, you'll want to spend several days. It's almost impossible to accurately describe the area, because the canyons, cliffs, mesas, and water are so beautiful they defy description. Locals who visit Lake Powell regularly always come home with stories of new spots they found, fishing holes they discovered, and a better appreciation of all the Glen Canyon National Recreation Area has to offer.

The visitor center operates from 7 A.M. to 7 P.M. Memorial Day through Labor Day, and from 8 A.M. to 5 P.M. the rest of the year.

Annual Events

January
February
March
April
May
June
July
August
September
October
November
December

You will find something fun for the family to do whenever you visit the Four Corners. From four-wheel-drive trails and mountain biking to cultural activities, it's all available at some time of the year. The events listed in this chapter are by no means all of them. This is just an idea of what you'll find when you travel to this wonderful part of our country. Most of the events listed are for the entire family—the Four Corners believes in family values, and you'll find most events are targeted for family fun. Events are arranged by month, then alphabetically, for your convenience. I encourage you to participate in as many of these events as you can when you visit the Four Corners, for the things we do here are typical of the kind of life we lead—fun, interesting, and always exciting.

January

Colorado

Snowdown
Durango
www.snowdown.org

This popular winterfest puts an end to the winter blues by offering great fun and lots of things to do. Ski joring (a horse and rider pulling a skier through a professionally designed course with electronic timing), ski softball, waiter-waitress race, cookie eating contest, scavenger hunt, dating game, hula hoop contest, pool tournament, bed races, snow sculptures, worst dressed fashion show, parade, and snow games for kids are just some of the activities offered.

February

New Mexico

Shiprock Balloon Rally
Shiprock
(800) 448–1240

Balloonists from throughout the Four Corners participate in this colorful rally when they take their balloons over the majestic Shiprock pinnacle. The highlight of this rally is when all balloons fly around the Shiprock, which is an incredible spectacle of color and great Native American history.

Utah

Moab Repertory Theater
Moab
(435) 259–6727

This has become a popular annual event in Moab. It provides an intimate setting for innovative works. A dessert reception follows the performance, with cast members attending. Some performances are strictly for an adult audience, so call for information before taking the family.

Arizona

Flagstaff Winterfest
Flagstaff
(800) 842–7293
www.flagstaff.az.us

Winterfest features more than 100 events, including sled dog races, Nordic and alpine skiing competitions, snowboard and snowshoe events, snowmobile drag races, stargazing, special children's activities, concerts and cultural events, outdoor walks and talks, and other family entertainment highlights. Winterfest has been named a "Top 100 Winter Event in North America."

Winter Events
Flagstaff
(520) 779–1951
www.arizonasnowbowl.com

The Arizona Snowbowl and the Flagstaff Nordic Center host many winter events, including the Mountain Sports Cup, Arizona Citizens' Cup, Arizona Special Olympics Winter Games, and the Grand Canyon State Winter Games. Most of the events offered at the Snowbowl and Nordic Center are free to those who want to watch

March

Utah

Canyonland 5 Mile Run and Half Marathon
Moab
(435) 259–4525

This is a great run, and offers divisions for youngsters 11 and younger to more seasoned runners 70 years of age and older. A special wheelchair division is also offered. Proceeds are donated to charity—recently for scholarships to two high school track stars.

Arizona

Archaeology Day
Flagstaff
(520) 774–5213

Special activities and events for children and adults about Southwestern archaeology are held at the Museum of Northern Arizona. Gallery interpretations and hands-on activities about archaeology are highlights on Archaeology Day. Kids of all ages will enjoy it.

Arizona Ski and Golf Classic
Flagstaff
(520) 779–1951

The third weekend in March has teams competing in a four-person-scramble golf tournament in Sedona on Saturday and a modified giant-slalom ski race at the Arizona Snowbowl on Sunday. Spectators enjoy this event almost as much as the participants do.

Voices from the Past
Flagstaff
(520) 774–2096

Staff of Lowell Observatory recreate the lives of famous astronomers of the past, including Galileo, Copernicus, Caroline Herschel, and Maria Mitchell, then lead visitors on a tour of the night sky. This is an event everyone who enjoys astronomy and the stars of the sky will want to return to again and again.

Insiders' Tip

Desert areas are in full bloom by late April or early May, while high alpine tundra is still snow-covered.

April

New Mexico

Badlands Battle Mountain Bike Race
Farmington
(800) 448–1240

Racers from around the Four Corners take on the high desert terrain in a race of agility and skill. This isn't a race for the novice, as the terrain offers challenges not found elsewhere.

Colorado

Durango Meltdown
Durango
(970) 385–7547

A bluegrass festival is held at various places in downtown Durango, including the Durango & Silverton Narrow Gauge Railroad and the Strater Hotel. There are three venues for the Meltdown, all within walking distance of each other in historic downtown Durango. Events include a Super Jam, a Celtic Jam, and a Sunday morning gospel set. Maximum audiences are 250, which gives performers the opportunity to interact with those attending. This is a great event for those who love bluegrass. Tickets are $25 for the weekend, $20 for Saturday, and $15 for Sunday.

Utah

Annual Green River Trail Ride
Moab
(435) 564–8112

B.Y.O.H. (Bring Your Own Horse) and join a wonderful family ride through the beautiful San Rafael Swell area of the Green River. A chuck wagon dinner and breakfast is provided, and you'll have the opportunity to ride through the desert, around canyon rims, and through the bottom of the canyons just like the cowboys and prospectors did hundreds of years ago.

May

New Mexico

Farmington Invitational Balloon Festival
Farmington
(800) 448-1240

Dozens of hot air balloons take to the air and participate in a splash and dash at Farmington Lake. The splash and dash is always exciting and spectators love seeing if the balloons can really "splash the water and dash back up into the sky!" It's a colorful event, with balloons from all over the Four Corners participating. Be prepared to get up early for this festival since the best balloon flying is done just

Balloon Festival, Farmington, New Mexico.
PHOTO: ELIZABETH ATTEBERY

after sunrise. It's well worth the effort, however.

Riverfest
Farmington
(800) 448–1240

One of Farmington's biggest celebrations, Riverfest offers fun for the entire family. Raft rides, music, and a 10K and 5K run/walk highlight the event. This is a kick-off of summer event and northern New Mexico is always ready to enjoy the food, music, fine arts, and activities at Riverfest.

Shiprock Marathon
Shiprock
(800) 325–0279

This is a popular annual event in the Shiprock area. Runners from around the country enjoy participating in this event, which takes runners by Shiprock in all its majesty. There are categories for men and women, ages 15 and older. There is a $30 entry fee for the marathon and a $25 fee for a fun walk.

Colorado

Durango & Silverton Narrow Gauge Railroad,
Durango
(888) 872–4607
www.durangotrain.com

The Durango & Silverton Narrow Gauge Railroad (D&SNG) begins its season as it takes passengers through the San Juan Mountains. The train runs daily through the warmer months, and has a daily, shorter ride to Winter Cascade Canyon from late November through the first of May. Special rides are held at Christmas

Durango & Silverton Narrow Gauge Railroad.
PHOTO: ROBERT ROYEM

and New Year's. Tickets are $53 for adults May through October, $27 for children ages 5 to 11. Group rates are available; call for information. More information can be found on the D&SNG RR in the Attractions section and the Close-up in the Colorado chapter.

Hopi Pueblo Dancers
Mesa Verde
(800) 449–2288

Watch these beautiful dances performed by the Hopis. The Hopi dancers are primarily men, dressed in colorful costumes and accompanied by drums. There's no special reason for them to perform at this particular time.

Iron Horse Bicycle Classic
Durango
(970) 259–4621
www.ironhorsebicycleclassic.com

This is a classic 47-mile road race against the Durango & Silverton Narrow Gauge Railroad (yes, you actually race the train) over two mountain passes. The weekend also includes mountain bike rides, kid's races, a run, a swim, a free pasta dinner, and more.

Pueblo to Pueblo Run
Cortez
(970) 565–1151

An 11-mile run and a 2-mile walk begin at the Anasazi Heritage Center and end at the Cortez Cultural Center, with proceeds going to the Cortez Center. This is a great

race, with most of the top local runners participating.

Utah

Annual Green River/Moab Friendship Cruise
Green River
(435) 564–8144

The cruise begins in Green River and floats down the river to the confluence of the Colorado River, then travels up the river to Moab. The trip is 184 miles and usually takes two to three days. Stops are made so participants may explore the many natural and historic sites along the route. This is a wonderful experience the whole family will enjoy.

Migratory Bird Day Festival and National Wetlands Day
Moab
(435) 259–4629

This is a great way to introduce children of all ages to the wonders of bird watching. Resource specialists, naturalists, and face painters all join in to make this celebration of the journeys of migrating birds and the processes of wetlands a fun, educational, and memorable event.

Arizona

A Celebration of Native American Art
Flagstaff
(520) 774–5213
www.musnaz.org

This is a celebration to honor the creativity of Native American and Hispanic

artists and the Museum of Northern Arizona's legacy of support for the native arts of the Colorado Plateau. The exhibit features arts and crafts of the Hopi, Navajo, Pai, and Zuni and runs through September.

June

New Mexico

Aztec Fiesta Days
Aztec
(505) 334–9551

Aztec celebrates summer with a parade, the burning of Old Man Gloom, lots of food, and arts and crafts. Old Man Gloom depicts winter, and a dummy "old man" is burned to say farewell to cold weather and welcome to summer.

Outdoor Summer Theater
Farmington
(800) 448–1240

Original plays are performed in a natural sandstone amphitheater at Lions Wilderness Park, with an optional Southwest-style dinner served prior to each performance. The event continues into mid-August. These plays are traditionally

about the early days of northern New Mexico, focusing on the trials, tribulations, joys, and successes of the pioneers and early Native Americans. The beautiful outdoor stage is the perfect backdrop for these wonderful plays, many of which are being performed for the first time.

San Juan County Sheriff's Posse Rodeo
Farmington
(800) 448–1240

Northern New Mexico's largest open rodeo is held at the San Juan Rodeo Grounds. An open rodeo allows anyone to enter competition, as opposed to rodeos that are sanctioned by organizations and only allow members of that organization to participate.

San Juan Open Golf Tournament
Farmington
(800) 448–1240

Professional and amateur golfers hit the links at the San Juan Country Club in a tournament that benefits local charities. While prizes range from golf apparel to a new car for a hole-in-one at a designated hole, it's the bragging rights that are most sought after. This course is carefully cared for and this tournament is much anticipated by local amateurs and professionals alike.

Colorado

Animas River Days
Durango
(800) 525–8855

Two days of kayaking races on the Animas River.

Mountains by Moonlight
Durango
(970) 247–2733

Enjoy the Durango & Silverton moonlight train to Cascade Canyon. The train leaves at 7:30 P.M. and returns at 11 P.M. The moonlight ride continues through August.

River Raft Day
Dolores
(800) 807–4712

Enjoy raft rides on the beautiful Dolores River. The Dolores River is a Class III+ river, with white water rapids just waiting to be tamed. The Snaggletooth Rapid, said to be the most famous in southwestern Colorado, is located on the Dolores River.

Ute Mountain Bear Dance and Tribal Activities Pow Wow
Towaoc
(970) 565–6485

A wonderful opportunity to see Ute dances.

Utah

Annual Rod Benders Car Show
Moab
(435) 259–8942

Anybody who appreciates the classic cars of days gone by will really enjoy this great car show. Rod runs, a movie night, and great dance music from the past will keep you busy and entertained. These classic automobiles are polished and much loved and their owners are more than willing to tell you the story behind their favorite car.

PCRA Rodeo
Moab
(435) 259–6226

Watch some of the country's best ropers, bull riders, barrel racers, and bucking bronc riders participate in one of the best rodeos in the Four Corners. Competition is tough, the participants are tougher, and the ride is fast and furious! Great wild west fun for the whole family.

Arizona

Chili Cook-off
Flagstaff
(520) 526–4314

This annual all-day event is a qualifier for the World Championship Chili Cook-off, a competition for no-beans chili. Cooks from throughout northeastern Arizona vie for the priviledge of going on to the World Championship Chili Cook-off, an honor not taken lightly in this part of the Four Corners. This chili must be created without beans, and recipes are rarely exchanged. The cook-off is held in conjunction with the Route 66 Celebration, which provides fun for the entire family and great music.

Concerts in the Park
Flagstaff
(520) 774-4505

Concerts are held every Wednesday during June between 6 and 8 P.M. Sponsored by the Flagstaff Parks and Recreation Department, concerts offer a variety of music and are enjoyed in the beautiful mountain air. Bring your lawn chairs, a blanket, and a picnic for an evening of great entertainment.

Flagstaff Heritage Days
Flagstaff
(800) 842-7293
www.flagstaffheritagedays.com

Enjoy twelve days of fun in Flagstaff at this annual event. Festival highlights include a Route 66 Festival and car show, Arizona Dream Cruise, and Route 66 Car Rally.

Flagstaff's Historic Walk
Flagstaff
(520) 774-8800

This entertaining tour, led by two local historians dressed in period costumes, provides a colorful and interesting picture of Flagstaff's early days. Tours are scheduled

through September. The tour takes visitors through about eight blocks of downtown Flagstaff. The couple who lead the tour are knowledgeable about the early days of Flagstaff (in the early 1800s) and their love of the city is shared with their guests.

Gem and Mineral Show
Flagstaff
(520) 779-2741

Rough rocks to gemstones are displayed at this show, along with minerals, jewelry, beads, crystals, tools, and equipment.

The Great Fiesta Del Barrio and Fajita Cook-off,
Flagstaff
(520) 526-3186

Held the second Saturday of June, this popular event celebrates the customs and culture of the Hispanic community. The highlight is a fajita cook-off.

Pine Country Pro Rodeo
Flagstaff
(520) 774-3446
www.pinecountryprorodeo.com

Top rodeo contenders compete. Additional events include barn dances, street dances, and a rodeo mixer where rodeo contestants have the opportunity to get to know each other and share rodeo tales.

Summer Plant Sale and Garden Fair
Flagstaff
(520) 774-1442
www.thearb.org

More than 200 uncommon varieties of plants, including hardy and hard-to-obtain natives, perennials, trees, shrubs, herbs, and vegetable starts, are offered for sale. Gardening lectures and a variety of family activities are also included. Activities will vary, and you can be assured of a day of wholesome fun for the family at this popular sale and fair

Wool Festival
Flagstaff
(520) 774-6272

Held the first weekend in June, this festival features a sheep wagon from the Arizona Historical Society Pioneer Museum; sheep, goat, and llama shearing; and live-stock and fleece judging. Food is cooked in Dutch ovens and on griddles, just like at a sheep camp. Felting, spinning, dyeing and weaving demonstrations are held all weekend.

July

New Mexico

Freedom Days
Farmington
(800) 448-1240

The Fourth of July is celebrated in grand style with a variety of special events, including fireworks, an auction, parade, and triathlon.

Northern New Mexico Street Rodders
Annual Land of Enchantment Rod Run
Farmington
(505) 326-6202

An annual event where car enthusiasts show off their classic cars and visitors drool over them.

Colorado

Annual Parade of Boats
Dolores
(800) 807-4712

A fun event, with many boats participating in this unusual parade, held at McPhee Marina. Fishing boats, houseboats, speedboats, and sailboats take part in this parade.

Montezuma County Fair
Cortez
(970) 565-1000

Exhibits, events, judging, and more at the Montezuma County Fairgrounds.

Music In the Mountains
Durango
(970) 385-6820
www.musicinthemountains.com

This three-week classical series features musicians from major symphony orchestras and other chamber music programs. The event is held under a festival tent at Purgatory Ski Resort.

Utah

Canyonlands Film and Video Festival
Moab
(435) 259-4663

This great festival began in 1995 and has become an annual event for independent film makers from around the world. The festival strives to provide high quality independent films to visitors in a friendly, small-town atmosphere. In addition to giving audiences the opportunity to view wonderful films and visit with directors and producers, the festival also gives film-makers the opportunity to work toward their professional goals.

Arizona

Coconino County Horse Races
Flagstaff
(520) 774-5130

Held each Fourth of July weekend at Fort Tuthill Downs, the event features thoroughbred and quarterhorse racing. Race distances range from 350 yards to one mile. Pari-mutuel wagering is offered.

Festival of Arts and Crafts Extraordinaire
Flagstaff
(520) 779–1227

This is a major fundraiser for Northland Hospice, and offers a variety of entertainment, food, children's activities, and arts and crafts.

Flagstaff's Fabulous 4th Festivities
Flagstaff
(800) 842–7293
www.flagstaff.az.us

This old-fashioned community parade has floats decorated using paper napkins, just like in days gone by. Expect music; animals; and important people of Flagstaff to be in the procession.

Independence Day Festival
Flagstaff
(520) 774–6272

A weekend of living history and demonstrations: crafts, cannon firings, a mountain man encampment, woodsman's skills, quilting, spinning, woodworking, candle dipping, blacksmithing, and pottery making.

August

New Mexico

Connie Mack World Series
Farmington
(800) 448–1240

Some of the best amateur baseball players from throughout the country and Puerto Rico take part in this tournament. These players are the cream of the crop of high school baseball teams. Each year, this series attracts more national and international attention, and has been spotlighted on the ESPN television network. Many major league stars have gotten their start at the Connie Mack World Series, which attracts scouts from all of the major and minor league teams.

San Juan County Fair
Farmington
(800) 448–1240

The largest county fair in New Mexico provides livestock shows, exhibits, a pa-rade, arts and crafts booths, a food midway, carnival, and free entertainment.

San Juan River Bi-Fly Tournament
Farmington
(505) 325–0255

A tournament held on the Quality Waters of the San Juan River benefits the Four Corners Home for Children.

Pie eating contest at the San Juan County Fair.
PHOTO: DOROTHY NOBIS

Colorado

Escalante Days
Dolores
(800) 807–4712

This is a celebration of the town's history and is attended by almost everyone who lives in Dolores. Great fun for the family in a wholesome atmosphere, plus a barbecue, games, and arts and crafts.

La Plata County Fair
Durango
(970) 247–4355

Livestock show and auction, barbecue dinner, dances, tractor pulls, flower and vegetable show, and lots of competition for honors in baked goods, jellies, quilting, photography, woodworking, and more.

Main Avenue Juried Arts Festival
Durango
(970) 259–2606

This art show features artists from several states, with art in every medium. Enjoy art, entertainment, and a variety of great food.

Utah

Grand County Fair
Moab
(800) 635–6622

Want to know who makes the best apple pie in the county? Want to see some of the best livestock in the Four Corners? Want to return to a world where cotton candy is one of the basic four food groups, where there are no long lines at carnival rides, and where family fun reins supreme? Then come on to the Grand County Fair, where you'll find families competing, eating, laughing, and sharing their lives during the county fair.

Arizona

Flagstaff Summer Fest
Flagstaff
(888) ART–FEST
www.888artfest.com

This three-day celebration of fine arts and crafts features 200 juried artists from across the country. More than 40 musicians from throughout the West perform on three stages, and great food is offered. A hands-on activity area for children is also provided.

September

New Mexico

Hispanic Festival
Farmington
(800) 448-1240

The Hispanic Festival is a celebration of the Hispanic culture, arts, and people who live in San Juan County. Entertainment, arts, and crafts, and the heritage of the Hispanic community will be offered.

Totah Festival
Farmington
(800) 448–1240

Totah means "the meeting place of the waters," which signifies the meeting of the Animas, the San Juan, and the La Plata rivers. The festival features Native American fine arts and crafts and a marketplace. The event includes an Indian rug auction.

Colorado

Annual Share the Trails Triathlon
Durango
(970) 385–1210

A day of non-competitive fun on public lands includes runners/walkers, mountain bikers, and horseback riders on the Colorado Trail.

Durango Songwriters Expo
Durango
(970) 382–9966

The Expo is a songwriter's showcase with workshops, listening sessions, and entertainment.

Four Corners Iron Horse Motorcycle Rally
Ignacio
(888) 284–9213
www.fourcornersrally.com

Biker bull riding, bands and entertainment, biker field events, arm wrestling contest, and tattoo row highlight this annual event, which attracts motorcycle enthusiasts from throughout the country.

Gallery Walk
Durango
(970) 247–8277

Hosted by the Durango Gallery Association, local galleries host a reception and stroll through each gallery.

Mancos Fall Festival
Mancos
(800) 873–3310

An annual event with lots of activities for the family.

Western Movie Festival
Durango
(970) 259–6145

This movie celebration highlights Western films with entertainment, a gala dinner with stars from the old Westerns, and a marketplace featuring art, crafts, and Western film nostalgia.

Utah

Moab Points and Pebbles Rock Hounding Club
Moab
(435) 259–7661

Once a month, this group gets together to discuss geology and rock hounding. Weekend field trips are scheduled regularly, and they love including visitors in their trips and discussions. If you enjoy geology and rocks, you'll find this group warm and friendly and willing to share some of the geological wonders of the Four Corners.

Arizona

Annual Bed Race
Flagstaff
(520) 523–642

The bed race includes a parade, banquet, silent auction, and racing competition. Teams from businesses and community groups push "beds" down Aspen Avenue.

Coconino County Fair
Flagstaff
(520) 774–5130

The largest county fair in northern Arizona features exhibits, livestock, entertainment, a demolition derby, and carnival.

Insiders' Tip

Fall colors in the Four Corners are extraordinary and peak in mid- to late-September. The colors remain until the first frost, which usually occurs in October.

Labor Day Arts and Crafts Festival
Flagstaff
(520) 779–6176

Family-oriented arts and crafts festival featuring a variety of local and regional artists, entertainment, and food. No alcohol is allowed.

Shoot-Out-in-the-Pines
Flagstaff
(520) 556–9573

A sports festival that features a 3-on-3 basketball tournament involving more than 100 teams of all age and skill levels. The event benefits Toys for Tots.

October

New Mexico

Renaissance Fair
Farmington
(800) 448-1240

The Renaissance Fair is a popular event that attracts more people each year. Participants dress in period costumes and enjoy games, arts, and the social aspects of the 14th–16th centeries.

Road Apple Rally
Farmington
(800) 448–1240

An annual mountain bike race and tour offers a 30-mile test of skill for beginners, veterans, and professionals. The Road Apple Rally Junior encourages youngsters' participation in the sport.

Shiprock Fair
Shiprock
(800) 448–1240

The annual Northern Navajo Nation celebration that includes a parade, a fair, a rodeo, arts and crafts, a powwow, and traditional songs and dancing.

Colorado

Durango Cowboy Gathering
Durango
(970) 259–2165

A celebration of American cowboy culture, including Western trapping exhibits, Western art show, poetry, storytelling, and a rodeo.

Indian Summer Run
Cortez
(970) 565–3414

A 5-mile run, 2-mile run/walk, and a great celebration.

Utah

Canyonlands Fat Tire Festival
Moab
(800) 375–3231

This is the end of the season event for mountain bikers from around the world. Racers, manufacturers, and journalists join enthusiastic bikers as they celebrate the sport they love. Rides are scheduled in several locations, so call for the latest information. If you love mountain biking, you'll want to attend the Fat Tire Festival.

Arizona

Flagstaff Festival of Science
Flagstaff
(800) 842–7293
www.scifest.org

The Flagstaff Festival of Science includes ten days of family-oriented learning experiences with field trips, interactive exhibits, and open houses of observatories, museums, and other scientific facilities.

Flagstaff Symphony's Elegant Affair
Flagstaff
(520) 522–0549

A silent auction to benefit the Flagstaff Symphony comes with champagne served butler-style, followed by a luncheon. A fashion show with prizes is included. Members and families of the board of directors and volunteers model the latest styles.

Halloween Tours at the Riordan State Historic Park
Flagstaff
(520) 779–4395

The staff of the Riordan State Historic Park guides visitors through the mansion with tales, folklore, and stories of Halloween. Timothy and Michael Riordan built the mansion in 1904. The beautiful 5,000 square feet house includes 40 rooms. The Riordans were the owners of Flagstaff's logging company and their wives were sisters. Reservations are necessary and children younger than ten are not encouraged to attend.

November

Colorado

Caroling Procession
Durango
(970) 247–0313

Enjoy an old-fashioned welcome from Santa Claus as he walks down historic downtown Durango while singing holiday carols and enjoying cookies at the Durango & Silverton Narrow Gauge Railroad train depot.

Arizona

Annual Holiday Lights Festival
Flagstaff
(800) 435–2493

More than 2 million lights twinkle on trees, with a lighting ceremony the Saturday following Thanksgiving. Cookies, hot cider, Santa, and entertainment offered.

Handel's *The Messiah*
Flagstaff
(520) 523–5661

Northern Arizona University's concert hall plays host to the annual performance of *The Messiah*, with student soloists, chamber orchestra, and chorus.

December

New Mexico

Christmas Parade
Farmington
(505) 325–0279

A parade of lights follows Santa Claus downtown on Main Street.

Navajo Live Nativity
Farmington
(800) 448–1240

Presented by the children at the Four Corners Home for Children, this annual living nativity scene uses Navajo costumes and live animals.

San Juan College Luminarias
Farmington
(505) 599–0214

The college hosts the largest luminaria display of a non-profit entity in New Mexico.

Colorado

Annual Parade of Lights
Cortez
(970) 565–8939

An annual kick-off to the holiday season.

Christmas in Dolores
Dolores
(800) 807–4712

The community of Dolores takes great pride in its rich Western history. Christmas in Dolores reflects that pride, and offers a simple, family-style holiday.

Luminaries at Mesa Verde National Park
Mesa Verde
(970) 529–4632

Luminarias light up the beautiful cliff dwellings and ruins at Mesa Verde.

Moonlight New Year's Eve Train
Durango
(888) 872–4607

All aboard the Durango & Silverton Narrow Gauge Railroad for a spectacular ride through the San Juan National Forest on this special night. Appetizers and entertainment offered, followed by a party at the train depot museum.

Olde Fashioned Christmas
Mancos
(800) 873–3310

Christmas celebrated like families of years ago includes sleigh rides, lots of caroling, trimming the tree with simple, homemade ornaments, and remembering what the holiday stands for.

Utah

Electric Light Parade
Moab
(435) 259–7814

Kick off the holidays with an electrifying event. The annual Electric Light Parade lights up the streets, the trucks, the floats, and the band members, including everybody and everything that enters. This is a fun and festive way to get in the holiday spirit.

Arizona

Holiday Plant Sale
Flagstaff
(520) 774–1442

Plants in decorative pots, unique gifts, and the work of local artisans.

New Mexico

Hotels and
Motels
Bed and
Breakfasts
Campgrounds
and RV Sites
Restaurants
Shopping
Trading Posts
Kidstuff
Recreation
Attractions
Arts

On January 6, 1912, New Mexico became the 47th state in the Union. The fifth largest state, following Alaska, Texas, California and Montana, New Mexico encompasses 121,599 square miles. Known as the Land of Enchantment, the state has attracted many people who have chosen to call it home. The exceptional climate, endless landscape, colorful history, and great New Mexican chile have created an environment many consider second to none.

Santa Fe is the state capital, and is the oldest government seat in the United States. Recognized for its beauty, many artists have traveled to the city to work, only to find they cannot leave. The state flower is the Yucca plant, the state bird is the roadrunner, and true to its emphasis on great cuisine, the state vegetables are the chili and frijoles (pinto beans), with the biscochito the state cookie.

In World War II, the U.S. military used Navajo "code talkers," who used their native language as a top-secret wartime code that the Japanese could never break. The code talkers are considered legends in the state, and their efforts in fighting the war have been greatly recognized in recent years.

The Four Corners area of the state includes the major communities of Farmington, Aztec, Bloomfield, Shiprock, and Gallup. Aztec is the county seat of San Juan County, a distinction that did not come without controversy. The Territorial Government appointed Aztec as the county seat in 1887. However, the citizens of Farmington, Junction City, Largo, and Mesa City protested the appointment, each community believing it should be the county seat. In 1890, an election was held to decide the controversy. Junction City received 255 votes; Aztec, 246; Farmington, 1; and Mesa City, none. In 1891, a judge ordered the city of Aztec to move county records to Junction City, where the county seat remained—but not for long.

Aztec officials declared the election illegal and took their case before a presiding judge in the district, who investigated the election process and found discrepancies and illegal activities surrounding the election. The judge ordered the county seat distinction be returned to Aztec in August of 1892. Ironically, within a year, Junction City was no longer a city, and that area eventually became part of Farmington.

In the 1900s, Aztec was an agricultural community and a canvas of color with fruit orchards and vegetable farms. By 1905, however, the Denver and Rio Grande Railroad completed construction of a railroad, and Aztec became the shipping point for sheep and cattle. Today, Aztec is a bedroom community for Farmington, but has a flourishing downtown retail area and strives to make the city a destination for tourists.

A community rich in history, the people of Aztec take great pride in their heritage and each September celebrate Founders Day with old fashioned "gun fights," a melodrama, ice cream socials, and a party in the park. Many of the buildings and homes in the community are listed in the Historic Register, and a tour of them is available. While fruit orchards no longer add color to the town, citizens and business owners work together to make sure flowers and shrubbery create an atmosphere that encourage Insiders and tourists alike to stop, smell those flowers and enjoy the quality living of small town Aztec.

Bloomfield, too, was primarily a farming community when it was established in 1877. Incorporated in 1956, the city describes itself as "The Hub of the Four Corners" because of its accessibility to most of the major attractions in the Four Corners. The town is known as the "Gas Capital of the United States" because of the large production of natural gas from the area.

Also a bedroom community to nearby Farmington, Bloomfield is home to less than 10,000 people, but offers a quality of life those residents prefer and enjoy. There is no "downtown" to Bloomfield, with the business district spread throughout the community. Residential areas are frequently interspersed with local businesses, although city officials continue to strive to create a business district that is separate from residential areas.

People in Bloomfield find living in a community where almost everybody knows your name is a pleasant and welcome change from being nameless in a larger community. As the city continues to grow, working to attract more businesses and residents, the focus remains on retaining the rural atmosphere that residents and businessmen alike have come to expect and appreciate.

Junction City lost its hope for being the county seat of San Juan County, and it eventually lost its identity as well when the town was renamed Farmingtown. In later years, the "w" was dropped and Farmington assumed a new and ever-increasing status in the Four Corners.

With three rivers converging in Farmington—the Animas, San Juan, and La Plata—the Navajos call the city "Totah," the meeting place of the waters. Incorporated in 1900, Farmington was, like its sister cities Aztec and Bloomfield, primarily a farming and ranching community. Fruit orchards dotted the area, and cattle and sheep sales helped the economy. In 1950, however, a new economy base began taking form, as oil and gas development began. The oil and gas boom brought in thousands, with Farmington increasing in size by nearly 736 percent in one short decade. Many Insiders remember the boom and eventual bust the oil fields brought to the area, but those oil and gas companies who survived and prospered remain the heart of this important Four Corners industry.

Today, oil, gas, coal, and power generating industries continue to support the local economy. Farmington has become known in recent years, however, as the retail hub of the Four Corners, attracting large national companies as well as supporting the hundreds of small, local businesses that offer personal service.

Shiprock, some 20 miles northwest of Farmington, is on the Navajo Reservation. The town is named for the Shiprock pinnacle, a large rock formation that rises up from the desert and is sacred to the Navajo people. The Navajo call Shiprock "Tse 'Bit'a'i," meaning rock with wings. Rock climbing and hiking are prohibited on the rock. The town of Shiprock has been made famous by mystery writer Tony Hillerman, who bases his Jim Chee-Joe Leaphorn novels in this Navajo community. I'll talk more about Shiprock in the Navajo Indian Reservation chapter of this book.

Gallup is located almost directly south of Shiprock and is considered the largest American Indian center in the Southwest. In 1880, when the Atchison, Topeka, and Santa Fe Railroad was moving westward, David Gallup, a paymaster, established a small company headquarter along the projected right-of-way. Rail workers began "going to Gallup" to collect their pay, and when the railroad tracks were finally laid through the area in 1881, the settlement was formally named after the paymaster.

For the first half-century of its existence, Gallup relied on coal mining for its economy. Today, the city serves as a major trading center for the some 210,000 Native Americans who live in the 17.5-million-acre Navajo Nation. Many Navajo artisans depend on businesses in Gallup to sell their works of art.

Historic Route 66 travels through Gallup, and novelties and souvenirs of the famous route are plentiful.

The history of the New Mexico fourth of the Four Corners is as rich as its heritage, and as you travel through the area, you will find many points of interest that will take you back to a time when cowboys and Indians did, indeed, ride these plains, and time was not told by the watch on your arm, but the sun in the sky.

Hotels and Motels

Price Code
The price is based on the coast of a standard room for two adults for one night.

$ . . . . $40–$60
$$ $61–75
$$$ $76–100

If you plan to base your visit to the Four Corners out of New Mexico, you'll find many fine hotels and motels anxious for you to call them "home" for your stay. Most of them are in Farmington, but you'll find comfortable places to stay in Bloomfield, Aztec, and Gallup as well.

The tourist season in northwest New Mexico begins Memorial Day and lasts through Labor Day. While there are many rooms available, be advised that the Connie Mack World Series and the San Juan County Fair attract thousands during the month of August, so make your reservations early if you plan to arrive during that time. The High School National Finals Rodeo will also be held in late July beginning in 2002, and thousands more tourists are expected, so be prepared to have a little more difficulty in obtaining rooms if you haven't made reservations well in advance. All hotels and motels are wheelchair accessible unless otherwise noted. Pets are not always welcome, so please check with the staff when you make reservations about accommodations for your pet. Room rates are noted, but dates, special discounts, and availability of rooms are adjusted regularly. Please call the numbers provided for current rate information. All major credit cards are accepted unless otherwise noted.

While major chains of hotels and motels are prominent in the area, there are smaller, locally owned places that will offer you the comforts of home with a local flair. Whichever you choose, choose well. If you have young children and need room service, be sure to ask when you call for reservations. If you have family pets that you're bringing along, ask if they, too, are welcome in the hotel or motel of your choice. And be prepared to unpack your bags and make yourself at home because the adventure of the Four Corners awaits you.

Farmington

Anasazi Inn $
903 W. Main
(505) 325–4648

This is a pleasant motel that has 60 rooms and eight suites. A restaurant, lounge, and liquor store are also on the premises. The rooms here are very nice, especially if you plan to stay in the area for several days.

Best Western Inn and Suites $$$
700 Scott Ave.
(800) 528–1234

The 192 rooms in this motel were recently remodeled. Kitchenettes are available. An indoor swimming pool, restaurant, and lounge are on the premises.

Comfort Inn Motel $$
555 Scott Ave.
(800) 228–5150

An outdoor swimming pool, 60 rooms, and 19 suites are available at the Comfort Inn, which also serves a free limited breakfast to guests.

Courtyard by Marriott $$
560 Scott Ave.
(800) 321-2211

A new motel in Farmington, the Courtyard has an outdoor swimming pool, weekly rates, 123 rooms, and two suites. Breakfast is available to guests in the in-house restaurant and lounge. The outside patio looks over the Animas River and is a lovely place to unwind after a busy day.

Holiday Inn $$
600 E. Broadway
(888) 327–9812

The Holiday Inn has an outdoor swimming pool, 149 rooms, and an excellent restaurant and lounge. A free airport shuttle is provided for guests.

Holiday Inn Express $$
2110 Bloomfield Blvd.
(800) HOLIDAY

A newer addition to the area, the Holiday Inn Express offers a free continental breakfast to guests, an indoor swimming pool, and 66 rooms.

La Quinta Inn $$
675 Scott Ave.
(800) 531–5900

The La Quinta is an established motel in Farmington and offers an outdoor swimming pool, complimentary continental breakfast to guests, and 106 rooms.

Microtel Inn and Suites $
1901 E. Broadway
(800) 823–4535

Another recent addition to motel choices, the Microtel has 54 rooms, 9 suites, kitchenettes, weekly rates, and offers a limited free breakfast to guests.

9 Inns $
5915 E. Main
(505) 326–1555

This motel offers 32 rooms and weekly rates.

Ramada Inn $$
601 E. Broadway
(800) 228–2828

The Ramada has 75 rooms, several lovely suites, weekly rates, and an outdoor swimming pool. It also has one of the best restaurants in town.

Super 8 Motel $
1601 Bloomfield Hwy.
(800) 800–8000

With 60 rooms and weekly rates, this motel also offers a free continental breakfast to guests.

Travelodge $
510 Scott Ave.
(505) 327–0242

The Travelodge has renovated its 98 rooms, and also has an outdoor swimming pool, weekly rates, and provides a free continental breakfast to guests. A restaurant is located next door and a refrigerator and microwave oven are available in some rooms.

Insiders' Tip

The largest group of Native Americans in New Mexico is the Navajo, with more than one third (about 77,000) of our country's Navajo people living here.

Bloomfield

Bloomfield Super 8 Motel $
525 W. Broadway
(505) 632–8886

The newer of two motels located in Bloomfield, the Super 8 is clean and comfortable. It offers a free continental breakfast to guests and is conveniently located to routes to all Four Corners attractions.

Bloomfield Motel $
801 W. Broadway
(505) 632-3383

A long-time establishment in Bloomfield, this motel offers daily and weekly rates, refrigerators, and microwaves.

Aztec

Enchantment Lodge $
U.S. Hwy. 550
(505) 334–6143

An American owned motel, the Enchantment Lodge has been providing lodging for tourists for many years. It offers laundry facilities, a picnic area, and morning coffee to guests. Pets are not welcome at this motel.

The Step Back Inn $$
103 W. Aztec Blvd.
(505) 334–1200

The Step Back Inn has 40 rooms, each named after one of Aztec's pioneer families who settled the community in the 1800s. Large rooms have beautiful Victorian furniture and photos of Aztec's early days. While the rooms are meant to take you back in time, they do not lack modern conveniences. Each room has a chiffonier, and behind the doors, you'll find a television. The bathrooms have hair dryers, and a beauty salon is located in the hotel for those who want a cut and shampoo. The Parlor Restaurant offers country style cooking, fresh baked breads, freshly made desserts, and always, owner Tweeti Blancett says proudly, fresh vegetables.

Gallup

Best Western Inn and Suites $$$
3009 W. U.S. Hwy. 66
(800) 528–1234

An enclosed garden and heated pool delight visitors to this motel, which has 126 rooms. A free continental breakfast is provided and a dining room is also available.

Holiday Inn $$
2915 W. U.S. Hwy. 66
(800) 432–2211

The Holiday Inn, which has 212 rooms, a pool, and a dining room, provides a complimentary hot breakfast to its guests.

The El Rancho Hotel $$
1000 E. U.S. Hwy. 66
(800) 543–6351

This historic hotel has hosted celebrities who enjoy the ambiance and service the hotel provides. It has 75 rooms, an Indian shop, a dining room, and pool. Next door to the hotel is the El Rancho Motel, which has 24 rooms.

Best Western Red Rock Inn $$
3010 E. U.S. Hwy. 66
(888) 639–7600

This motel has 77 rooms, a swimming pool, and provides a free continental breakfast to guests.

Comfort Inn West $$
3208 W. U.S. Hwy. 66
(888) 722–0982

This motel offers 51 rooms, a free continental breakfast, and a swimming pool.

Days Inn Central $
603 W. U.S. Hwy 66
Days Inn West
3201 W. U.S. Hwy 66
(800) DAYS–INN

There are 78 rooms available at the Days Inn Central and 74 rooms at the Days Inn West. Both motels offer a free continental breakfast to guests and a swimming pool. Both motels are nice places to stay and are close to area attractions.

Economy Inn $
1709 W. U.S. Hwy 66
(800) 255–3050

This motel offers 50 rooms, and an indoor sauna, spa, and heated pool.

Holiday Inn Express $$
1500 W. Maloney Ave.
(888) 570–6300

With 70 rooms, this Holiday Inn offers a free continental breakfast to guests and has a swimming pool.

Ramada Limited $
1440 W. Maloney Ave.
(800) 2–RAMADA

The Ramada has 60 rooms, a pool, a restaurant, and serves free continental breakfast each morning for the convenience of its guests.

Red Roof Inn $
3304 W. U.S. Hwy 66
(800) 633–8300

This motel has 104 rooms, and a pool. It offers breakfast, a complimentary coffee bar, data port phones, wonderful walk-in showers, and a guest laundry.

Sleep Inn $$
33820 E. U.S. Hwy 66
(800) 753–3748

Located next to a family restaurant, the Sleep Inn has 61 rooms, a pool, and offers a free continental breakfast to guests.

Bed and Breakfasts

Price Code

Prices are based on a standard room for two adults for one night.

$ . . . . $60–$75
$$ . . . . $76–$100
$$$ . . . . $101–$200

Bed and breakfasts continue to enjoy popularity in the Four Corners. If you prefer a bed and breakfast to a hotel or motel, you're sure to find one that will be just right for you. All major credit cards are accepted, unless otherwise noted. All rooms are wheelchair accessible if not otherwise stated.

The Casa Blanca Bed and Breakfast $$
505 E. La Plata St., Farmington
(800) 550–6503
www.farmingtonnm.lodging.com

The Casa Blanca Bed and Breakfast was once home to one of Farmington's distinguished families, and was built and decorated by them—Miriam and Merrill Taylor. The couple planned their dream home in the early 1940s while living and working as traders among the Navajo Indians. Casa Blanca sits on top of a bluff, which overlooks Farmington, and is surrounded by beautiful gardens and lush, green lawns. After a day of sightseeing, guests often find themselves on the patio of Casa Blanca, where they rest and recount their day. Casa Blanca has five rooms. The Sequito is upstairs and has a sun porch, a king size bed, two sofa sleepers, a tiled double bath, and a breakfast room. The Caballero has a king size bed and a tiled double bath. French doors lead to a private patio. The Chino has a patio view and a queen size bed, plus a French style day bed. The Aztec also has a queen

Kokopelli's Cave Bed and Breakfast. PHOTO: KOKOPELLI'S CAVE

size bed and a patio view. The Casita is a private two-bedroom cottage. A queen size bed with fireplace and large marble shower comprises one bedroom, while the other has a king size bed and a jetted tub big enough for two. Each room has a separate bath, entrance, and courtyard.

While the accommodations are luxurious, the atmosphere at the Casa Blanca is decidedly informal. Breakfast is served in the formal dining room and the hosts cater to your every need. Fresh fruit and chilled fruit juice begin your morning repast, which is followed by European blended coffee, a variety of fresh homemade baked goods, local jams and jellies, and an ever-changing menu of entrees, including popular Southwestern specialties. If you like, breakfast will be served to you on the patio or, for total luxury, in bed.

Casa Blanca is the consummate host, and offers tea every afternoon, complete with freshly baked goods, teas, and other beverages.

If you find it necessary to conduct business while staying at the Casa Blanca, a spacious living room, dining room, and

den/library are available to you. Staying at Casa Blanca is an experience you will enjoy so much, you may not want to leave. Personal touches and care are important to the owners of Casa Blanca and you'll be treated in the manner you so richly deserve.

Kokopelli's Cave Bed and Breakfast $$$
206 W. 38th Ave., Farmington
(505) 325–7855
www.bbonline.com

One of the most unique bed and breakfasts in the area, or even in the country, is sure to be Kokopelli's Cave. Kokopelli's Cave is the culmination of a long-held dream of Bruce and Margie Black of Farmington. Originally planned as an office for geologic consulting, Kokopelli's evolved into a guesthouse and finally into a bed and breakfast. It was excavated in 1981 into the Ojo Alamo Sandstone. Bruce and his son did almost all of the construction, except the initial blasting, cabinetwork, and carpeting. Margie and the couple's daughter decorated Kokopelli's, which is comfortable and appealing.

Kokopelli's Cave is located two miles north of Farmington. This wonderful "house in a hill" is accessed only by hiking in. While not a difficult hike, the Blacks discourage visitors who aren't up to the physical aspect of getting to the cave. All guests are required to sign a waiver of liability against potential accidents, which are possible on the cliff face if common sense and good judgment do not prevail, or cave rules are not followed. Children younger than 12 are also discouraged from staying at Kokopelli's.

The kitchen in Kokopelli's Cave is stocked with a variety of cereals and pastries, as well as milk, orange juice, and coffee—a continental breakfast. A gas barbecue grill is available for those who want to cook outside and enjoy the incredible view. Swallows, hawks, and golden eagles soar along the cliffs, and you won't want to miss any of them in their "flight pattern."

Staying at Kokopelli's Cave will definitely add to the excitement of your trip to the Four Corners. Bring your camera because you'll have a hard time convincing family and friends that you did, indeed, stay in a cave, and that it was a unique and pleasurable experience. Because of the location of Kokopelli's Cave, it is not accessible by wheelchair.

Silver River Adobe Inn Bed and Breakfast
$$
3151 W. Main St., Farmington
(800) 382–9251
wwwcyberport.com/silveradobe

The Silver River Adobe Inn Bed and Breakfast sits on a sandstone cliff where the San Juan and La Plata rivers join. It is landscaped with natural vegetation, and the cottonwood trees are home to birds that live along the river. Exposed adobes and rough sawn timbers add to the charm of this bed and breakfast, and an eclectic library provides a wonderful backdrop to the large dining room table, where conversations between guests often linger well into the evening.

Miss Gail's Inn $
300 S. Main St., Aztec
(505) 334–3452
www.southwestdirectory.com/Miss GailsInn

In Aztec, Miss Gail's Inn is a bed and breakfast housed in the first hotel built in the community by George Stone in 1907. Miss Gail's is on the state register of historic landmarks and offers country charm in a homey atmosphere. All rooms are furnished and have private baths, and several rooms have kitchenettes. A restaurant and gift shop complete this nicely appointed bed and breakfast, and you won't regret spending your time there.

Campgrounds and RV Sites

Camping, whether it is in a tent miles away from civilization or in a campground where public restrooms and showers are available, is a popular way to enjoy the natural beauty of the Four Corners. For it is under the stars, around a campfire, or roasting marshmallows with the kids that a family can reconnect and re-establish lines of communication without the interruption of television, computers, or the telephone. There is something about being in the outdoors, listening to the sounds of Mother Nature, and inhaling the wonderful aromas of pine trees and campfire cooking that unites people like nothing else.

Here, in the Four Corners, the skies are endless, unbroken by skyscrapers or the sound of jets roaring overhead. The sunsets are incredible, as are the sunrises—and you can appreciate them here, where four states connect, like no place else in the United States. It is in the Four Corners where, in the early morning light, you may awaken to find the skies above you bright with hot air balloons, drifting quietly and slowly, taking advantage of gentle winds and coloring the sky with cheerful crayon hues.

In New Mexico, national and state parks provide a multitude of campsites, and these will be covered later in the Attractions section. There are a few private RV parks in this part of the Four Corners. Plus there are acres and acres of federal land here, much of which is available to campers so you won't have difficulty finding a place to park your RV or to pitch your tent.

As you travel through northwestern New Mexico, you will find other campgrounds and campsites that may entice you to stop and stay. Take advantage of them and enjoy your visit, but only after you are certain of the safety of the grounds and the area.

Bloomfield

Bloomfield KOA Kampground
1900 E. Blanco Blvd.
(505) 632–8339

KOA campgrounds have a reputation for providing clean and affordable camping opportunities. The Bloomfield KOA Kampground is run by a couple that takes to heart the importance of treating their guests well. The grounds are lovely, punctuated by brightly colored flowers and yards of green grass, which are always appreciated in this dry, desert climate. There is an adults-only hot tub, a game room, pet park, playground, and security-gate closure. This KOA also has one of the nicest gift shops in the area, with wonderful Native American art and reasonable prices. There are 75 full hookups, priced at $20 to $25, shaded grass tent sites for $18 to $20, and Kamping Kabins for $30.

Restrooms, showers, and laundry facilities are also available.

Downs RV Park
U.S. Hwy. 64
(800) 582–6427

Halfway between Bloomfield and Farmington on U.S. Highway 64, is the Downs RV Park. A Good Sam Park, the Downs offers gravel sites, shade trees, a laundry room, playground, and clean restrooms. Be forewarned, however, that during the fall live horse racing season at nearby Sun Ray Park and Casino, this RV park can be full. There are 31 full hookups at a cost of $15 for two people. Tent spaces are $10 per site for two people, and the park offers a ten percent discount for Good Sam Park members.

Aztec

Ruins Road RV Park
312 Ruins Rd.
(505) 334–3160

On the road to Aztec Ruins National Monument, Ruins Road RV Park is a nice little park nestled in a country setting within walking distance of Aztec's historic downtown. There are 30 full hookups, which cost $15 per night. If you don't need hookups, the cost is $6 per night.

San Juan Mobile Home Park
305 N. Light Plant Rd.
(505) 334–9532

Also located in Aztec is San Juan Mobile Home Park, which offers 12 hookups for campers. The spaces include full hookups and are $15 per night. This is a pleasant campground, but is primarily a mobile home park.

Farmington

Dad's RV Park
202 E. Pinon
(888) 326–DADS

In Farmington, try Dad's RV Park. Dad's provides 15 full hookups at $15 per night,

asphalt parking, propane, security fence and gates, and security lighting. Dad's also has a wonderful miniature train that railroaders of all ages will enjoy, and a toy shop that will delight young and old kids alike.

Kirtland

Paramount RV Park
4336 U.S. Hwy. 64
(505) 598-9824

West of Farmington heading toward Shiprock is Paramount RV Park. Full hookups, cable TV hookups, pull-throughs, a security fence, and public telephones are available. Paramount offers daily rates of $15, and has special weekly and monthly rates for visitors who plan an extended stay. There is an 18-hole golf course just 1.5 miles from this campground in case you want to play a round or two while you're here.

Gallup

KOA Kampground
2925 W. U.S. Hwy. 666
(505) 863-5021

The Gallup KOA Kampground is open all year. It provides a swimming pool and is located near area restaurants. Another nice KOA campground, this park has over 90 spaces, and charges $24.95 for full hookups. Hookups without sewer are $22.95. A movie theater and playground will keep youngsters happy, and Mom and Dad can do laundry at two facilities.

Red Rock State Park
5 miles east of Gallup
(505) 722-3829

Also in Gallup is Red Rock State Park. This campground is at the base of some of the most beautiful red cliffs imaginable, and is definitely worth a look and a stay if you're in the area. Currently, this campground is primitive, only offering restrooms, but park officials say they plan improvements to the park and added attractions, especially for youngsters. There are 103 spaces and fees are $14 with hookups and $10 without.

Restaurants

Price Code

The price code is based on the cost of two dinner entrees, and does not include appetizer, desserts or alcoholic beverages.

$	less than $15
$$	$16-$25
$$$	$26-$50
$$$$	$51-$75
$$$$$	$76 and up

For many Insiders, the true value of a vacation depends on the quality of restaurants enjoyed. Many a short and long trip by Insiders is determined by the best places to eat and the time they open. I'm pretty sure most tourists share our interest in local cuisine, and I'm anxious to share our favorite spots with you. A reminder—as usual—the Insider can only list some of the best places to eat. As you travel about the Four Corners, you'll find others that you will remember for great appetizers, fine wine, entrees, or desserts. Dining in northwestern New Mexico is a culinary delight, and I encourage you to try new dishes as well as take comfort in your favorite stand-bys.

Mexican food is the fifth food group for most New Mexicans and we are finicky about how it is prepared. As you travel throughout the Four Corners, you will find places that tout New Mexican food as well as Mexican food. While this Insider has never really figured out the difference, you will enjoy both, if you like your dishes hot and spicy.

Aztec

HiWay Grill $$
401 N. Aztec Blvd.
(505) 334–6533

If you're in Aztec, make plans to stop at the HiWay Grill. This is another favorite of Insiders because of the good menu selection, and because the staff works so hard to make sure your meal is an enjoyable experience. Mexican food, great sandwiches, really good steaks, and salsa made from a family recipe are just some of the great food you can enjoy at the HiWay. The kids will enjoy this restaurant because it's done in '60s style and the HiWay staff enjoys serving up ice cream sundaes to the kids as much as they do dinner and drinks to Mom and Dad.

> **Insiders' Tip**
> Casual dress is the norm in New Mexico. Even in finer restaurants, blue jeans and cowboy boots are usually acceptable attire. New Mexicans enjoy a less hectic pace, and that casual attitude affects the way they live, the way they play, the way they dine, and, sometimes, the way they respond to schedules!

Bloomfield

Five Seasons Restaurant $$$
1100 W. Broadway
(505) 632–1196

Those who enjoy horse racing know it's the fifth season, and the Five Seasons Restaurant enjoys those who enjoy horse racing. This is a local favorite that provides great steaks and Mexican food. The atmosphere is comfortable and kids are welcome.

Roadside Restaurant $
319 S. Bloomfield Blvd.
(505) 632–9940

Locals know if you want really good Mexican food and chile, the Roadside is one of the best places to go. Recently remodeled and enlarged to accommodate its ever-increasing customer base, the Roadside caters to the family. While the Mexican food is one reason to stop here, that Southwestern favorite, chicken fried steak, is really good too. It's open for breakfast, lunch, and dinner and is worth a stop.

Farmington

Ann's Restaurant $
1003 W. Broadway
(505) 325–6065

If you need a good breakfast to get your day started, Ann's Restaurant is the place to go. Insiders know that Ann's serves up some of the very best biscuits and gravy anywhere and skimping on portions is unheard of. If you're not a big eater, you might want to consider sharing a breakfast—neither of you will go hungry.

Arches $$
1770 E. 20th St.
(505) 327–1351

Golden Dragon $$
2324 E. Main
(505) 325–5100

If you're hungry for Chinese food, Farmington has two of the best restaurants around and they're owned by the same hard working couple. The Golden Dragon and Arches have basically the same menu, which is extensive. In the more than 15 years I have has eaten at these restaurants, a bad meal has never been served. The crab Rangoon appetizers are the best ever, as are the dumplings. A full bar compliments both restaurants. The Golden Dragon and Arches also offer a lunch buffet with a great selection. Because the food is so good and the buffet is reasonably priced, expect to spend a little longer enjoying your lunch.

Bagel Conspiracy $
3030 E. Main
(505) 564–8888

If you want something a little faster, but don't want fast food, go to the Bagel Conspiracy. You'll have a tough time deciding which of the many different bagels to have, which really good cream cheese to top it with, and which flavored coffee will start you off. The Bagel Conspiracy also offers an excellent breakfast bagel, as well as bagel sandwiches. This is one of the best places to go in Farmington for bagels.

Insiders' Tip

While autumn brings the end of summer and the changing of the colors in New Mexico, it also means green chile roasting season. You will find vendors roasting green chiles wherever you go in New Mexico, and New Mexicans use green chile in their cooking much like the Italians and French use wine—in almost everything!

Chatters $$$
601 E. Broadway
(505) 325–1191

Another Insiders favorite for steaks, chicken, seafood, and almost anything else is Chatters. This is a small but lovely restaurant that offers exceptional food. The barbecued shrimp is a great way to start off your meal, but be warned that the shrimp is very spicy and is enough to serve two or maybe three hungry adults. Entrees at Chatters vary from wild game to a seafood linguini that is sinfully good. Each meal comes with warm bread to be dipped in seasoned olive oil—reason enough to dine here. Chatters also has a full service bar and a great wine selection, but this restaurant may be too much for tired youngsters.

Deli Factory $
412 W. Broadway
(505) 327-2333

If you're looking for a sandwich and a bowl of soup, the best place to go in Farmington is the Deli Factor. This little restaurant is packed at lunch time, so plan to go a little early or a little late, or expect a wait. However, the food and homemade soup is worth the 10 to 15 minutes you may have to wait for a table. The Deli Factory's soup is a meal in itself, but combined with one of its original sandwiches, it's even better.

El Charro $
737 W. Main
(505) 327-2464

El Charro is a small restaurant that is always full, especially at lunch time. There are specials offered each day, and Insiders have never gotten a bad meal there. Service can sometimes be slow, but the food is always worth the wait.

K.B. Dillons $$$
101 E. Broadway
(505) 325-0222

If you're hankerin' for a good steak or a wonderful chicken dish, K.B. Dillons in Farmington is a great place to go. Insiders love K.B.'s Chicken Louisiana, chicken covered with a wonderful seafood sauce, and the steaks here are tender and well seasoned. K.B.'s also has the best green chili chicken soup you've ever eaten, so be sure to order at least a cup. K.B. Dillons has a full bar and a comfortable atmosphere, but may not be the best place to take restless children. K.B.'s is also open for lunch and has a good lunch menu.

Señor Peppers $$
1300 W. Navajo
(505) 327–0436

In Farmington, there are several great Mexican restaurants. Señor Peppers, located at the Four Corners Regional Airport, offers really good Mexican food and has been featured in flight magazines and in national food magazines. Señor Peppers Mexican pizza is a huge tortilla topped with spicy ground beef, cheese, jalapeño peppers, and seasonings that create a wonderful dish big enough to be shared. Order a Pepper's margarita and your meal is complete.

Si Señors $
4015 E. 30th St.
(505) 324–9050

Si Señors is another Insiders' favorite. Si Señors offers not just salsa to dip tortilla chips in, but a wonderful sour cream dip that's hard to beat. The chicken enchiladas are great here, as are most of the dishes offered on the extensive menu. Beer and wine are served and the service is always good.

Something Special Bakery and Tearoom $$
116 N. Auburn
(505) 325-8183

For something special, Insiders know one of the best places to go is the Something Special Bakery and Tearoom, located in an older home. Charlene Barnes has transformed the house into a lovely little restaurant. Charlene's son, Dean, is the baker at Something Special. The pies, cakes, cookies, brownies—everything he bakes—make it worth a trip across the

> **Insiders' Tip**
>
> A Navajo taco is an open-faced taco that has lots of fresh lettuce, tomatoes, refried beans, guacamole, sour cream, and your choice of red or green chile. All that is served up on fry bread, a Native American food that closely resembles the Mexican sopaipilla.

country. Two entrees are served each day, and whatever they might be, rest assured the food is wonderful. Insiders don't just go to Something Special for the lunch; they go for the dessert. And this is probably the only restaurant Insiders go to where dessert is NOT shared—at least not halved. Everyone wants their own slice of bakery heaven, and "tastes" are shared. For those who just can't get enough of the baked goods, Dean also makes cookies, breads, and pastries you may buy to take home. Something Special also serves up a wonderful ambrosia and offers fruity iced teas as well as coffee to compliment what will be a meal you won't soon forget.

Three Rivers Eatery and Brewhouse $$
101 E. Main
(505) 324-2187

For a great lunch or dinner, try Three Rivers Eatery and Brewhouse. Three Rivers brews its own beer and has many beer selections for you to taste and enjoy. Located in downtown Farmington, Three Rivers is where everyone loves to go for lunch—the chicken Caesar's salad is wonderful. Reasonably priced, Three Rivers is a non-smoking restaurant, and its menu offers something to tempt even the most finicky diner.

Don Diego's Restaurant and Lounge   **$$**
801 W. U.S. Hwy. 66
(505) 722–5517

Don Diego's Restaurant and Lounge is another Insiders favorite. Don Diego's offers great Mexican food, and the Southwestern and American food is just as good. A full bar is available to compliment your meal.

Ranch Kitchen   **$**
3001 W. U.S. Hwy. 66
(505) 722–2537

In Gallup, Insiders like the Ranch Kitchen. This restaurant has been a favorite of Insiders for some 40 years, and its barbecue is some of the best you'll find anywhere. The rustic atmosphere of the Ranch Kitchen makes you want to linger, so take a minute to visit the two gift shops while you're there.

Shopping

You simply cannot take a vacation without doing a little shopping. Your visit to the Four Corners, unfortunately, will mean doing more than a "little." There simply are too many wonderful shops to visit and too many trading posts to explore. The shops and trading posts this book lists are just a sampling of what is available to you. You are encouraged to give in to the urge to shop and take advantage of any opportunity to discover local arts and crafts—you'll find an abundance of gifts for friends, family, and you.

Animas Valley Mall
4601 E. Main St., Farmington
(505) 326–5465

Insiders know that the Animas Valley Mall is the place to go for large department stores and one-stop shopping. The mall has about 60 stores, anchored by Sears, JC Penney, and Dillard's. Other specialty shops are also housed in the mall, as are a four-screen movie theater and several restaurants.

Added Touch
405 W. Broadway, Farmington
(505) 325–6573

Added Touch is a great place to find a gift. Baby items, collectibles, cards for every occasion, and a wonderful selection of cigars are offered at Added Touch. A party room upstairs will provide you with everything you need for birthdays, weddings, anniversaries, and special occasions.

DeNae's Ladies Apparel
3030 E. Main St., Farmington
(505) 326–6025

DeNae's is a great place for the fashion conscious to find the latest in style trends.

The shop is not a large one and is not packed so tightly with merchandise that you can't get a garment off the rack. Quality ladies wear, with an eye to the young and the trendy, is available in this fun shop, along with one of the friendliest clerks in town.

Dusty Attic
111 W. Main St., Farmington
(505) 327–7696

Farmington's downtown is enjoying a resurgence, with many antique and specialty shops thriving. The Dusty Attic has three levels of booths, offering everything from antiques to hand-crafted items. This is a wonderful place to find an inexpensive gift for someone who's difficult to buy for, and the choices will amaze you. Plan on spending at least an hour in the Dusty Attic, for it will take you at least that long just to take a peek at all it has to offer.

Farmington Downtown Association
208A W. Main St., Farmington

There are many antique stores in downtown Farmington, and all within walking distance of each other. If you're into collectibles and antiques, you'll find lots to choose from. The Downtown Association is creating an atmosphere in downtown Farmington that attracts tourists and locals alike.

MMoose
119 W. Main St., Farmington
(505) 325–7800

MMoose is nestled in downtown Farmington amongst the antique stores and arts and crafts shops, and is as unique as its neighbors. Fun fashions for men and women are offered here, although the focus is on women on the move. A wonderful array of jewelry is available, and handbags and great accessories are tucked into every nook and corner. There is a sale room in the back of the store where customers find lots of fashion for less money. The sales clerks at MMoose allow customers to browse and are helpful without hovering.

Panache
4250 E. Main St., Farmington
(505) 327–2215

Panache is a lovely little shop where the coffee's always on and cookies are always on the table. The emphasis here is on quality, detail, and careful selection of fashion. The sales staff understands the importance of honesty and if an outfit doesn't fit right or look right, the staff will tactfully suggest another style or color. You'll find the perfect earrings or necklace to accessorize your outfit, and if alterations are needed, they will be done quickly and at no or little cost. A great shop with great clothes in a great atmosphere.

Aztec Main Street Program
110 N. Ash St., Aztec
(505) 334–9551

Aztec Main Street Program continues to work with merchants to make the historic downtown area a great place to do business and to shop. There are several antique shops along Aztec's downtown stretch of Main Avenue, so take your time and see what treasures you can find. New shops and new merchandise arrive all the time in downtown and it's worth a stop to seek out new treasures.

Echoes Gifts and Antiques
103 S. Main Ave., Aztec
(505) 334–9302

Echoes carries a little bit of everything, and is a great place to spend both time and money. Teddy bears, stuffed animals, candles, Fenton glass, and other collectibles fill the shelves of this unique shop.

Kokopelli's Gift Shop
112 N. Main Ave., Aztec
(505) 334–4009
www.kokopel.com

In Aztec, downtown is the place to go for browsing and buying. Kokopelli's Gift Shop has beautiful Indian creations, as well as collectibles, t-shirts, and souvenirs. The shop sells Hopi kachinas by Hopi and Navajo artists, and pottery by Navajo and Pueblo artists. The owners limit the number of artists they work with and know each of the artists personally, allowing them to share their knowledge of the art and artists with shoppers.

Navajo Spirit Southwestern Wear
815 Coal Ave., Gallup
(800) 377–6837
www.navajospirit.com

Navajo Spirit Southwestern Wear is a unique store with home decorating items, gift items, blanket coats, moccasins, leather belts, and some of the most beautiful Southwest velvet fashions you'll find anywhere. Virginia Yazzie-Ballenger designs many of the beautiful fashions, and is often in the shop to help you with your selections.

The Rio West Mall
1300 W. I-40 Frontage, Gallup
(505) 722–7281

The Rio West Mall in Gallup provides major mall shopping, and discount stores are close by. It is downtown Gallup where you'll find unique stores carrying unique items. Shops carrying Route 66 memorabilia are everywhere and are fun places to browse.

Two Grey Hills Trading Post

There is no neon sign flashing to attract customers, and no billboards encouraging tourists to look for the treasures it holds. It's not located in a trendy shopping mall or a re-developed downtown. In fact, the directions to the Two Grey Hills Trading Post in Toadlena, New Mexico, are vague, at least to someone who has never visited this century-old establishment.

"From Shiprock," reads the directions offered on the Two Grey Hills Trading Post web site, "travel 29.7 miles south on U.S. 666 to milepost 59.3. Turn right, west, toward Toadlena, on Navajo Highway 19, which is a blacktop road. After seven miles, pass a housing project on the right. Turn left, south, through the cattle guard onto the new blacktop. After three miles, pass the chapter house and buildings on the right, see the back of the trading post at the top of the hill. Continue across the wash, through another cattle guard, to a left turn onto the old road to Newcomb, and take another left into the rutted front parking lot."

If the directions seem primitive in today's techno-based world, wait until you step through the door of the Two Grey Hills Trading Post. You won't find computer checkouts here, and you won't find cappuccino being served. What you will discover, however, are incredible rugs, woven by Navajos who live in the area, and who have learned the art of creating these world renowned rugs at the looms of their mothers, grandmothers, and great-grandmothers. The rugs are recognized by the trademark colors—grays, browns, white and black—and are woven from wool shorn from the sheep raised in this primitive area of the Four Corners.

Les Wilson is the proprietor of the Two Grey Hills Trading Post, and is proud of the simple store he owns and operates. Wilson buys some wool from the Navajos, but is careful to purchase only the highest quality, which he then sells or trades to the weavers who come to the trading post. A room adjacent to the store has wool stacked in piles, each stack offering a different shade of brown or gray, plus white and black wool. Another room, located behind the "post office," offers the finished work of the weavers, many of whom have been selling their rugs at the Two Grey Hills Trading Post for generations.

"I like to buy the finest rugs, just like everyone else does," Wilson said. He picked up a lovely rug, unfolded it to show the Two Grey Hills design, and explained, "This one was done by a young woman named Stella. She's 21 now, and I've been buying her rugs since she was about 7. She's very talented." In fact, as Wilson goes through the hundreds of rugs he offers for sale, he has stories about most of the women who have woven them. He has watched many of them improve and mature in their craft, and takes great pride in their accomplishments, just as he does of Stella.

While Wilson is not a Navajo, his wife is, and he has embraced the Navajo as his own people. "I like living with the Navajos and I love my trading post life," Wilson said. "The Navajos have gotten to know me and know I'm going to treat them right." When asked if he'd mastered the Navajo language, which can be difficult to learn, Wilson laughed and shook his head. "I'm pretty fluent in "store Navajo," he said, "but that's about it."

Being miles away from town, Wilson said he enjoys the slower pace and lifestyle he has at the trading post. He and his wife live in a mobile home located just steps away from the back door of the store. "I'd rather live here than in Farmington," Wilson admitted. "It's quieter, although not always quiet. Any kind of violence or trouble can erupt here, and if you call the police, it will be at least 45 minutes before they get here."

Trouble isn't a constant visitor at the trading post, however, and the Navajos who trade there don't use their Visa's or MasterCard's to purchase the goods they need. "I still extend credit, but mostly to the elderly people who pay when their social security checks come. A few weavers have credit against their rugs, and some of those rugs are worth thousands of dollars," Wilson said. He remembers a time, however, when he had more than 200 credit accounts, which would be paid when the Navajos brought in rugs, livestock or other arts and crafts to settle up their bill.

"Many trading posts are closing because people now shop off the reservation," Wilson said sadly.

Leo Wilson at the Two Grey Hills Trading Post.
PHOTO: DOROTHY NOBIS

The Two Grey Hills Trading Post is listed on the New Mexico State Register of Cultural Properties. With the beautiful rugs Wilson offers to tourists and collectors, he admits he enjoys the "other side" of the trading post as well. The store, which looks as if it were created for a Hollywood movie, offers a look back to a time when the pot-bellied stove was the focal point of a store, and when penny candy still cost a penny. This isn't a store where you'll find Starbucks coffee all ground and packaged to take home, or where you'll find every flavor of Ben and Jerry's or even several flavors of Blue Bunny ice cream. You'll find the potato chips and snacks favored by the Navajo people, fresh mutton for mutton stew, and disposable diapers. But you'll also find jewelry created by talented Navajo artists, mud toys, and wedding baskets. You'll find a post office, where mail can be picked up or mailed off, and you'll find an owner who appreciates his customers, their culture, and their talents, and who proudly calls them his friends.

The hundred-year-old structure has changed little over the years, and continues to offer some of life's basic necessities to people who live a life in tune with nature and each other. While the pickup trucks that park outside may be newer, and movie videos are now rented inside, the Two Grey Hills Trading Post remains a reminder of days when a trip to town was a cause for celebration and paved parking lots were only found "uptown."

Les Wilson leaned against the counter in the post office section of the trading post, greeted several customers when they entered the store, and looked around his piece of history with some wistfulness. "There aren't many of us left," he said of trading posts. "We do the best we can to run a small store, but nationwide, small stores are becoming a thing of the past. Here, we're just a little neighborhood store that's been open for more than one hundred years. I just hope I can extend that a little while longer."

Yazzie's Indian Art
236 W. U.S. Hwy. 66, Gallup
(No phone number available)

Yazzie's carries the most exquisite gold and silver, contemporary inlaid jewelry you've ever seen. In addition, Colina Yazzie is a Navajo weaving instructor and gives lessons and offers instruction on how to care for your woven purchases.

Trading Posts

A trip to the Four Corners isn't complete without visiting some of the many trading posts in the area. The New Mexico part of the Four Corners offers many top-notch trading posts, some of which are highlighted here. But again, there are countless other reputable trading posts in the area that offer great art that will forever remind you of your trip to the Indian reservations.

As you travel throughout northwestern New Mexico, you'll find other trading posts, and you're encouraged to stop and browse. Every trading post has its own personality and those personalities, like the people they represent, are unique and wonderful in their own right.

The Fifth Generation Trading Post
232 W. Broadway, Farmington
(505) 326–3211

The Fifth Generation Trading Post is well named. Five generations of the Tanner Family have been trading since 1875. Handmade Navajo rugs, alabaster sculptures, drums, kachinas, pottery, jewelry, and Navajo sand paintings are just some of the arts and crafts Fifth Generation Trading Post has to offer.

The Hogback Trading Co.
3221 U.S. Hwy. 64, Hogback
(505) 598–5154

The Hogback Trading Co., located just west of Farmington, was established in 1871 by Joseph Wheeler. The trading post quickly became an institution in the daily lives of the Navajo people of the area. Tom Wheeler, Joseph's great-grandson, continues the family tradition of encouraging Native American sculptors and artists by purchasing alabaster art. Hogback Trading Co. is the principle alabaster sculpture dealer in the West, and its upstairs gallery and personal collection show a wide range of young and mature Navajo artistisans. In addition, Hogback has traded in silver jewelry since 1871, buying, selling, and providing pawn services to the Navajo.

For more than 125 years, the Hogback Trading Co. has maintained a reputation for its extensive inventory of Navajo rugs. The shop has 10,000 square feet of Indian art and is definitely worth a stop.

Ellis Tanner Trading Co.
1980 NM Hwy. 602, Gallup
(800) 469–4434

Ellis Tanner Trading Co. is a fourth generation trading post. It offers original Native American art and jewelry, and fea-

Insiders' Tip

Native Americans in New Mexico often sell their arts and crafts to area pawn shops and trading posts. Many collectors and smart shoppers make visiting trading posts and pawn shops a priority. The beautiful jewelry, rugs, weavings, sand paintings, and other Native American art available is often priced at much less than in art galleries or tourist attractions.

tures a large selection of unclaimed pawn jewelry and paintings by award-winning Native American artists. The Tanner family is highly respected by the Native Americans and the company's customer base has grown from about 250 its first year in 1967 to the tens of thousands of customers throughout the world today.

Shush Yaz Trading Co.
1304 W. Lincoln, Gallup
(505) 722–0130
Shush Yaz Trading Co. is owned by Don Tanner, one of the fourth generation of Tanners to own a trading company in the Southwest. Shush Yaz features a general

store where you can buy locally made Navajo rugs, Navajo squaw skirts, Indian jewelry, and Native American arts and crafts.

Tobe Turpen's Trading Post
1710 S. Second St., Gallup
(800) 545–7958
www.tobeturpens.com
Tobe Turpen's Trading Post has been trading for more than 80 years. With more than 11,000 square feet of space, Turpen's offers jewelry, rugs, kachinas, baskets, buffalo hides, feathers, beading supplies, and one of the largest displays of Indian crafts in the area.

Kidstuff

Northwestern New Mexico puts an emphasis on the family, and as such, communities work hard to provide activities for their youngsters. Because life moves a little slower here than in large metropolitan areas, there are more opportunities to spend time with the kids. There are plenty of quality events and activities for them to enjoy.

For many youngsters, just having the opportunity to be with family, be in the outdoors, and enjoy the more simple pleasures of a vacation is fun itself. Sitting around a campfire, roasting marshmallows and hot dogs, listening to the sounds of coyotes as they communicate during the dark of night, and discovering new places can provide memories your children will share with their children and grandchildren. Check out the Camping and RV Sites section for more information about camping with your children. Wherever you go in the Four Corners, you'll find Insiders who are more than happy to give you tips on where to take the kids and which events, attractions, and retailers are kid-friendly. Don't be afraid to ask the friendly waitress in the restaurant or the helpful host at the motel.

Playgrounds and tennis courts can be found throughout the city of Farmington. Call the city's recreation center at (505) 722-2619 for information.

Aquatic Center
1151 N. Sullivan, Farmington
(505) 599–1167
The weather here is mild, and water and water sports play an important part of most family's entertainment. The city of Farmington, recognizing the need for a swimming pool for kids of all ages, built an aquatic center in the mid-1990s. A beautiful facility, the Aquatic Center provides recreational and lap swimming throughout the year. Lap swimming and open swim sessions are available several times during the day. A 150-foot waterslide and playground located in the leisure pool area

is a favorite of youngsters, and squeals of delight and shouts of glee provide background "music" as kids splash and swim. Kids ages 3 to 12 can swim in the 50-meter pool for $1.75, the slide/leisure area (which includes a playground) for $3, or both for just $3.25. Youngsters ages 13 to 18 will pay $2 for the 50-meter pool, $3 for the pool and slide/leisure area, and $4.50 for both. Adults can splash and play with the kids for $2.50 for the 50-meter pool, $3 for the slide/leisure area, or $5 for both. Red Cross swimming lessons are provided throughout the year, and special classes are offered for infants and their parents, as well as for adult "kids." The Aquatic Center can accommodate private parties on some evenings from 7:30 to 9:30 P.M.

Brookside Pool
1901 N. Dustin, Farmington
(505) 599–1188

The Aquatic Center isn't the only pool available to youngsters, however. The Brookside Pool is an outdoor pool open from June through August. This pool is located in Brookside Park, one of the loveliest parks in the area. Playground equipment and a skateboard area are also provided in this park. Adults will enjoy the beauty while the kids expend youthful energy and have a wonderful time. Admission to this pool is $1 for kids 12 and under, $1.50 for those 13 and older.

Neighborhood Center Pool
400 W. Princeton, Gallup
(505) 722–2619

The Neighborhood Center Pool offers outdoor water fun from June through August. The pool is open from 8 A.M. to 9 P.M. during the week, and from 9 A.M. to 5 P.M. on weekends. Lap swimming is offered during the morning hours. Admission is $1 for youngsters, $2 for adults, and $1 for senior citizens.

Harold Runnels Pool
707 E. Wilson, Gallup
(505) 722–2619

Harold Runnels is an indoor facility with an Olympic-sized pool, a therapy pool, weight room, diving tank, and a steam room. The pool is open year-round from 5 A.M. to 9 P.M. during the week, and from 9 A.M. to 5 P.M. on weekends. Admission is $1 for youngsters, $2 for adults, and $1 for senior citizens.

E3 Children's Museum and Science Center
302 N. Orchard, Farmington
(505) 599–1425

Farmington's E3 Children's Museum and Science Center is a wonderful place to stimulate a child's imagination while having a great time. Special educational programs are offered regularly at the museum. Staff members are as enthusiastic about working with children as the children are about learning and enjoying the company of other kids. Youngsters enjoy string games and fun with bubbles, as well as other fun programs. In addition, Stuffee, an anatomically correct doll, allows youngsters to remove its organs to see what they look like and what job they perform in the human body. The museum is open from 12 P.M. to 5 P.M. Wednesday through Friday, and from 10 A.M. to 5 P.M. on Saturday. Admission is free and the kids are sure to love this museum.

Exhibit Barn of Harvest Grove Farm and Orchards
Animas Park, Browning Expressway, Farmington
(505) 599–1422

The Exhibit Barn of Harvest Grove Farm and Orchards is located in Animas Park. Displayed are a variety of antique tractors and early agriculture equipment. This can be especially fun for youngsters who don't have the opportunity to watch fields being plowed or worked for fruits and vegetables. Located near Harvest Grove's Exhibit Barn is the Riverside Nature Center, where youngsters may observe birds and animals from big windows that overlook areas where food and water attract wildlife. Special programs for children are held throughout the year. Hours vary by season and events, so call for information.

San Juan College Planetarium
4601 College Blvd., Farmington
(505) 326–3311
www.sjc.cc.nm.us

San Juan College has a wonderful planetarium that kids of all ages are sure to enjoy. The shows are family-oriented, with most shows held at 7 P.M. on Friday nights. A 24-foot diameter dome highlights the planetarium and children especially enjoy the night sky shows, which include wonderful sound effects. There's no admission charged, and the planetarium is open only during show times. Special events are held regularly, but you should call for more information.

Family Funland
200 Scott Ave., Farmington
(505) 324–0940

While not Six Flags or Disneyland, the Family Funland in Farmington offers carnival rides and go-karts for kids to enjoy at rates that will fit comfortably in your vacation budget. Youngsters, young and old, will enjoy miniature golf, bumper cars, rollercoasters, a roll-o-plane, and the Octopus. Funland is open from 1 P.M. to 10 P.M. May through September, with limited hours in the fall and winter months.

Bowlero Lanes
3704 E. Main, Farmington
(505) 325–1857

Bowlero Lanes gives the kids an opportunity to strike or spare, with Mom and Dad joining in on the fun or simply watching. Youngsters will especially like bowling on the bumper lanes, where balls never go in the gutter, allowing them to hit more pins. Starting at 9 P.M. on Saturdays, Bowlero offers Cosmic Bowl, where the house lights are dimmed, black lights come on, and everything glows in the dark. A jukebox adds a little atmosphere and young people really enjoy it. Some video games are available, as is a pool table. Shoe rental is $1.50, and lanes may be rented for $1.75 during the week and $2.50 on weekends. A snack bar helps fill hungry tummies and a full-service bar is available for adults. Call Bowlero for lane availability.

Civitan Golf Course
2201 N. Dustin, Farmington
(505) 599–1194

Civitan Golf Course is a three-par, nine-hole golf course that's situated in the heart of Farminton. It is a city facility, and is popular with young golfers, inexperienced golfers, and those who just want to brush up on their game. Families are often found here, enjoying the beautiful course. Civitan park is adjacent to the course, which encourages family participation.

Pinon Hills Golf Course
2101 Sunrise Pkwy., Farmington
(505) 326–6066

Youngsters hoping to be the next Tiger Woods will love Pinon Hills Golf Course, rated one of the best public golf courses in the nation by *Golf Digest*. This beautiful and popular course is sure to challenge and delight kids of all ages. For more information on this golf course, check out the Recreation section.

Skateway USA
2101 Bloomfield Hwy., Farmington
(505) 327–7756

Rollerskating has enjoyed a comeback amongst youngsters and Skateway USA has a nice rink for kids to enjoy. Special events are scheduled regularly at Skateway USA, so call for information. Many youngsters enjoy their birthday parties at the rink, which makes the moms happy. Parties are just $3 per person, and include a hot dog and drink for each child. Sundays are Family Day at the rink, and a family of four can spend just $10 to skate, as long as Mom or Dad stay too. Admission varies, but includes skate rentals. Rollerblades may be rented for just $2. Hours are seasonal, with longer hours during the summer and school breaks, so call for information.

Recreation

The incredible scenery of the Four Corners lends itself to outdoor recreation, and Insiders take advantage of it. Hiking, biking, fishing, and water sports are counted as hobbies for most Insiders, and the mild climate allows us to enjoy the outdoors almost all year long.

Mountain Biking

Insiders always encourage each other and visiting bikers to wear the appropriate safety equipment, take along plenty of water, and to respect the land. It's also interesting to note that there are more unpaved roads in San Juan County than there are paved roads in the entire state of New Mexico. Remember to wear a helmet at all times.

Lions Wilderness Park
5800 College Blvd., Farmington
(505) 599–1197

Lions Wilderness Park, located on the northeast side of Farmington, offers ever-increasing challenges to the mountain biker. The Road Apple Rally, the oldest continuously run mountain bike race in the world, is held each spring and attracts professional as well as amateur bikers. Several divisions allow novices to compete against each other while giving professional bikers the opportunity to challenge each other on the course. There is even a division for those who bike only for the fun of it.

The Rally course goes through the Glade area of Farmington. The Glade is a pretty area, but it is easy to become disoriented. Watching for landmarks will help keep you from getting lost. There is no water available in the Glade, either, so make sure you take enough for your ride, especially if you're biking during the warm summer months.

Pinon Mesa Trails
3 miles north of Main St. on
NM Hwy. 170, Farmington
(800) 448–1240

There is another challenging trail network, Pinon Mesa Trails, north of Farmington on the La Plata Highway. As with any course, before you attempt it, contact one of the bike shops in the area for advice and additional information. You may call Cottonwood Cycles at (505) 326-0429; Havens Bikes and Boards at (505) 327-1727; or the Bicycle Express in Aztec at (505) 334-4354.

Hiking

The city regularly adds parks as neighborhoods develop. The city of Farmington is noted for its emphasis on the family, and parks are always a priority in city development and planning.

Walkers will find equally pleasant paths in almost every park in San Juan County and in Gallup. Hikers will find paths of differing challenges in the foothills, and state and national parks.

Angel Peak Recreational Area
20 miles south of Bloomfield via
NM Hwy. 44
(505) 599–8900

Insiders love to hike and walk the many trails of the Four Corners. From primitive trails in the Angel Peak area to the beautifully maintained trails along the river corridor, you'll find a path that challenges your skills as well as satisfies your appetite for outdoor activities.

River Corridor
Two locations: Off Browning Pkwy. south
of the Animas River and Scott Ave. and
San Juan Blvd., Farmington
(505) 599–1400

The city of Farmington has created a river corridor that attracts many to the pleasant paths that weave around the Animas River. There are benches to rest upon, water fountains aplenty, and restrooms strategically placed. Many senior citizens choose the River Corridor for their daily exercise, joining speed walkers and others who stroll the corridor with babies in carriages and toddlers in tow. There are more than 5 miles of interconnecting walking paths. Two pedestrian bridges cross at several observation areas offering wonderful opportunities to view the river's wildlife. The area also is a haven for bird watchers.

Brookside Park
Dustin Ave. and 20th St., Farmington
(505) 599–1197

Brookside Park is a pretty and popular place for field trips, company and family picnics, and warm weather enjoyment. A swimming pool, picnic tables, basketball court, skateboard bowl (increasingly popular with area skateboarders), play-grounds, and restrooms make Brookside a great place to spend a few hours.

Citivan Park
Between Dustin Ave. and Butler Ave., north of 20th St., Farmington
(505) 599–1197

Civitan Park is also home to the 9-hole golf course, Civitan Golf Course, and offers picnic tables, a playground, shelter, and restrooms. This is a popular neighborhood park, and you'll find youngsters playing with their dogs, senior citizens enjoying the weather and the neighbors, and golfers enjoying a quiet moment before heading home or to the links.

Golf

No matter where you play golf in northwestern New Mexico, you'll find courses that will challenge you and offer a pleasant golfing experience.

Pinon Hills Golf Course
2101 Sunrise Pkwy., Farmington
(505) 326–6066
www.farmington.nm.us

If golf is your game, your visit to the Four Corners will no doubt include a visit to popular Pinon Hills Golf Course in Farmington. A public municipal golf course, Pinon Hills was first opened in 1989 and was almost immediately recognized by popular golf magazines as a premier course. *Golf Digest* rated it the number one course in New Mexico for six years. Golfers from throughout the country proclaim Pinon Hills as challenging, beautiful, and a best golf bargain. There is a pro shop, snack bar, and driving range available, and the course is open year-round, weather permitting. Green fees are $20 during the week for 18 holes and $25 on the weekends. Carts are available at a rental cost of $16 for 18 holes.

Civitan Golf Course
2201 N. Dustin Ave., Farmington
(505) 599–1194

Civitan Golf Course is a par 3 course and is located in the heart of Farmington. A municipal course, it offers nine holes and provides a great opportunity to practice and improve your game. No tee times are taken, so you may drop in any time and play this carefully groomed course. Green fees for this course are $3 for nine holes. Rental carts are not available, but pull carts may be rented for just $2.

Riverview Golf Course
69 Rd. 6500, Kirtland
(505) 598–0140

Riverview Golf Course was funded through monies from the Central Consolidated School District in Kirtland and San Juan College in Farmington. The course offers one of the largest driving ranges in the Southwest, and a state of the art golf academy for youngsters interested in the sport. Its 18 holes are challenging and the course is well kept and manicured with pride. Green fees are $13 during the week and $14 on the weekends. Rental carts are available.

Hidden Valley Golf Course
29 Rd. 3025, Aztec
(505) 334–3248

This 9-hole course has recently been completely re-developed, with a new clubhouse, a more challenging course, and additional upgrades. Green fees are from $10 to $15.

Gallup Municipal Golf Course
1109 Susan St., Gallup
(505) 863–9224

The city of Gallup is in the process of reconstructing many of the tee boxes on this 18-hole course, making it more challenging and beautiful for golfers. A pro shop is available, and green fees are $10 on weekdays and $14 on weekends. Rental carts are available for $8 per person for 18 holes.

Fishing

When you talk fishing, you're talking the language of the Four Corners. There is no better fishing than in this part of the country and Insiders and tourists alike will attest to that. Fishing licenses in New Mexico are $6 for five days for residents and $16 for non-residents; a one-day license is $8 for residents and non-residents. For youngsters ages 12, 13, and 14, a five-day license is $5 for residents and $18.50 for non-residents. Youngsters younger than 12 don't need a license to fish.

Because there are so many avid anglers in the Four Corners, if you ask any Insider, you're apt to discover a favorite fishing hole not mentioned here. The Quality Waters has attracted people from throughout the world. They love the area and the fishing. Be prepared for lots of company when you fish those waters, and you'll find companionship almost anywhere you choose to wet a line.

San Juan River
30 miles east of Farmington
(505) 632–1770

The tree and brush lined San Juan River has invited countless footsteps of anglers who walk the banks and wade into the river to wet their favorite fly or lure. The river was created by the construction of Navajo Dam in 1962. The average temperature of the water is between 25 and 42 degrees—that consistent temperature and the high mineral content of the water provide a basic food chain that feeds an incredible trout population.

Beginning at the base of Navajo Dam and continuing for 3.75 miles downstream, an area has been designated as "Quality Waters," which is specially regulated. The first 0.25 mile below the dam is "catch-and-release" fishing. In the next 3.5 miles, trout measuring 20 inches or more may be kept, but only one fish per day per person. In the Quality Waters, only lures or flies with single barbless hooks may be used.

Below the Quality Waters, the normal limit of fish may be kept. Rainbow trout dominate the upper three miles of the river, with brown trout appearing in greater numbers downstream, along with a smaller number of Snake River trout.

There are several guide services, that will take you to the best fishing holes and help you master the Quality Waters. Some of them include Born 'n Raised on the San Juan River, Inc., (505) 623-2194; Four Corners Guide Service, (800) 669-3566; Rainbow Lodge Guide Service, (888) 328-1858; San Juan Troutfitters, (505) 324-8149; and Mountain States Guide Service, (505) 327-6004. Other guide services are available—call the Navajo Lake State Park's office at (505) 632-2278.

Navajo Lake
45 miles northeast of Farmington on U.S.
Hwy. 550
(505) 632–2278

For bass anglers, or those who hanker to hook a crappie, bluegill, Kokanee salmon, pike or catfish, in addition to those great trout, Navajo Lake offers all that and more. The lake is one of the largest in New Mexico and extends into southern Colorado. Snagging for salmon is a popular sport during the late summer. One word of warning—Navajo Lake is also a popular spot for water sport enthusiasts. Therefore anglers share the water with jet skis, water skiers, party boats, and recreational boaters. Summer months, especially afternoons on the weekends, find the dock crowded with boats and jet skis anxious to get in the water to enjoy the sunshine and the lake.

Morgan Lake
15 miles west of Farmington on
U.S. Hwy. 64
(520) 871-6451
Offers good fishing. An adjacent power plant keeps the water of Morgan Lake warm, making it a popular fishing spot during the cooler winter months. Bass, crappie, and catfish abound in these waters. A special permit is required to fish all lakes on Native American land. Fishing permits range from $5 to $15 per day; less for junior anglers. While no swimming is allowed in the lake, it is known for fantastic windsurfing. The water remains a warm 75 degrees year-round.

Jackson Lake State Waterfowl Area
5 miles northwest of Farmington on U.S.
Hwy. 170
(505) 841-8881
Eight hundred forty acres of land and lake along the La Plata River, offers year-round trout fishing.

Attractions

If you're looking for reasons to visit the Four Corners, you're going to find a multitude of them. Insiders are proud of the things we have to offer visitors and we're equally pleased to show them off. For it is here where you can learn the history of the nation's earliest Native Americans, enjoy traditional events all but lost in today's focus on the latest technology, and realize that the 60 minutes in the hour can be savored like great chocolate and enjoyed like fine wine.

As you go through the list of attractions in northwest New Mexico, keep in mind that some of the special events are held at the same time each year, and you might want to plan your trip to the Four Corners around that schedule. Most of the wonderful things we have to offer here can be enjoyed year-round, so pick your favorite events, make your travel plans, and get ready for the time of your life.

Again, these are just some of the attractions Insiders think you should include in your visit to the New Mexico portion of the Four Corners. You're sure to find more, which will add to your scrapbook of your trip.

Indian Ruins

One of the most popular attractions in the Four Corners is the multitude of Indian ruins, which depict a life thousands of years ago.

Chaco Culture National Historic Park
54 miles south of Bloomfield on
NM Hwy. 544
(505) 786–7014

The distinctive architecture of Chaco Canyon attracts thousands of tourists each year. Monumental public buildings, straight roads, and ceremonial kivas highlight the unique Indian ruins. Pueblo Bonito is the most magnificent of the buildings, which towered four stories tall and contained more than 600 rooms. Because of the remoteness of Chaco, the recommended access route is from the north, via U.S. Highway 550. Turn off the highway at County Road 7900, three miles southeast of Nageezi and about 50 minutes west of Cuba. The route includes five miles of paved road and 16 miles of dirt road. The roads are generally maintained, but rain and snow can make them impassable, so please call ahead for road conditions before you begin your trip back to the area.

As stated in the Four Corners Attractions chapter, there are no services available at Chaco—no food, gas, lodging or auto repair—so plan ahead. Bring a picnic lunch and plenty of water, and make sure your gas tank is full. The six major Cha-

home and outbuildings remain standing near the ruin. San Juan County purchased the 22-acre tract containing Salmon's homestead and the ruins in 1969, and in 1970, Salmon Ruins was named to the National Register of Historic Places and the New Mexico State Register.

The archaeological digs at this site continue to unearth scientific samples and artifacts, with archaeologists and students from around the country arriving at the site regularly to continue the search for more information about these early people. Aside from the park's demonstrations, tours, and special children's activities, the Salmon Ruins gift shop is especially intriguing. More information about the Salmon Ruins can be found in the Four Corners Attractions chapter.

coan cultural sites consist mainly of ceremonial rooms and smaller living quarters. These sites are accessed via a nine-mile paved loop. You can see the ruins from the road in your car, but park and walk the short, self-guided trails to the sites to really experience this incredible site. It's best to plan to spend 45 minutes to an hour at each site. Allow enough time because all trails and Chacoan cultural sites are closed from sunset to sunrise.

For more information on the Chaco Culture National Historic Park, check out the Four Corners Attractions chapter.

Salmon Ruins and Heritage Park
6131 U.S. Hwy. 64, Bloomfield
(505) 632–2013
www.more2it.com/salmon

Salmon Ruins and Heritage Park is located just outside of Bloomfield. Its inhabitants descend from or had close ties to the people of Chaco Canyon and those of the Mesa Verde area.

George Salmon homesteaded the property in the late 1800s. Salmon was a farmer and recognized the value of the ruins, which fostered his great care and concern for the area. His family protected the ruin from vandals and treasure seekers for more than 90 years, and the family

Aztec Ruins National Monument
Ruins Rd., Aztec
(505) 334–6174
www.nps.gov/azru/

Aztec Ruins National Monument located on Ruins Road, about 0.75 mile north of New Mexico Highway 516 and just outside of Aztec, features awe-inspiring dwellings that beg the question, "How did they do that?" The visitor center offers exhibits and a 25-minute video, *"Hisatsinom—The Ancient Ones,"* to help answer that question. You may also purchase books, postcards, slides, posters, and videos of the ruins.

A 0.25-mile self-guided trail winds through the West Ruin. Park rangers help guide you through the tour. Rangers are nice, knowledgeable people who will answer your questions and who take great pride in these ruins.

It will take you about 1.5 hours to see the exhibits and the video, and to walk the paved trail. The monument is open from 8 A.M. to 6 P.M. Memorial Day through Labor Day, and from 8 A.M. to 5 P.M. the rest of the year. It is closed Thanksgiving, Christmas Day and New Year's Day.

For more information on the Aztec Ruins, see the Four Corners Attractions chapter.

Zuni Pueblo
34 miles south of Gallup off NM Hwy. 53
(505) 782–4481

Zuni Pueblo, 38 miles south of Gallup on New Mexico Highway 602, is said to be the largest inhabited pueblo in the United States. It was built upon the ruins of the ancient site of Halona, one of the fabled "Seven Cities of Gold." Our Lady of Guadalupe Mission, located near the center of the pueblo, was originally constructed in the early 1600s and was rebuilt in 1968.

Zuni remains home to approximately 8,000 people. They dwell in regular homes, but still use the ancient dwellings for ceremonial purposes. The income of the native people is derived from farming and sheep and cattle ranching. Many of the artists of the Zuni work in their homes, creating the beautiful Zuni silver work that is inlaid with turquoise, shell, and coral.

Visitors are not allowed to take pictures of the Zuni without a permit, which may be obtained at the Zuni Tribal Headquarters, located on the main street of the pueblo. Visitors will also enjoy spending time in the shops along main street and the great food offered in the pueblo's restaurants.

State Parks

Navajo Lake State Park
1448 NM Hwy. 511 #1, Navajo Dam
(505) 632–8645
www.navajolake.com

Navajo Lake State Park is located on the San Juan River, 40 miles east of Farmington, and includes three separate recreation areas. Pine River, the most developed area along the lake, includes a visitor center with interpretive exhibits. Sims Mesa is across the lake, accessible by New Mexico Highway 527.

Insiders know that Navajo Lake is a true treasure of the Four Corners. Anglers and water sport enthusiasts crowd the lake and the park during the summer months, and those willing to brave the chill enjoy the area almost all year long. It is a home away from home for Insiders as well as tourists, who enjoy the pleasant camping and picnic areas as well as the lake.

Navajo Lake is fed by melting snow pack from the surrounding mountains and hills. When filled, it covers 15,610 acres. Boaters will find marinas, docks, and launching ramps at the Pine River and Sims Mesa areas. Those who plan to camp along the lake may do so anywhere along the New Mexico side. Colorado allows camping in designated areas only. For those who want to boat to a camping site, there are many great spots not far from the marina. Firewood is plentiful and campfires are permitted, unless a fire danger exists. Check with a park ranger before heading out.

Those who choose to camp in the campgrounds at the park won't be disappointed either. The staff works diligently to provide clean camping spots and you won't find friendlier or more courteous people anywhere. The more developed sites include shaded areas and picnic spots, and electricity and water sites are available. For those who want to rough it, undeveloped campsites are also available and are equally clean and nice.

The Pine River area has a marina with a store that offers fishing equipment and tackle, grocery items, liquor, and general merchandise. Rental boats and gasoline are also available. Houseboats are available for rent, but the demand is high, so make your reservation early. Fishing boats, pontoon boats, ski boats, and personal watercraft are also available for rent. The marina also provides boat slips, both for long-term use and for short stays. Call (505) 632-5345 for information.

Whether you plan to take advantage of the lake or simply camp and enjoy short hikes and beautiful scenery, your visit to Navajo Lake State Park is sure to be a highlight of your trip to the Four Corners. While Insiders would like to keep the park a local secret for their own use, its popularity increases each year, with more and more people discovering this great spot.

Red Rock State Park
P.O. Box 328, Church Rock
(505) 722-3839

Red Rock State Park is located 4.5 miles east of Gallup via I-40 and New Mexico Highway 566. Incredible red rock cliffs frame this park, and a short hike into any of the canyons surrounding the park will offer spectacular sandstone bluffs. The park is the setting for many events, including the Inter-Tribal Indian Ceremonial held in June and the Red Rock Balloon Rally held annually the first weekend in December. The park has campsites and a visitor center and is a beautiful place to visit. Include it in your tour of the Four Corners.

New Mexico Specialties

Downtown Gallup in itself is another attraction you won't want to miss. The 12-block downtown area has turn-of-the-century architecture as well as trading posts and galleries.

El Morrow Theater
207 W. Coal, Gallup
(505) 863-4131

You'll want to check out the El Morro Theater, which is one of the finest examples of decorative Spanish Colonial Revival style. The new Gallup Cultural Center, located in the restored historic railroad station on Route 66, should also be included in your tour of downtown. A project of the Southwest Indian Foundation, the center includes the Ceremonial Gallery, the Storyteller Museum, a visitor center, and the Kiva Cinema. You'll also want to visit the Museum Shop and the El Navajo Café, where organic espresso drinks, homemade sandwiches, soups, and breakfast burritos are served up with flair.

El Malpais National Monument and
Conservation Area
P.O. Box 939, Grants
(505) 285-4641

The El Malpais National Monument and Conservation Area, located northeast of Gallup on New Mexico Highway 53, has lava beds, cones, and caves. The 376,000-acre preserve resembles a moon landscape and the kids are sure to love it. La Ventana (The Window) formation is one of the Southwest's largest freestanding natural arches. This park is primitive, so bring lots of water and supplies.

El Morro National Monument
NM Hwy. 53 south of Gallup
(505) 783-4226

South of Gallup on New Mexico Highway 53, you'll find El Morro National Monument, another attraction you'll want to see. The 200-foot-high Inscription Rock is the most remarkable feature of the park. Don Juan de Onate, the first Spanish colonial governor of New Mexico, made his mark on the rock in 1605. Walking trails and a campground are available.

Ice Cave and Bandera Volcano
12000 Ice Caves Rd., Grants
(888) ICE-CAVE

Between El Malpais and El Morro, you'll discover Ice Cave and Bandera Volcano. "The Land of Fire and Ice" features lava trails leading to Bandera Volcano, one of the finest, most accessible examples of an erupted volcano, and the Ice Cave, a natural ice box located in part of a collapsed lava tube, in which the temperature never rises over 31 degrees and the ice floor is about 20 feet thick.

Special Events

Special events abound in the Four Corners. There are many attractions you'll want to include in your trip to the area. Insiders especially enjoy the ones listed below, but new events and special attractions are scheduled regularly, so for up-to-date information on what's happening, call the Farmington Chamber of Commerce at (800) 325-0279 or the Gallup Convention and Visitors Bureau at (800) 242-4282.

Connie Mack World Series
Ricketts Park
1101 Fairgrounds Rd., Farmington
(800) 448-1240

The Connie Mack World Series is held each August in Farmington and attracts the best young amateur baseball players in the world. Farmington is known as the "Amateur Baseball Capital of the World" and for just cause. The series brings in thousands of visitors each year from as far away as Puerto Rico and Canada. Baseball players 16 to 18 years of age compete for the championship, which takes an entire week of daily and nightly play to determine.

Former Connie Mack World Series players who have gone on to great achievements on the professional baseball diamond include Ken Griffey Jr., Manny Rameriz, Duane Ward, and Ben Grieve. Festivities include a welcoming parade and Home Run Derby prior to opening ceremonies of the game, and a "Balls of Fame" baseball exhibit, where local artists use baseballs as canvases.

The Connie Mack World Series has been held in Farmington since 1965, and because of the continued popularity of the event, city officials are building a new ballpark to handle the ever-increasing crowds. If you love baseball, you'll want to schedule your trip to the Four Corners to include at least some of the games of this series.

Farmington Invitational Balloon Rally
Farmington
(800) 448-1240

In May the Farmington Invitational Balloon Rally attracts colorful balloons and their pilots from throughout the country. Activities include a splash and dash over Farmington Lake. If you love hot air bal-loons, this attraction is one you'll want to include in your travel plans.

Freedom Days
Farmington
(800) 448-1240

The Fourth of July is celebrated in Farmington in fine style. Freedom Days includes a spectacular fireworks display, an auction, food and arts and crafts booths, entertainment, a parade, and a triathlon, which is the highlight of this event. There is no age limit to compete in the triathlon, but usually only hardy, healthy, and enthusiastic teens and adults attempt the challenge. The event begins at Farmington Lake, where participants swim 1.5 miles, then don running shoes and run 6.2 miles across the beautiful vistas around the lake. A 40K bike race follows, and the survivors are met with an enthusiastic entourage when they've completed this segment.

San Juan County Fair
McGee Park
41 Rd. 5568, Farmington
(505) 325-5385

Another popular event held the week after the Connie Mack World Series is the San Juan County Fair, the largest county fair in New Mexico. An average of 100,000 people attend this week-long event, which highlights the efforts of kids of all ages. Livestock exhibits, arts and crafts exhibits, a photography contest, a pie-eating contest, commercial booths, a carnival, and great entertainment all add to the fun of a county fair. Gates open at 8 A.M. and close at 10 P.M., except for Friday and Saturday nights of the fair, when the gate remains open until 11 P.M. You'll find great food, lots of activities and wonderful exhibits when you visit the San Juan

County Fair. The fair offers a taste of Americana that is missing from much of our country, and Insiders know it's a great place for families (no alcohol is allowed on the fairgrounds) and the food on the midway is reason alone to attend.

Riverfest
Berg Park, Farmington
(800) 448–1240

Riverfest is held in May, and is one of Farmington's biggest celebrations. Riverfest offers activities that include raft rides, music, and a 10K and 5K run/walk around the Animas River and pretty Berg Park.

SunRay Park and Casino
41 Rd. 5568, Farmington
(505) 325–3844

SunRay Park and Casino offers live horseracing in the fall and simulcast racing throughout the year. SunRay is located seven miles southeast of Farmington at McGee Park and also has slot machines for those who wish to play.

Northern Navajo Nation Fair
Shiprock
(800) 448–1240

In October, Shiprock has its annual Northern Navajo Nation Fair, which includes a parade, fair, rodeo, arts and crafts, powwow, and traditional song and dance at the Shiprock Fairgrounds. This is an opportunity to see the Navajo people celebrate their heritage—don't miss it.

Arts

While northwest New Mexico is considered rural, cultural arts are anything but. While country music stars attract large crowds at concerts and line dancing and the two-step are popular at local bars, the people of the Four Corners don't lack the opportunity to enjoy professional ballet, symphonies, and theater productions. The people who live in this part of the country have chosen the area for the quality of life it provides for their families. When they move here, however, they bring their love of fine arts with them, and there is a conscious effort to promote the arts and bring the best of them to the community.

The groups and events I've highlighted here are but a sample of what is available. Concerts, plays, and dance performances are scheduled regularly. For updates call the Farmington Chamber of Commerce at (800) 325–0279. The chamber staff is helpful, courteous and "in the know" of almost everything that goes on in the area.

Performing Arts

Lions Wilderness Park
5800 College Blvd., Farmington
(877) 599–3331
www.farmingtonnm.org

The city of Farmington has a beautiful amphitheater that has been used for many years to showcase the talents of local actors in original productions. The Lions Wilderness Amphitheater is the setting for outdoor theater during the summer months. Original plays have been presented in the past, and an optional Southwestern style dinner is offered before the play begins. Dinner and the theater are $19 for adults; $17 for senior citizens 62 years and older and for students 13 to 18 years old; and $13 for youngsters 2 to 12. If you aren't interested in dinner, tickets for the performance are only $11 for adults; $9 for senior citizens and students; and $6 for children 2 to 12. Children and adults will enjoy this outdoor production, so make plans to include it during your trip to the Four Corners. This is as popular with the locals as it is with tourists, so call ahead for reservations.

Theater Ensemble Arts
4601 College Blvd., Farmington
(505) 327–0076

Farmington also has an amateur theater group that performs regularly. The Theater Ensemble Arts (TEA) includes an enthusiastic team of actors, directors, and support staff who strive to provide theatergoers with great entertainment at a nominal cost. TEA also encourages the participation of young adults and students in the arts, and strives to provide them with opportunities to display their theatrical talents. Three productions are offered each season, which runs from October through April. Tickets are $8 for adults and $6 for senior citizens and students.

Gallup Area Arts Council/Red Mesa Art Center
105 W. Hill, Gallup
(505) 722–4209

Gallup also has an active performing arts group. The Gallup Area Arts Council/Red Mesa Art Center offers a monthly Artist Talk Series, "Art, Chat and Coffee." The GAAC promotes all art forms created by regional and local artists. It encourages artists to interact with audiences and to share their love of the arts as well as their talent of their chosen art. The GAAC strives to give artists every opportunity to perform and aggressively promotes the arts in the Gallup area.

Museums

There is no lack of quality museums in the area, which provide an Insiders insight into the culture and the history of this most unique area.

Farmington Museum
3041 E. Main, Farmington
(800) 448–1240

The Farmington Museum offers Four Corners history, San Juan Basin geology, and exhibits. The museum consists of four facilities—the Gateway Museum and Visitors Center, Harvest Grove Farm and Orchards Exhibit Barn, Riverside Nature Center, and the E3 Children's Museum and Science Center. Each center is unique and the Parks and Recreation Department of the city of Farmington is justifiably proud of this wonderful complex. The Harvest Grove Farm and Orchards includes a variety of antique tractors and early agriculture equipment. This exhibit offers visitors a glimpse of the early days of San Juan County, when orchards and farms were the economic base. The Riverside Nature Center allows visitors to observe birds and animals from big windows that look over areas where food and water attract wildlife. Exhibits in the center feature the plants and animals of the area.

Weekly bird walks help visitors identify birds of the area. The E3 Children's Museum offers hands-on exhibits that allow children to use an early telephone, "ride" a bicycle that has only one gear, and shell corn with a corn sheller. Children love this museum and local schools include it in their field trip plans. The Gateway to the Four Corners is a new facility, and the city of Farmington has provided area residents and tourists a beautiful place in which to look back at the history of the area and to look forward to the challenges of the future. Admission is free. The museum offers special events throughout the year.

Bolack Museum of Fish and Wildlife
3901 Bloomfield Hwy., Farmington
(505) 325–4275

The Bolack Museum of Fish and Wildlife is located on the B-Square Ranch and Experimental Farm in Farmington on U.S. Highway 64. This museum offers hundreds of exotic animals and wildlife in a beautiful setting. The late former New

Mexico governor Tom Bolack established this museum and his family continues to expand and improve it. The museum also has a wonderful aquarium that will delight exotic fish lovers. Bolack's son, Tommy, has always had an interest in electricity and has created a museum that explores the subject. Adults and children will find it interesting. The museum is open from 9 A.M. to 3 P.M. Monday through Saturday. It is closed Sundays and holidays. Admission is free.

Aztec Museum
125 N. Main, Aztec
(505) 334-9829

The Aztec Museum is a jewel in the desert and quite possibly one of the best-kept secrets in the Four Corners. This wonderful little museum is a delight to visitors and to the many area residents who continue to visit and monitor the always improving exhibits. In the main museum, you'll find a mineral and fossil display, Southwest artifacts, tools, arrowheads, and dolls; china, silver, and salt and pepper collections; authentic Hummel figurines; an early telephone exhibit; a barber shop complete with bathing facilities; ladies and children's early fashions; copies of the Aztec newspaper from 1906 to 1988; hundreds of photographs; farm and ranch tools; and a quaint little gift shop that offers everything from coffee mugs to cookbooks.

The museum also offers a Pioneer Village, which includes a sheriff's office, Aztec's first jail, a judge's office, a one-room school house, a general store and post office, a bank replica, a doctor's office, a pioneer cabin, a blacksmith shop, a church, and a Denver & Rio Grand narrow gauge caboose. The Pioneer Village takes visitors back in time, and the museum's volunteer board of directors and director take great pride in making sure things are authentic to the era. The village is the site of a melodrama and "shoot out" during Aztec's Founder's Day festivities in the fall. Kids will love this little town and adults will appreciate the history it offers.

An oil field exhibit is also included at the museum complex. A 1920s cable tool oil rig, an oil well pumping unit, an oil-field "doghouse" and tools, core samples, and a pictorial history give visitors a look at the oil and gas industry, which has provided an important economical foundation to this area.

In the Atwood Annex, visitors will see authentically furnished pioneer rooms, quilts and sewing items, heavy farm equipment, sleighs, buggies and wagons, and an early movie projector. Again, museum officials oversee each of these exhibits and are rightfully proud of their efforts.

Admission to the museum is $2 for adults and $1 for children ages 11 to 17, with children younger than 11 admitted free. It is worth the small admission to see this complex. Summer hours are from 9 A.M. to 5 P.M. Monday through Saturday. Winter hours are from 10 A.M. to 4 P.M. Monday through Saturday. The museum is located in historic downtown Aztec. Don't miss this museum—it's sure to be a highlight to your trip to the Four Corners.

Red Rock Museum
4.5 miles east of Gallup via I-40 and NM Hwy. 566, Gallup
(505) 863-1337

In Gallup, the Red Rock Museum is also worth taking the time to visit. Located in Red Rock State Park, the museum offers an overview of the American Indian cultures in the Gallup region. Pottery, weaving, jewelry making, and carving exhibits are on permanent display. The museum also includes a Zuni "waffle garden," an agricultural technique that makes use of each drop of precious water in the desert. Admission is $1 for adults and $.50 for children.

Rex Museum
300 E. U.S. Hwy. 66, Gallup
(505) 863-1363

Those interested in the railroad and mining industries in the area are sure to enjoy the Rex Museum. Operated by the Gallup Historical Society, the museum includes history exhibits on the railroad and mining in the Gallup area.

Libraries

The city of Farmington has an excellent public library, as does San Juan College. Smaller libraries are provided in Aztec and Bloomfield.

- Farmington Public Library, 100 W. Broadway, Farmington, (505) 599–1270
- Aztec Public Library, 201 W. Chaco, Aztec, (505) 334–3658
- Bloomfield Public Library, 333 S. 1st, Bloomfield, (505) 632–8315
- Octavia Fellin Public Library, 115 W. Hill Ave., Gallup, (505) 863–1291

Music

Music abounds in the Four Corners, with the strains of Bach mixing with the horns of Brassworks.

Brassworks 4 and Showcase Concerts
San Juan College Little Theater
4601 College Blvd., Farmington
First United Methodist Church
808 N. Monterey, Farmington
(505) 327–1700

Brassworks 4 and Showcase Concerts highlight the music of many very talented local musicians. The concerts are held at the San Juan College Little Theater and at First Methodist Church and are more than music to the ears, they're music for the soul. Brassworks 4, which includes four professional musicians who have been together for almost a decade, has entertained audiences from coast to coast. These talented guys and one gal provide music, laughter, and great fun to audiences, and Brassworks 4 is a mainstay of music in northern New Mexico. The Showcase Concerts not only offer great music to the Four Corners, but encourage young musicians to pursue their love of the art. Eight concerts are presented each year, with tickets ranging from $10 for adults to $4 for students 6 to 18 years old. Seating is on a first-come, first-served basis, but no matter where you sit, the view is good.

Farmington Community Concerts
Farmington Civic Center
200 W. Arrington, Farmington
(505) 326–7672

Farmington Community Concerts hosts concerts September through May at the Civic Center.

San Juan Symphony
San Juan College Performance Hall
4601 College Blvd., Farmington
(505) 599–1148

The San Juan Symphony offers music from the masters beginning in the fall and continuing through early spring. A dedicated group of volunteers strives to bring great music by the very best musicians from San Juan County and Durango, and it does an excellent job. These concerts are usually sell-outs, so call for ticket availability. A month's notice is usually adequate.

Gallup Community Concerts Association
Red Rock State Park
4.5 miles east of Gallup
(505) 863–3075

In Gallup, the Gallup Community Concerts Association presents music in beautiful Red Rock State Park. The concerts are held in the Red Rock Convention Center, where there are no bad seats. Concerts are usually held in January, February, March, and April. A variety of concerts are presented to assure each performance is music to the ears.

Dance

Farmington Chamber of Commerce
203 W. Main, Farmington
(800) 325–0279
www.farmingtonnm.org

Several Farmington dance studios offer performances of students, many of whom are excellent dancers. Schedules vary, so call the Farmington Chamber of Commerce for listings. Most of the studios focus on teaching youngsters, although there are limited lessons for adults. Ballet and tap dancing are most popular here in northern New Mexico, and many talented youngsters enjoy performing on stage.

New Mexico Ballet Company
Farmington Civic Center
200 W. Arrington, Farmington
(505) 599–0462

The New Mexico Ballet Company gives residents and tourists great dance performances. The schedule varies, but the *Nutcracker* is a popular holiday performance. The New Mexico Ballet Company tours all over the state to bring professional ballet performances to more rural communities who would not otherwise have the opportunity to attend the ballet. The *Nutcracker* is an annual performance in Farmington, and draws large audiences each year. The company occasionally returns to the area at other times of the year as their touring schedule permits.

Colorado

Hotels and
Motels
Bed and
Breakfasts
Campgrounds
and RV Sites
Restaurants
Shopping
Trading Posts
Kidstuff
Recreation
Attractions
Arts

The boundary lines of Colorado create an almost perfect rectangle, but for the millions of people who call Colorado home, the state itself is considered almost perfect. With mountains, plateaus, canyons, and plains, Colorado offers scenes everyone can enjoy. The eastern half of the state has flat, high plains and rolling prairies gradually rising westward to the Front Range foothills and the higher ranges of the Rocky Mountains. The western half of the state, which is where this guide will focus, consists of alpine terrain, with wide valleys, rugged canyons, high plateaus, and deep basins punctuating the landscape.

For most people, the altitude and the mountains of colorful Colorado are reason enough to visit the nation's highest state. The lowest elevation of Colorado is 3,350 feet at the Arkansas River, near the town of Holly in the southeastern part of the state. Colorado's highest peak is Mt. Elbert, at 14,431 feet. Mt. Elbert is also the 14th highest peak in the United States. In addition, there are 54 mountain peaks in Colorado over 14,000 feet and more than a thousand peaks over 10,000 feet.

The eastern, western, and south central parts of the state are noted for agriculture, with many different crops grown. In the southwestern part of the state, fruits such as apples, peaches, cherries, grapes, and apricots are grown and enjoyed. During the fall months, roadside stands offer freshly picked fruits, and Insiders and visitors alike take advantage of the offerings.

About 350 miles southwest of Denver, the capital city of Colorado, is Durango. It was founded in 1880 by the Denver and Rio Grande Railroad when it extended its line from Durango to Silverton to haul precious metals from the high country mines. A beautiful city nestled in the Animas River valley, Durango no longer depends on the railroad for its survival. Instead, tourism feeds the pockets of those who live here, and the city takes its responsibility of being a good host to visitors very seriously. You will find people helpful in Durango, anxious to share information about local "hot spots," and proud of the historic community in which they live.

There is much to love about Durango. The Historic Strater Hotel, completed in 1887, remains one of the best places to stay, and its Diamond Belle Saloon is one of the best places to quench a hearty Western thirst. A visit to Durango isn't complete without a ride on the Durango & Silverton Narrow Gauge Railroad, or a stop at the Palace Restaurant, next door to the train depot. (The Close-up in this chapter highlights a vibrant lady who has worked for the Durango & Silverton Narrow Gauge Railroad for many years.) Downtown Durango offers a plethora of quaint shops, where Insiders go for great gifts and visitors find souvenirs for themselves and others.

There is no lack of great dining in Durango, either. Whether it's the Olde Tymer's Café, with its wonderful wooden booths and great old bar, or the Red Snapper, where the service is overshadowed only by the food, you'll find something to whet your appetite no matter what that might be.

About 50 miles west of Durango is Cortez, which proclaims itself as the gateway community to Mesa Verde National Park. The Navajos called Cortez "Tsaya-toh,"

Insiders' Tip

The high altitude in Colorado affects people differently. Avoid altitude sickness by drinking plenty of water and eating light meals that are high in carbohydrates, and don't overexert yourself during the first couple of days of your Colorado vacation. Altitude sickness may include headaches, nausea and dizziness. If symptoms persist longer than a few days, see a physician

meaning "rock water." The stream of water that the Navajos' sheep drank from also attracted ranchers to the area. The stream was then known as Mitchell Springs. The name was changed in 1886 when the town of Cortez was founded.

Cortez is a meeting place of two major Indian tribes, the Navajo and the Utes. The beautiful art work of both tribes may be found in trading posts throughout Cortez. During the summer months, visitors may enjoy Native American dances, storytelling, and other cultural programs six nights each week at the Cortez Cultural Center.

Eight miles north of Cortez is the town of Dolores, which took its name from the beautiful river that flows through it. The valley's first colonial settlement, in 1877, was at Big Bend, about 1.5 miles downstream from today's Dolores. Big Bend was abandoned when the Rio Grande Southern Railroad was scheduled to bypass the settlement, and residents moved next to the tracks at the site now known as Dolores. The Rio Grande Southern's Galloping Goose Number 5, located just feet from where the railroad once ran, is a major tourist attraction in the little town.

Dolores is a beautiful town, and Insiders know that when peace and tranquility are sought, the banks of the Dolores River and the hospitality of the town that shares the river's name, can't be beat. Campers, hunters, anglers, and those who enjoy a slower pace make Dolores a destination that almost always guarantees a pleasant time.

Mancos, nine miles southeast of Dolores, is the third of the cities that comprise Mesa Verde Country. The first white men to discover Mesa Verde rode there from their Mancos Valley ranch in search of stray cattle. The people of Mancos have succeeded in keeping the flavor of the West strong for visitors and Insiders alike. The incredible sunrises and sunsets are reason enough to visit this quaint little town, where folks are as hospitable now as they were when stagecoaches and horses, not automobiles, brought visitors to the front door.

As you travel through southwestern Colorado, you'll be awestruck by the beauty of the area. You will find yourself pulling off the road to photograph incredible views and catching your breath at the site of the wildlife that roam the area. There are many trails off the beaten path that you will be tempted to follow, and many of them will take you to streams rarely fished, towns where only the memories of better days still linger, and meadows that are a carpet of wildflowers. Some of the more memorable spots will be highlighted in the Recreation and Attractions sections of this chapter. You will enjoy the lifestyle of this part of the Four Corners, and if you're tempted to pack up and move here, you will join countless others who have made the move and have embraced a way of life that's a little less demanding and offers a lot of opportunities. More information on moving to Colorado can be found in the Relocation chapter.

Hotels and Motels

Price code

The price code is based on the cost of a standard room for two adults for one night.

$ . . . . .less than $50
$$ $51–75
$$$ $76–100
$$$$ . . . .$101 and up

You won't have any difficulty finding quality accommodations while traveling the Colorado portion of your trip through the Four Corners. Most major hotel chains have nice places for visitors to stay, but if you're looking for something that's a little out of the ordinary, southwestern Colorado has wonderful options for you.

All hotels and motels accept major credit cards unless otherwise noted, and all are wheelchair accessible unless stated otherwise. Pets are welcome during some seasons, so please check when you make your reservations.

General Palmer Hotel $$$$
567 Main Ave., Durango
(800) 523–3358
www.generalpalmerhotel.com

Built in 1898 and restored in 1982, the General Palmer is just steps away from the Durango & Silverton Narrow Gauge Railroad. Each room at the General Palmer is decorated with antique furniture and offers an ambiance that encourages guests to put their feet up and enjoy the luxury the rooms offer. You'll find wonderful handmade chocolates by the bed when you arrive, and delicious homemade muffins awaiting you when you wake up in the morning. A suite with three beds is available for the family, and a beautiful bridal Victorian queen suite is just waiting for the latest bride and groom.

The Historic Strater Hotel $$$$
699 Main Ave., Durango
(800) 247–4431
www.strater.com

Durango is rich in history and its marvelous historic hotels reflect the spirit of the Old West. The Strater, originally built in 1887, remains one of the great old hotels. Henry H. Strater was just 20 years of age when he managed to raise $70,000 to build the Strater, which has never closed its doors since it first opened. The rooms in the Strater reflect a Victorian charm, and are decorated exquisitely. Marble and granite tabletops, $55-a-roll wallpaper, and polished brass appointments highlight the rooms. Wonderful dressers, armoires, and headboards encourage dreams of a time gone by. Each room has a diary, where guests may enter their thoughts and appreciations of the accommodations. While the luxury of the rooms may make you not want to leave them, a visit to the Strater isn't complete without going to the Diamond Belle Saloon. Gals in dance hall costumes and bartenders ready to mix your drink the Western way will delight you, as will the wonderful ragtime piano players who perform regularly. Your stay in the Strater will likely be one of your fondest memories of your trip to the Four Corners.

Insiders' Tips

The Historic Strater Hotel, located in downtown Durango, was completed in 1887 and houses the largest collection of antique walnut furniture in the world.

Jarvis Suite Hotel $$$$
125 W. 10th St., Durango
(800) 824–1024

You don't get a room when you stay at the Jarvis—you get a suite, and a sweet suite it is. Newly renovated, each suite offers a complete kitchen, sitting and sleeping areas, and hookups for your laptop, if you must work or check your e-mail while on vacation. Studio, one- and two-bedroom suites (some with lofts) will make your stay in southwestern Colorado so wonderful you may never want to go home. There are just 22 suites in the Jarvis, so you're assured of receiving personal attention. This hotel is on the National Register of Historic Places and will provide you with a memory of your visit to the Four Corners that will register tops in your memory book.

Rochester Hotel $$$$
726 E. Second Ave., Durango
(800) 664–1920

The Rochester Hotel is located just off Main Avenue in Durango. Built in 1892 and wonderfully renovated, the Rochester offers 15 spacious rooms with high ceilings and a décor reminiscent of the Old West. Rooms are named after the many movies that have been filmed in the Durango area, and include the Butch Cassidy and the Sundance Kid room, the City Slickers room, and the How the West Was Won room. A full gourmet breakfast is included with your room, which you won't want to miss. Morning glory muffins, sour cream orange pecan bread, banana walnut French toast, Havarti dill scrambled eggs with potato chive cake, and pepper Jack scrambled eggs with country seasoned potatoes are just some of the wonderful dishes offered for your morning repast. A social occurs every afternoon in the lobby. Hot and cold tea and homemade cookies will tide you over until dinner. The Rochester is a non-smoking hotel.

Mesa Verde Motel $
191 Railroad Ave., Mancos
(800) 825–6372
www.mesaverdemotel.com

Located just seven miles from the entrance to Mesa Verde National Park, the Mesa Verde Hotel is a nice place to stay while visiting the park. You won't find anything fancy when you visit this pleasant little motel, but you'll find clean, comfortable rooms that will offer a relaxing place to put up your feet after a day of sightseeing and touring. The motel offers a hot tub where guests can soak and enjoy the wonderful mountain air of colorful Colorado.

Far View Lodge $$$
1 Navajo Hill
Mesa Verde National Park
(800) 449–2288

The Far View Lodge is located 15 miles inside Mesa Verde National Park and is a pleasant place to stay while you enjoy the sites of the park. The lodge offers private balconies, from which you can soak in the beautiful scenery and see for up to one hundred miles. The lodge provides archaeological site tours on a seasonal basis, and guided bus tours for half-day or full-day trips. Be prepared to enjoy your companions when you stay at the Far View Lodge, however, for there are no telephones and no televisions.

Bed and Breakfasts

Price code

The price code is based on the cost of a standard room for two adults for one night.

$ . . . .$75–$100
$$ . . . .$101–$150
$$$ . . . .$151 and up

For those who prefer the more intimate bed and breakfast when they travel, Colorado offers some of the finest anywhere. The hosts and hostesses of these fine bed and breakfasts take great pride in providing their guests with personal touches that make the difference between a hotel room and the warmth of a guest bedroom. While the bed and breakfasts I've listed here are wonderful, there are many others throughout southwestern Colorado and you're encouraged to enjoy the hospitality of those hosts and hostesses, too. Pets are not always welcome at bed and breakfasts, so please ask before you bring Fido along. All major credit cards are accepted unless otherwise noted and all are wheelchair accessible unless otherwise stated.

Apple Orchard Inn $$
7758 C.R. 203, Durango
(800) 426–0751
www.appleorchardinn.com

The Apple Orchard Inn was voted "Best of Colorado" and for good reason. This wonderful farmhouse has four guest rooms and six cottages for its guests with private baths, a vanity with a second sink outside of the bathroom, featherbeds and wonderful comforters. A fireplace dominates one guest room, a view of the old apple orchard highlights another; guests in another room enjoy looking at the inn's gardens and ponds, and the fourth room offers picture postcard views of the mountains. The cottages are just as unique. Fireplaces, bay windows, views of the area are highlights of these beautiful little "homes." One cottage complies with the Americans with Disability Act. The full breakfast offered guests may include homemade jam and baked goods, French toast, breakfast burritos, and hazelnut waffles. Complimentary wine and beer, soft drinks, lemonade and iced tea are offered guests each afternoon and evening, and are accompanied by snacks. Gourmet dinners are also available with advance reservations, with guests helping determine the menu. Dinners are served in a private dining room or on the lovely patio. Children are welcome at the Apple Orchard Inn, but pets are not. The inn is a non-smoking facility, but guests who want to smoke outside may do so.

Country Sunshine Bed and Breakfast $$
35130 U.S. Hwy. 550 N., Durango
(800) 383–2853
www.countrysunshine.com

The Country Sunshine Bed and Breakfast overlooks the Animas River and is on three beautifully wooded acres. Six guest rooms await tired tourists, each room uniquely decorated with color and furnishings. Several of the rooms are perfect for families, with trundle beds and day beds along with king and queen size beds. A hearty breakfast is offered, and complimentary drinks and snacks are always available. After a busy day of sightseeing or enjoying outdoor activities, you'll want to put your feet up at the large stone fireplace while the kids enjoy a video or watch television in a separate area.

Waterfall Bed & Breakfast $
4138 C.R. 203, Durango
(970) 259–4771
www.waterfallbb.com

The Red Cliffs and the only waterfall in the Animas valley await guests of the Waterfall Bed & Breakfast. You may sit in the orchard and enjoy the view before you start your day, or following a busy one. There are only two guest rooms at the Waterfall, each with cable television, king size beds, and private baths. A private entrance, sitting/dining area, and a lovely deck are provided for guests. A deluxe continental breakfast is served in the guest dining area, and is likely to include home baked muffins or breads, juice, fresh fruit, coffee, and tea. Upon your return to the Waterfall after a busy day, you may want to relax in the Jacuzzi, warm and bubbling, waiting to soothe those tired muscles. Smoking is not allowed at the Waterfall and pets are not welcome. Children over the age of 13 are welcome.

Kelly Place $$
14663 Rd. G, Cortez
(800) 745–4885
www.kellyplace.com

Kelly Place has been described as both an outdoor educational center and unique bed and breakfast. Located 10 miles west of Cortez in McElmo Canyon, Kelly Place is the culmination of efforts of George and Sue Kelly, horticulturists from the Denver area. They created a beautiful area of orchards, gardens, and courtyards at the base of Sleeping Ute Mountain. There are more than 25 documented Anasazi Indian sites on the one hundred acres of Kelly Place, and guests may enjoy a self-guided tour to any of them. The lodge at Kelly Place is an adobe-style building with courtyards that was built in the mid-1960s.

Seven guest rooms and three adobe-styled cabins await guests. Some of the cabins have kitchenettes, fireplaces, and Jacuzzis. All rooms have private baths. Guests may enjoy horseback riding, archaeology or botany/ethno botany talks and tours, or primitive pottery making while staying at Kelly Place. With so much to do at Kelly Place, and the wonders of the Four Corners, too, it may be difficult to leave this beautiful home away from home. A full country-style breakfast is served daily and babysitting services are available.

Campgrounds and RV Sites

As always, you're apt to find other great campgrounds as you tour the Four Corners. Inspect them for cleanliness and security and enjoy your stay. There's nothing like the great Colorado air to clear your mind and heighten your senses.

Durango

Durango East KOA
30090 U.S. Hwy. 160
(800) KOA–0793

Insiders know that rarely does a traveler go wrong when they select a KOA campground for their stay, and the ones in southwest Colorado are no exception. This campground has cabins, 112 spaces, electricity, water and sewer, showers, tent spaces, a swimming pool, and a small grocery store.

Durango N. Ponderosa KOA
13391 C.R. 250
(800) KOA–2792

Another good campground, this one has 147 spaces (41 with utilities), showers, small store, tent spaces, and swimming pool, and offers fishing too.

Cortez

Cortez-Mesa Verde KOA
27432 E. U.S. Hwy. 160
(800) 562–3901

Another good KOA, this campground offers 100 units, cabins, tent spaces, grills, a laundry, showers, and RV hookups.

Lazy G Campground
U.S. Hwy. 160 and CO Hwy. 145
(970) 565–8577

There are 38 spaces in the Lazy G, spaces for tents, grills, a hot tub, laundry, outdoor pool, RV hookups, and showers.

Mesa Oasis Campground
5608 U.S. Hwy. 160/666
(970) 565–8716

There are 125 spaces at the Mesa, with spaces for tents, grills, laundry facilities, RV hookups, showers, and fishing.

> ## Insiders' Tip
> There are more than 440 species of birds in Colorado and more than 900 species of wildlife.

Dolores

Cozy Comfort RV Park
1501 Central Ave.
(800) 757-1723

This pleasant campground offers great service and an affable staff. There are RV spaces and tent sites, restrooms, laundry facilities, and showers, and the beautiful Dolores River is close by.

Dolores River RV Park and Cabins
18680 CO Hwy. 145
(800) 200-2399

Another great park in wonderful Dolores. The Dolores River RV Park and Cabins is a full-service park, with cable TV (if you want it), housekeeping cabins, sleeper tent sites, heated restrooms with hot showers, laundry facilities, a community room, a store with RV supplies, groceries and gifts, and old-fashioned ice cream parlor and lunch counter. The park observes "Quiet Hours," and also offers a special walking area for pets.

Mancos

A&A Mesa Verde RV Park
34979 U.S. Hwy. 160
(800) 972-6620

This campground is more than just a place to park your RV or pitch your tent— this is a camper's shopping mall. Located on 30 acres in the heart of Mesa Verde Country, A&A has more than 70 sites (some are big pull-throughs), shaded sites with fire pits, group camping spots, a heated pool, hot tub, 18-hole miniature golf course, mini-van rentals, and nightly bonfires. In addition, the park offers restrooms and showers, a recreation hall, playground, laundry facilities, grocery and gift shop, low-cost access to the internet on the camp computer, fossil hunts, wagon rides, and—the ultimate—a pet sitter.

Echo Basin Ranch
43747 C.R. M
(800) 426-1890

Echo Basin is another campground that's more than a campground. There are more than 70 sites in the RV park, and utilities are available. There are barbecue pits, bath houses near the park, a heated swimming pool and hot tub, laundry room, a fitness center, general store, a steakhouse for nights you don't feel like cookin' up your own, and a saloon where adults can dance and enjoy refreshments. The park also offers more primitive camping for those who like to rough it.

Restaurants

Price code

The price code is based on the cost of two dinner entrees, and does not include appetizers, desserts, or alcoholic beverages.

$ . . . . less than $10
$$ . . . . less than $25
$$$ . . . .$50 and up

Dining in southwestern Colorado is worth a trip to the Four Corners. You'll find restaurants to suit any dining pleasure and the atmosphere in this part of the country is decidedly casual. Clean jeans and a pressed white Western shirt are considered "formal" here, so leave the three-piece suits and high-heeled shoes at home. The restaurants highlighted in this chapter are but a few of the many great places to eat in this part of the Four Corners. You'll find fast food restaurants almost everywhere, and cozy little diners pop up regularly as more and more great cooks discover the Southwest. I urge you to try some of those places—you're sure to find a friendly atmosphere, food seasoned the Southwestern way, and new dishes you'll want the recipes for. Enjoy!

All major credit cards are accepted unless otherwise noted and all establishments are wheelchair accessible unless stated otherwise.

Ariano's $$$
150 E. College Dr., Durango
(970) 247-8146

Ariano's is a wonderful Italian restaurant that Durango residents rate as one of the best. Pastas and ravioli are made daily and you'll find veal, ginger shrimp, and steaks on the menu, as well as daily specials. You won't be disappointed with anything you order at Ariano's, and you'll find a good wine selection to complete your meal. If you've got room, homemade desserts, which vary, will satisfy your sweet tooth, and a great cappuccino or espresso will top it off. Reservations are not accepted at Ariano's, but if you don't have them and have to wait for a table, the bar area is comfortable and its surroundings are as lovely as the rest of this fine restaurant.

Bar D Chuckwagon Suppers $$
8080 C.R. 250, Durango
(970) 247-5753

You won't want to miss the Bar D Chuck-wagon Suppers, or the Western Stage Show, when you visit the Four Corners. Located about 15 minutes north of Durango, the Bar D offers good wholesome food and entertainment. The menu is almost always the same—roast beef or chicken breast simmered in barbecue sauce, baked potato, baked beans, home-made biscuits, applesauce, spice cake, and coffee or lemonade. The delicious food is the prelude to a wonderful evening of entertainment. The kids will especially enjoy this "restaurant," and can take a ride on the Bar D train, watch a blacksmith at work, shop in the gift shop or leatherworks store, or stock up on premium chocolate at the Chocolate Factory shop. This is family dining and entertainment at its best.

Carver Brewing Co. $$
1022 Main Ave., Durango
(970) 259-2545

Carver's is a popular place where locals gather for great home brewed beer. But it's not just the suds people enjoy—it's just about everything. Carver's offers a great breakfast, serving up some of the best pancakes this side of the Continental Divide. Homemade soups, served in bread bowls, are enough to fill you up at lunch time, and the dinner menu varies enough to always provide something new to try. Seating is limited at Carver's, so if you're planning to have lunch, arrive before noon to get a table. The restaurant is usually full of folks waiting to purchase the many homemade pastries and bread and that can create a bottleneck of customers at the front door. It's worth the wait to get through, however, because you can be assured of a great meal at a great price at Carver's.

Francisco's Restaurante y Cantina $$
619 Main Ave., Durango
(970) 247–4098

Francisco's is Durango's oldest restaurant and the Garcia family continues to offer some of the best Mexican food anywhere. The atmosphere is colorful and relaxing and the service is great. While it's the Mexican food that attracts most people, Francisco's also offers steaks, fresh fish, chicken, and pasta that are equally good. The carnitas, tenderloins of beef grilled and served with green chile, beans and rice, is wonderful, and Francisco's serves up some of the best margaritas you'll find anywhere. A special "Little Amigo's" menu is available for the kids.

Olde Tymer's Café $
1000 Main Ave., Durango
(970) 259–2990

The Olde Tymer's is a wonderful restaurant, which clings to the past with wooden floors, old-fashioned booths, and a great old bar. Comfortably casual and great for families, the Olde Tymer's serves Durango's best burger, if you believe the locals. You won't find a fancy menu here, but you will find food carefully prepared and served up by a friendly staff. Daily specials are offered, as are daily drink specials. This is a fun place to eat, but it's packed at lunch time so arrive early. You'll be treated like family at the Olde Tymer's, but it's a fun family, and you'll be glad they included you.

Palace Restaurant $$$
505 Main Ave., Durango
(970) 247–2018
www.palacerestaurants.com

You cannot visit Durango without enjoying the great food and wonderful atmosphere of the Palace, which is located right next door to the Durango & Silverton Narrow Gauge Railroad. Two dining rooms reflect the turn of the century in Durango and the restaurant is proud of its wheelchair accessibility. The restaurant, located in the original Palace Hotel, was built in the early 1890s. A popular eatery for years, the citizens of the Four Corners were disappointed when its doors were closed in 1996. The spring of 1997, however, found the Palace under new ownership, and a million-dollar renovation of the facility took place. The Palace re-opened in the fall of '97, and has served carefully prepared food in luxurious surroundings since. You'll find classic American dishes on the menu, with an emphasis on quality of ingredients and pride in presentation. The patio is open for lunch, dinner, and cocktails during the warmer months and is a popular place for locals and tourists alike to gather after a long day. An extensive wine list is offered, and kids are sure to find their favorites on the children's menu. Smoking is not allowed in the dining rooms, but smokers are welcome in the Quiet Lady Tavern, where live music is offered as well as a television for those wanting to catch their favorite sports team in action.

Red Snapper $$$
144 E. 9th St., Durango
(970) 259–3417

The residents of Durango consistently rate the Red Snapper as one of the best places in town to eat. A 100-year-old building is home to this popular seafood restaurant, located just a block away from Durango's Main Avenue. Aquariums filled with exotic fish highlight the décor of the Red Snapper, which offers elevated dining booths as well as tables arranged so diners can enjoy conversations while dining on quality seafood, prime rib, and steak. The Snapper also boasts one of the best salad bars in the area, and offers an extensive wine list. The only problem you may find at the Snapper is which dinner entree to select. And if that's not tough enough, the dessert menu of this restaurant offers sweet concoctions from Death by Chocolate to a sublime Key Lime pie. The Red Snapper accepts reservations, which are encouraged, and youngsters are welcome. Smoking is not allowed in the restaurant.

Scoot'n Blues Café and Lounge $$
900 Main Ave., Durango
(970) 259–1400

If you're a biker, you'll love Scoot'n Blues. The vintage motorcycle collection is worth the visit, but it's the food here that will make you want to return again and again. Steaks, ribs, chicken, burgers, sandwiches, salads—you want it, they've got it at Scoot'n Blues. This is a fun place to spend a lunch hour or hours, and the kids will love it as much as the adults. A boutique features shirts, hats, jackets, and all the accessories you need to compliment your biker wardrobe.

Sweeney's Restaurant $$$
1644 C.R. 203, Durango
(970) 247–5236

Sweeney's is a local favorite, but has been discovered by the thousands of tourists who make a point to visit this great restaurant whenever they're in the Four Corners. With more than 30 entrees that include steaks, seafood, and daily specials, the food is wonderful, and the service provided by Sweeney's wait staff is five-star. The décor is rustic and comfortable and a private cigar room is available for those who want to enjoy a good smoke after dinner. Sweeney's is located just outside of the Durango city limits and every local will be happy to direct you to it.

Nero's Italian Restaurant $$$
303 W. Main St., Cortez
(980) 565–7366

Nero's is a wonderful Italian restaurant and offers some of the finest cuisine in the area. Many residents of the Four Corners make the trip to Cortez to Nero's regularly because the food is great and the servers are attentive. Lasagna, chicken Marsala, and spaghetti and meatballs—all the usual Italian dishes created with care in Nero's kitchen—are offered, as is a nightly special. The specials are excellent, and include Italian entrees as well as fresh fish and steaks. Wines from Australia, France, Italy, South Africa, and the United States are offered. Because of the many tourists who visit the restaurant, Nero's offers menus in French and German to cater to their guests. A children's menu and sandwiches are also offered. Nero's understands that tourists want to be comfortable, and because this is the West, you must never worry about "dressing for dinner" here. One word of caution, however, smoking is available only in the bar, where there are just three small tables. Unless you arrive early, call for reservations.

Shopping

Shopping in southwestern Colorado is an experience you won't want to miss. Countless crafters and artisans set up booths and shops seasonally, and as you travel through the Colorado portion of your trip, Insiders encourage you to stop and shop. It is at these little booths and kiosks that you're apt to discover gifts for family and friends that will be treasured for a lifetime.

Durango, in particular, has an abundance of great shops and quaint little stores. The ones I've listed are just a sampling of what's available. Take your time as you tour downtown Durango, slip into the shops and stores, and savor the taste of shopping that is truly Durango.

Cortez, Dolores, and Mancos also have cute little shops where you can find fun things to take home to remind you of your wonderful visit to the Four Corners.

The Durango Mall
800 S. Camino del Rio, Durango
(970) 259-3606

The Durango Mall is the town's largest mall, and is anchored by JC Penney and Kmart. There are about 40 stores to shop in and you'll enjoy your visit.

Durango Cat Company
60 Main Ave., Durango
(970) 247-4045

Cat lovers, friends of cat lovers, and cats all love the Durango Cat Company. Whatever your cat needs or your friends need for their cats, you'll find it and more here. From sun visors for your favorite feline to cat beds, cat dishes, cat clothes, cat everything—it's all here. Cisco, the cat, heads up the Durango Cat Company as the CEO, and supervises shoppers, shopping, and sales from his perch in the front office.

Main Avenue Marketplace
742 Main Ave., Durango
(970) 247-9519

Main Avenue Marketplace is a great place to shop. Cool things for the kitchen, heavenly candles, unique decorations for your home or vacation cabin, Colorado Christmas items, toys, ladies clothing, and t-shirts fill the 6,500 square feet of the Marketplace. It will take you some time to browse, but it will be time well spent.

The Main Mall
835 Main Ave., Durango
(970) 247-8448

The Main Mall offers a cookie shop, ladies clothing, cards and gifts, as well as other unique stores. Shoppers get variety and a lovely place in which to shop.

O'Farrell Hatmakers
563 Main Ave., Durango
(970) 259-5900

You may arrive in southwestern Colorado without a cowboy hat, but chances are you won't leave without one—especially after you visit O'Farrell's. But it's not just cowboy hats O'Farrell's offers its legion of

customers. Custom hats, panama hats, palm leaf hats, fedoras, beaded hats—whatever kind of hat you need, O'Farrell's will make one for you. The hat makers at O'Farrell's take great pride in the work they do, and that pride is evident in the hats they create. O'Farrell's also carries leather garments, Stubbs shirts, skirts, jackets, vests, belts, buckles, and jewelry for you to add to your purchases. This is an Insiders favorite place to shop—it smells wonderful, the staff is courteous and helpful, and the selection of great clothing and incredible hats is worth every trip.

The Rio Grande Trading Co.
519 Main Ave., Durango
(970) 259-1745

The Rio Grande Trading Co. is another Insiders' favorite. Here, you can find Christmas ornaments and decorations all year long, and the selection is wonderful. Unique t-shirts and sweatshirts and Mesa Verde pottery are also available. Whether you're shopping for others or for yourself, you'll find it at the Rio Grande Trading Co.

Rocky Mountain Chocolate Factory
561 Main Ave., Durango
(970) 259-1408

This place is a chocoholics dream come true. The Rocky Mountain Chocolate Factory has been creating melt-in-your-mouth candy since 1981, producing more than two million pounds of the stuff each year. Once, candy was sold only out of this store on Main Avenue, but then the word got out about the richness of the sweet stuff and the care that was put into its creation. Now, Rocky Mountain Chocolates can be found in more than 200 stores in the United States, Canada, and Asia. But the freshest are still found on the shelves of the Durango store. Don't miss this opportunity to make your sweet tooth think it died and went to heaven.

Dream Catcher
15 E. Main, Cortez
(970) 565–6456

In Cortez, Insiders like shopping at the Dream Catcher where all kinds of wonderful gifts and treats are available.

Folk Art of the Four Corners
343 W. Main, Cortez
(970) 565–7916

Folk Art of the Four Corners is another great shop. Here, you'll find Navajo folk art, Appalachian arts and crafts, and gourmet foods and baskets.

Wagons West
313 Railroad Ave., Dolores
(970) 882–0100

In Dolores, Wagons West offers teddy bears, wildlife rugs and throws, scented candles, and more fun stuff than you can imagine.

Joy's of Colorado
121 Railroad Ave., Mancos
(970) 533–1500

Joy's of Colorado offers gourmet foods, gift items, and flowers. The salsa that comes from Joy's is wonderful and you'll want to take some home with you.

Girl of the West
107 W. Grand Ave., Mancos
(970) 533–7070

Girl of the West has beautiful clothing, accessories, and gifts that really do capture the spirit of the West. This is a really fun store to shop.

Mattie's Attic
101 Grand Ave., Mancos
(970) 533–1760

Mattie's Attic has pillows, pictures, unique antiques, rugs, hand-painted furniture, and great floral designs.

Trading Posts

Mesa Indian Trading Company and Gallery
27601 U.S. Hwy. 160 E., Cortez
(800) 441–9908

This trading post has fine art, jewelry, Pueblo pottery, and Navajo weavings. This is a wonderful post with quality art.

Notah Dineh Trading Company and Museum
345 W. Main, Cortez
(800) 444–2024

Notah Dineh Trading Company and Museum has Navajo rugs and Native American arts and crafts. You won't believe the quality and beauty of these Navajo rugs.

Kidstuff

As you travel through southwestern Colorado on your tour of the Four Corners, you'll find outdoor activities the kids will enjoy—from panning for gold in the high country to camping and having dinner by the campfire. These are the trips youngsters will remember forever, and will share those memories with their children and grandchildren. Make sure you take your time as you travel this beautiful part of our country, and not rush the moment—the kids will appreciate it.

Just as the kids will enjoy Colorado, Colorado loves kids—the ones who live here and the ones who visit. That's why you'll find, almost everywhere you go, kid-friendly establishments. The activities listed below are family oriented, so when you think "Kidstuff," think "Familystuff," too.

Ron D View Ranch
1151 Anna Rd., Ignacio
(970) 563–9270

At the Ron D View Ranch the emphasis is on family. Summer and family pack trips, daily rides, and hay rides are offered. Rides will run about $15 for an hour's worth of fun. Call for complete information about daily rides and pack trips.

Animas City Rock Gym
1111 Camino del Rio, Durango
(970) 259–5700

Animas City Rock Gym offers 6,500 square feet of indoor climbing and instruction for kids of all ages. A day pass with gear for youngsters 11 years old and younger is $8; adults can join in the fun for just $12 for a day pass with gear.

Diamond Circle Melodrama
699 Main Ave., Durango
(970) 247–3400

Diamond Circle Melodrama is in the Strater Hotel and will give kids the giggles and a great show. This is professional melodrama and vaudeville at its best and is an event the entire family will enjoy. Tickets to the melodrama are $12 for children 12 and younger, and $17 for adults.

Durango Pro Rodeo
2500 Main Ave., Durango
(970) 247–1666

Kids love rodeos and this rodeo at the La Plata County Fairgrounds will thrill and excite them. Real Western rodeo competition is offered during June and August. Admission is $12 for adults and $5 for kids.

Miniature Golf/Go Karts
650 S. Camino del Rio, Durango
(970) 382–9009

Miniature Golf/Go Karts offers a patio/picnic area that overlooks the Animas River and bike path. But the fun for kids will be the mini golf, go-karts, and arcade. Prices will vary, but expect to pay about $3 for a round of mini golf. Go-kart fees are about the same.

Outlaw Rivers and Jeep Tours
690 Main Ave., Durango
(907) 259–1800

Outlaw Rivers and Jeep Tours will take you and the kids on a tour that will include ghost towns and mines. Not only will the kids love these tours, but they will surely bring out the kid in you too. A 2.5-hour jeep trip is $25 for youths and $35 for adults; four hours is $40 for youth and $60 for adults; and a whole day is $75 for youth and $98 for adults.

Insiders' Tip

Great names in the West spent time in colorful Colorado. Butch Cassidy robbed the Telluride Bank in 1889, taking with him $30,000. The town of Silverton hired Bat Masterson to bring law and order to it in the early days of the West. Doc Holliday wasn't particularly impressed with the weather in Leadville. Holliday is reported to have said, "Leadville has ten months of winter and two months of late fall!"

Rocky Mountain Whitewater
700 Main Ave., Durango
(970) 247–0807

Rocky Mountain Whitewater makes sure kids and adults have fun while rafting. You'll enjoy rafting for a half day for $25 for youngsters and $35 for adults. A two-hour trip is $15 for youth and $20 for adults; and a full day on the water is $50 for youth and $60 for adults.

Southwest Adventures
12th and Camino del Rio, Durango
(800) 642–5389

Southwest Adventures offers rock climbing and instruction. Your rock climbing experience will range between $50 to $190, depending on if you have a half-day, full-day, or multi-day climb.

Trimble Hot Springs
6475 C.R. 203, Durango
(970) 247–1250

Trimble Hot Springs offers a swimming pool kids will love, while offering a therapy pool and full service massage for the "older" kids. Youngsters 2 to 12 can soak for just $6, while adults will spend $8. Massage rates will vary; call for an appointment.

Recreation

Colorado is known for the wonderful recreational opportunities it provides. Your trip to the Four Corners won't be complete without taking advantage of some of them. Your biggest problem will be which ones to choose.

Fishing, horseback riding, glider rides, jeep tours, golf, rafting and kayaking, skiing—all await you when you visit the Four Corners. Stagecoach rides, hay rides and sleigh rides are some of the outdoor recreation that don't take much physical effort but provide a lot of fun and fond memories. Whatever kind of recreation you select, remember the altitude is high here in southwestern Colorado, and you may feel slightly winded or tire more easily. As much as you might want to rush to enjoy a little bit of everything southwestern Colorado has to offer, take your time and you'll have the time of your life.

Fishing

Durango Area Chamber Resort Association
111 S. Camino del Rio, Durango
(800) 525–8855

There are many opportunities to wet a line in southwestern Colorado. The Animas River in Durango, the Dolores River in Dolores, and McPhee Reservoir near Dolores offer great fishing. The Durango area has some of the best quality fishing in the United States. From the Animas River, which can be fished from the middle of town, to special spots in the high country, Insiders know fishing is its best in southwestern Colorado! To know what's biting on the rivers, your best bet is to contact one of the many great tackle and supply shops in the area, or a fishing guide.

San Juan National Forest, Dolores District
(970) 882–7296

The Dolores River has been named one of the 50 best trout streams in America by *Trout Magazine*. There are many access points along the river for an angler to drop a line. For information about fishing the Dolores, call the Dolores District of the San Juan National Forest and they'll give you great advice!

McPhee Reservoir Marina
25021 CO Hwy. 184, Dolores
(970) 882–2257

McPhee Reservoir, which stretches north and west from Dolores, is a favorite place to fish. The reservoir is the second largest body of water in Colorado and is unique because it offers both cold water and warm water fishing. It's a rare lake in Colorado where rainbow trout and good-sized crappies can be caught in the same water, but McPhee isn't your ordinary reservoir! A special strain of rainbow trout, the McConaughy, is the primary species, but Kokanee salmon can also be caught, as well as largemouth and smallmouth bass, pan fish, and catfish. There are regulations as to the size and number of fish to be kept, so check with the marina for details. McPhee offers more than 50 miles of shoreline and is best fished and enjoyed by boat. Boat rentals are available at the McPhee Reservoir Marina.

San Juan National Forest, Mancos District (970) 533–7716

Jackson Reservoir (Jackson Gulch to Insiders) and the Mancos River drainage are off Forest Service 561, just north of Mancos. The beautiful fishing spot has camping spaces and a boat ramp and is a wonderful place to camp overnight, catch a few fish for dinner, and enjoy the sights and smells of the great ponderosa pines. For information about Jackson Reservoir, call the Mancos District of the San Juan National Forest.

Fishing near Durango, Colorado.
PHOTO: PAUL PENNINGTON

Four-Wheeling

Colorado Welcome Center
928 E. Main, Cortez
(970) 565–4048

For those who prefer four tires under their backside, instead of the two of a mountain bike, a four-wheeler is just the ticket to see places far off the paved and beaten path. The miners of the San Juan Mountains opened an incredible part of the country for adventure-loving explorers. Mining roads and mule trails left behind by hopeful gold seekers remain today, offering today's off-roader the opportunity to enjoy views and see wildlife not possible from a two- or four-

lane highway. For more information, call the Colorado Welcome Center.

Durango Area Chamber Resort Association
111 S. Camino del Rio, Durango
(800) 525–8855

Durango also offers four-wheeling challenges and fun. Guides can provide tours of the San Juan Mountains, Colorado's wonderful and popular ghost towns, forgotten mines, and summits with a beauty your camera just won't be able to capture—but bring it anyway. Call the Durango Area Chamber Resort Association for information on jeep rentals and guide services.

Glider Rides

Durango Soaring Club, Inc.
3 miles north of Durango on
U.S. Hwy. 550
(970) 247–9037

For those who seek the freedom of flight without the noise of an engine, the Durango Soaring Club is the place to head. Glider rides over the beautiful Animas valley will thrill you and give you a wonderful Four Corners memory. A certified FAA pilot will take youngsters ages 6 to12 for a ten-minute flight for $50 and senior citizens 70 years of age and older for $75 for 25 minutes. Regular fee is $85 for 25 minutes. Lessons are available.

Golf

Dalton Ranch Golf Club
589 C.R. 252, Durango
(970) 247–8774

This 18-hole, par 72 golf course is one of the most popular in Durango. It offers championship golf challenges, and includes a complete practice facility. A pro shop, full bar, and grill will surely add to your golfing enjoyment. Green fees are $59 for 18 holes during peak season, and cart fees are $10 per person for 18 holes. Dalton Ranch is a spikeless golf course and collared shirts are required for men. Tank tops are not permitted on the course.

Sheraton Tamarron Resort
40292 U.S. Hwy. 550, Durango
(970) 259–2000

When Insiders want to impress clients and friends, they take them to Tamarron to play golf. A championship course, cared for by professionals who take great pride in their work, is as beautiful a course as you'll find anywhere. This award-winning course requires collared shirts and Bermuda shorts, and no denim is allowed. Shoes must not have metal spikes. Green fees for 18 holes are $129, which includes cart rental.

Conquistador Golf Course
2018 N. Dolores Rd., Cortez
(970) 565–9208

This 18-hole, par 72 course sits at 6,200 feet, and provides not only some of the best golf in the Four Corners but the best views as well. A driving range and putting green and a full-service pro shop are available, as are rental carts. Green fees are $15 for 18 holes. Private carts are allowed, but a fee is charged. Shirts and shoes are required.

Hiking

Visitor Information Bureau
P.O. Box HH, Cortez
(800) 253–1616

Some of the most beautiful hiking trails in Colorado are in the southwest part of the state. Many of these trails are not often used, and Insiders know that keeping trash picked up and not venturing far off the beaten trail will keep them beautiful for years to come. The trails range in altitude from 5,000 feet to more than 12,000 feet, and some people can suffer from high altitude sickness. Symptoms from slight to serious can accompany high altitude sickness, so allow yourselves a few days to get used to the altitude before attempting a hike. While you may be tempted to drink the cool, clear water of the streams and creeks you find along the trail, please don't. Giardiasis, a virulent amoebic dysentery, occurs in all open waters of the state and can cause extreme symptoms. Take along your own drinking water or pack a water purifier. Enjoy playing in and admiring the mountain water, but don't drink it! Call the Visitor Information Bureau for a brochure that will give you several hiking trails and the difficulty of each. You also can consult *Hiking Colorado* or *Hiking Colorado II,* just two of several hiking guides by The Globe Pequot Press. To see all their hiking titles from day hikes to overnight hikes, go to www.falcon.com.

Insiders' Tip

The 13th step of the state capitol building in Denver is precisely one mile above sea level, which explains why Denver is called the "Mile High City."

Horseback Riding

Durango Area Chamber Resort Association
111 S. Camino del Rio, Durango
(800) 525–8855

Colorado means the West and the West means horses. There are many professional horseback riding outfitters in the area, and the Durango Area Chamber Resort Association will be happy to tell you which ones are available and how to get in touch with them. Family pack trips, day trips, breakfast rides, sunset dinner rides—you can enjoy them all! Take your sunscreen, your hat, and your camera, for you'll find a use for all of them as you trot off into the great Colorado outdoors. For those unfamiliar with the "horsepower"

of four-legged transportation, guides will find you a horse you'll be comfortable with and will gear the ride to your level of experience.

Colorado Welcome Center
928 E. Main, Cortez
(970) 565–3414

Horseback rides are also available in the Cortez-Dolores-Mancos area. Local outfitters and guest ranches offer rides that will take you into the beautiful backcountry of southwestern Colorado, where you will find scenes and experiences few people have ever enjoyed.

Mountain Biking

Visitor Information Bureau
P.O. Box HH, Cortez
(800) 253–1616

Riders of all levels will enjoy the many adventures offered by riding a mountain bike through some of the most beautiful scenery on earth—here in the Four Corners. Trails into the San Juan National Forest or deep into the Dolores River Canyon will provide biking fun you won't soon forget. The Visitor Information Bureau offers a brochure that details several possible trails, and places where you can rent a bike if you didn't bring yours along. As always, Insiders ask that you respect our beautiful countryside while biking and pack out what you pack in. Remember to wear safety equipment and enjoy the ride—this is as good as it gets.

Mountain bike racing in the Durango area.
PHOTO: DURANGO AREA CHAMBER RESORT ASSOCIATION

Rafting and Kayaking

Durango Area Chamber Resort Association
111 S. Camino del Rio, Durango
(800) 525-8855

River rafting and kayaking are very popular in southwestern Colorado. The Animas River and the Dolores River offer great rafting thrills for river rafters and kayakers alike. If you're interested in two hours or two days on the river, the Durango Area Chamber Resort Association will help you find the right group for you. The kids will definitely consider a river raft trip or a kayaking trip a highlight of their trip to the Four Corners—and so will you. Reservations are suggested to make sure you get the trip you want. Rates will depend on the difficulty of the trip and whether you opt for a full day, half day, or shorter trip. Professional guides will be with you at all times, and you needn't be a swimmer to enjoy a day on the river.

Stagecoach Rides

Bartels Mancos Valley Stage Line
4550 Rd. 41, Mancos
(800) 365-3530

A trip to the West just wouldn't be complete without a stagecoach ride, and the Bartels Mancos Valley Stage Line will give you a ride you'll never forget. With a matched team of horses and an authentic reproduction of a classic stagecoach, just like the ones in the movies, this stagecoach will take you into a landscape dotted with sage and pinon, and into some of the most beautiful country you'll ever see—from a stagecoach or car. This means of transportation won't get you anywhere fast, but it is a trip you'll never forget—and you can bet there will be no "Are we there yet's?" from the kids. Groups of up to 45 people may be accommodated and rides range from a one-hour tour for $25 (kids 3 to 12 are half price) to a 3-hour steak dinner tour, which is $65 per person, with kids 3 to 12 half price. A 3-hour day trip will stop for lunch at a wonderful log diner. Reservations are required.

Winter Recreation

Skiing

You simply can't come to Colorado in the winter without checking out the skiing—or the skiers, from the comfort of a warm lodge. Cross-country and alpine skiing are popular here, and you'll find the perfect place to enjoy that wonderful Colorado snow.

Purgatory Resort
1 Skier Place (25 miles north of Durango), Purgatory
(970) 247-9000

Insiders know this is a great place to ski, and snowboard, and go snowmobiling and make snowmen, and . . . you're getting the idea. Purgatory offers lots of snow and sunshine, but not the long lift lines many skiers have come to expect at a great ski area. With 1,200 acres open for skiing, Purgatory is a favorite of locals and visitors alike. There are 11 lifts that will take you to 75 trails. With four miles of groomed trails, you'll find skiing that is perfect for you, whether you're a beginner or an experienced skier. Lift tickets are $43, and $23 for children 6 to 12. A childcare center is available on the premises. For those who'd rather not depend on two skis or one board to enjoy the snow, a tubing hill is a popular attraction at Purgatory.

Hesperus Ski Area
9848 U.S. Hwy. 160, Hesperus
(970) 259-3711

While not as big or as impressive as Purgatory, many Insiders go to this little skiing oasis for the lack of crowds and to improve their skiing skills. Hesperus also offers night skiing under the stars, with 80 percent of the area lighted. Lift tickets are $22 for adults and $15 for juniors ages 7 to 12; with night tickets $15 for adults and $8 for juniors. A first-timers ski package is available for $36 for adults and $30 for juniors, and includes a group lesson, lift tickets, and rental equipment. This is a limited ski area, with few trails, but is a popular ski destination for many. Hesperus isn't of the snow-making ilk, however, so call ahead to make sure there's snow to play in.

Telluride Ski and Golf Company
Telluride
(800) 525–3455

While technically not in the Four Corners area, you simply cannot discuss Colorado skiing without mentioning Telluride. With 12 lifts to take you to more than 1,050 skiable areas, serious skiers won't want to miss this experience. "The Air Garden," which was created for intermediate and advanced snowboarders, offers winter fun for those who've given up their skis for the board. Telluride is a beautiful community surrounded with some of the most beautiful scenery in the world. When the sun glistens on the snow in Telluride, you may feel like you've entered winter heaven, and you may be right. Thousands of people make Telluride their skiing destination each year because of the great skiing and snow sports, the historic atmosphere of the town, unique shopping opportunities, and the possibility of seeing major movie stars and other "beautiful people." Be sure to call for reservations before you begin your winter journey of the Four Corners.

Snowmobiling and Sleigh Rides

Durango Area Chamber Resort Association
111 S. Camino del Rio, Durango
(800) 525-8855

Winter in Colorado isn't all about cross-country and downhill—unless you're talking about taking a snowmobile across beautiful country and downhill some wonderful hills. Winter usually arrives in Colorado about Thanksgiving and remains until Easter or beyond. Snowmobiling is a popular sport and many Insiders have machines and are gone every weekend to explore the gorgeous winter backcountry of southwestern Colorado. Snowmobiles may be rented for about $40 for adults for a one-hour ride. You do not need a drivers license to use a snowmobile, but you must take care and stay on designated trails. You may purchase a topographic map of the area at Forest Service offices. Snowmobilers are also urged to respect the wonderful wildlife in the Four Corners and please don't disturb their natural habitat.

MayDay Livery and Carriage Rides
4432 C.R. 124, Hesperus
970) 385–6772

If you truly want a wonderful experience, you must take a winter sleigh ride with the great people at MayDay Livery and Carriage Rides. A picture-book sleigh, pulled with some of the most beautiful horses anywhere, will take you on a ride you won't ever forget. The La Plata Mountains are the backdrop for this memorable ride, and the cold winter air will bring color to your cheeks, but you'll be most comfortable and warm in the heavy blankets that are provided. Rides are from one to two hours and take you through the beautiful La Plata Mountains. The two-hour ride includes a stop at a rustic mountain cabin where hot chocolate and cookies prepare you for the return trip. Four adults or a family of five will ride comfortably in these wonderful sleighs. Prices will vary, but expect to spend about $25 for each passenger. The people at MayDay are true examples of Colorado hospitality and friendliness, and you'll be glad you made their acquaintance, as well as took the sleigh ride they offer. There are other businesses that offer sleigh rides and the Durango Area Chamber Resort Association, (800) 525-8855, will be happy to provide those names and numbers to you.

Attractions

It won't be easy, this Colorado portion of your trip to the Four Corners. You'll arrive, smell the wonderful Colorado air, bask in the high country sunshine, and breathe in the beauty of the area. You'll want to do nothing more than find a tree by a stream, sit back, and let your soul be revived and your heart restored. Insiders encourage this, since it's something they do regularly—but then they're fortunate enough to live here, and can enjoy the many attractions this colorful state has to offer any time they choose. Visitors likely don't have that luxury. In the pages to follow, I'll highlight some of the many things to see and do while you're in Colorado, mindful that while you'll want to see them all, you'll surely take time to smell the columbines.

As you travel about southwestern Colorado, you will find local events and attractions, and Insiders encourage you to participate in the ones that appeal to you. Coloradoans are wonderful hosts and will do whatever they can to make the Colorado portion of your trip to the Four Corners memorable.

Indian Ruins

Mesa Verde National Park
Far View Visitor Center
(970) 529–4313
www.nps.gov/meve

For many of the thousands of people who visit Mesa Verde National Park each year, exploring the ancient culture of the ancestral Pueblo people who made their homes in the beautiful cliff dwellings is a history class come-to-life. Visitors may hike or climb ladders in and out of the cliff dwellings, where they may truly savor the way the early Native Americans lived. But whether you choose to hike and climb or simply stroll through, you will discover why people return again and again to this

> **Insiders' Tip**
> Mesa Verde has been designated a World Cultural Heritage Site by the United Nations, and has been rated the number one "Historical Hot Spot" by *Historic Traveler* magazine.

historic area. For more on Mesa Verde National Park, turn to the Four Corners Attractions chapter of this book.

Hovenweep National Monument
Ranger Station
On Colorado/Utah border
(435) 459–4344
www.nps.gov/hove

If you're looking for a peaceful way to spend a day during your trip to the Four Corners and take in more of the great Native American history, you'll want to include a visit to Hovenweep National Monument. Hovenweep is out of the way, and rainy days can make road conditions to the monument nearly impassable, but it is worth waiting for dry weather to visit this wonderful place. Pack a lunch, fill up the car with gas (services are not available), and prepare for a day of contemplation and exercise—the best sites are accessed by driving on bumpy roads and taking a short hike. For more on Hovenweep National Monument, visit the Four Corners Attractions chapter of this book.

Cortez Cultural Center
25 N. Market St., Cortez
(970) 565–1151
www.cortezculturalcenter.org

The Cortez Cultural Center holds a wealth of information on archaeology and Native American culture. The center was developed to promote intercultural understanding and education and is a forum for arts, education, and Native American cultures. The center's museum offers interpretive exhibits on the Basket-maker and Pueblo periods of prehistoric communities. Displays from the Ute Mountain Ute, Pueblo, and Navajo tribes are also offered. The work of local artists is showcased in the center's art gallery. A Navajo hogan is located on the plaza of the center and, from Memorial Day through Labor Day, Native American dances are held every Monday through Saturday. Lectures, slide shows, and musical programs are offered September through May. You will want to visit the center before attending the Indian dances and cultural programs, which should take you about an hour. The Cortez Cultural Center is a wonderful place to take kids— there's usually a lot to see and do, and you can learn a little something, too.

Crow Canyon Archaeological Center
23390 C.R. K, Cortez
(800) 422–8975
www.crowcanyon.org

While youngsters may enjoy Crow Canyon Archaeological Center, it will be adults who really appreciate all this great center has to offer. A not-for-profit research and education center, Crow Canyon offers day tours and a variety of programs to expand participants' knowl-edge of the ancestral Puebloans who once lived in the mesas, mountains, and canyons near Mesa Verde centuries ago. On Wednesdays and Thursdays from June through September, Crow Canyon Archaeological Center offers a one-day program to individuals, groups, or fami-lies, and features a tour of a working exca-vation site. Tour groups are kept small, so feel free to ask tour leaders about the Puebloans and their activities. The tour also includes a hands-on activity with artifacts that demonstrate the chronology of the ancestral Puebloans and gives some insight into their very complex culture.

For those who want more than a day to explore and inquire, week-long excavation programs are available. Those programs include lodging on campus and meals. Reservations must be made for the day tour, as well as the week-long experience. If you're traveling to the Four Corners pri-marily to learn about the ancient Native Americans and how they lived and sur-vived here, Crow Canyon Archaeological Center will be a top spot in your travel plans.

Anasazi Heritage Center
27501 CO Hwy. 184, Dolores
(970) 882–4811
www.co.blm.gov/ahc/hmepge.htm

A federal museum, research center, and curatorial facility, the Anasazi Heritage Center introduces visitors to the prehis-tory of the Four Corners and offers hands-on activities that teach archaeological methods. Permanent exhibits display arti-facts, photographs, videos, illustrations, and descriptive text that detail the lifestyles of the ancestral Puebloan people. Some three million records, samples and artifacts from public lands throughout southwestern Colorado are housed in the Anasazi Heritage Center. Visitors are encouraged to interact with the center's computers, microscopes, corn grinding implements, loom and other weaving materials, and enjoy an orientation film, an archaeological test trench profile, and a partially reconstructed full-size pithouse. The center is adjacent to the Dominguez and Escalante sites, twelfth-century sites named after the Spanish Franciscan friars who were the first to record the presence of Native Americans in Colorado. A half-mile nature trail guides you from the museum to the sites, providing an incred-ible view of the Four Corners area.

Ghost Towns
Silverton Chamber of Commerce, Silverton
(800) 752–4494

As if there aren't enough things to see and do during the Colorado portion of your trip to the Four Corners, the wonderful old ghost towns of southwestern Colorado are a rich part of the history of the area and, for many, the most romantic. For years, the formidable Rocky Mountains ended the trek of many pioneers who were heading west, hoping to find their fortunes in gold. Long before trains chugged through the mountains, prospectors were picking away at the ground, looking for the bright yellow of gold. Many of them found their golden dream, and word of the discovery of gold in the mountains of Colorado spread quickly. Unfortunately, not everyone found the precious ore, and left the little towns they had established to the ghosts of lost dreams and fortunes. There are many ghost towns in southwestern Colorado, and Insiders love to visit them, see if there's any gold left in "them thar hills," and bask in the history of this beautiful area. The ghost towns of Howardsville, Eureka, and Animas Forks are all located within 14 miles of Silverton and are accessible by two-wheel-drive roads. Insiders encourage visitors to enjoy exploring these wonderful haunts and to listen to the ghosts who may (or may not!) remain, but do not enter old mines—they are not safe. We want you to enjoy our ghost towns, but not become a permanent part of them.

Colorado Specialties

Durango & Silverton Narrow Gauge Railroad
479 Main, Durango
(970) 247-2733
www.durangotrain.com

You simply can't come to Durango and not ride the train—it's unthinkable. Visitors from all over the world climb aboard the Durango & Silverton Narrow Gauge train to take a trip back through time, and enjoy the time of their lives. Excited passengers take their seats while the train whistle shrills the impending departure. The 119-year-old train belches out smoke, pulling the Victorian-era coaches out of the train depot, and begins the spectacular journey through some of Colorado's most beautiful mountains. The three hours on board the train as it travels to Silverton will pass quickly, and you'll arrive at your destination ready to relax and enjoy the old mining town of Silverton. The two-hour layover in this wonderful historic mining town is almost as much fun as the train ride there. The town prides itself on maintaining its rich history, and quaint shops and great restaurants await the tourist. If you'd like to sit in an open gondola car (the Insiders' choice), you must specify that when you make your reservations. Gondola cars have a roof and seats, but the sides are open, which allows more visibility but, if the weather chooses not to cooperate, it can get a little chilly. For those making the trip in the winter months, coaches are heated. The D&SNG has some events that will make your trip even more special—a Mountains by Moonlight ride, which offers hors d'oeuvres and cocktail specials; a Photographer's Special during the fall when the changing colors make the scenery even more spectacular; Silverton Salutations, which is opening day of the Silverton service, and passengers are encouraged to dress in Victorian or Old West attire; and a Cascade Canyon Winter Train caroling event, Santa Train, and New Year's Eve Moonlight Train. Call for schedules and reservations. Because this is such a popular attraction, the earlier you can make your reservations, the more assured you are of being able to get a seat on this most famous of train rides.

Rocky Mountain Colorfest!
(970) 247-0312
www.durango.org

Colorfest! is that time during September and October when Insiders and visitors alike celebrate the changing seasons and the beautiful colors of the high country.

All of southwest Colorado participates in Colorfest! with bicycle tours, river races, balloon rallies, jeep jamborees, Native American exhibits, dancers, art fairs, film and cowboy festivals, and more music than you can imagine! Communities throughout southwest Colorado plan activities and greet visitors like long-lost loved ones finally coming home.

San Juan Skyway
San Juan National Forest
15 Burnett Ct., Durango
(970) 247–4874
www.durango.org

For some of the most incredible scenery you'll see anywhere, plan on taking one full day and traveling the San Juan Skyway. This 236-mile drive is a photographer's dream and will take you through mountains and desert, and into historic mining towns and modern resort communities. Your trip will take you through Durango, Purgatory, and Molas Pass, where the wildflowers and crisp mountain air will encourage you to stop, stretch, and fill your spiritual soul with the beauty. Leaving Molas Pass, you'll enter Silverton, a historic mining community that takes pride in preserving its history. From Silverton, you will climb Red Mountain, a collapsed volcano cone that got its name from the lava flow and oxidized minerals within the rocky surface, including gold and silver. Insiders are accustomed to driving Red Mountain Pass, even during the winter months, when extreme care must be taken if the pass is open. The road is well maintained, but narrow, and Insiders and visitors alike should call the Colorado Department of Transportation (970-247-3355) for road conditions. Red Mountain Pass will take you into Ouray, a picturesque little town famous for its natural hot springs. Ouray should be another rest stop on your trip and you will find wonderful little shops and restaurants to make your stop worthwhile. Leaving Ouray, your trip will take you to the ranching community of Ridgeway, where the San Juan Skyway leaves U.S. Highway 550 and turns onto Colorado Highway 62. This road winds through beautiful fields before it changes to Colorado Highway 145 and drops into the deep box canyon where Telluride is located. Telluride is home to many famous people, but perhaps its most famous, short-term resident was Butch Cassidy, who robbed his first bank here on June 24, 1889. Leaving Telluride, you'll continue on the San Juan Skyway on Colorado Highway 145 over Lizard Head Pass, which gives you views of Mt. Wilson and Wilson Peak. You'll enter the little town of Rico, where you'll see beehive structures that were once used in the early parts of the primarily gold and silver smelting process. The road continues into Dolores, where you will find yourself on U.S. Highway 160, taking you into Cortez. The San Juan Skyway is designated as an All-American Road by the United States Department of Transportation and was awarded the distinction because of the rich culture, archaeology, history, scenery, and recreation the road offers. Take time to make this trip and, while it can be done in five to six hours if you don't stop, but please allow enough time to truly appreciate the drive by stopping often and experiencing the beauty you'll find.

Special Events

Iron Horse Bicycle Classic
Durango
(970) 259–4621
www.ironhorsebicycleclassic.com

Held each Memorial Day weekend, the Iron Horse Bicycle Classic attracts thousands of cyclists from throughout the country. It's road bikes against the Durango & Silverton Narrow Gauge Railroad, over two mountain passes and 5,500 feet of climbing. The race is 47 miles long. There will also be three days of mountain bike racing on a course in Durango. The kids' races are for bikers 3 to 16, with courses to fit all levels of

Soul-filling Job

Pat Gates considers herself to be one of the luckiest people in the Four Corners. As a member of the train crew for the Durango & Silverton Narrow Gauge Railroad, Gates fills her soul with the beauty of the Colorado Rockies all year long.

"It's like stepping back in time," Gates said of her job. "I relive the history of the area and of the train, which began in the early 1880s. I guess you have to appreciate history to really enjoy this."

Fortunately for Gates, she not only appreciates the history of the train and of the mining area it transverses, but she also loves sharing her appreciation with passengers. While she often works the Concession Car, serving snacks, lunch, and alcoholic beverages to passengers, Gates admitted she'd rather work the Parlor Car and the Cinco Animas Car. It is there that she has the time to share her love of the area with visitors and to get to know the people who board the train for a trip back in time.

"I really like working the Cinco and Parlor cars," Gates said. "I'm the only crew member there and I get to talk to the tourists and tell them about the different mines we pass by and about the history of the area. We go by Rockwood, where they filmed *Butch Cassidy and the Sundance Kid*, and I have a captive audience when I get to tell them all about it."

In the Concession Car, Gates said she waits on about 400 people, but in the Cinco and Parlor cars, it's just 28 passengers who get her total attention. While she enjoys all the passengers who ride the train, Gates said she is especially fond of those from Great Britain. "Most of the tourists are from Germany and France, and from all over the United States, but the most interesting group, and the nicest, are from Great Britain. They are very friendly and very nice people."

Many foreign countries film the train for commercial use, Gates added. "People come from all over the world to film here. There's great interest in the area and the train, and we play host to lots of film crews."

The train also attracts celebrities, especially during the Western Film Festival, held each fall in Durango. "Dennis Weaver rides a lot, and Michael J. Fox, Tom Selleck, and Bill Gates have all ridden the train," Gates said. "During the Festival, lots of the stars come and ride, and that's always a lot of fun."

Unfortunately, Gates said few people from the Four Corners ride the train. "I don't understand why because it's such a beautiful ride and such a fun trip," she said. "I'd like to see more local people on the train, but for some reason, they just don't come."

The train offers special rates to school children, Gates said, and yet few schools take advantage of the offer. "We have a group rate of just $7.50 per child and I don't know why the schools don't bring their kids up," she said.

It's not the movie stars or celebrities that keep Gates with the train crew, however. "It's the views," she admitted with a laugh. "I love the High Line, which took nine months and 1,500 Chinese people to complete. It's just beautiful. Every couple of weeks, we get to see a black bear, and the tourists really get a kick out of that."

In the wintertime, Gates said, ice crystals flow down the Animas River near the High Line. "It's beautiful," she said enthusiastically. "And I get to see elk, deer, bald eagles, and bighorn sheep. In the summer, I love the old silver mines on the way to

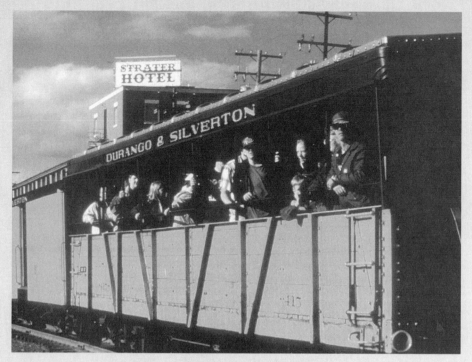

The open car of the Durango & Silverton Narrow Gauge Railroad. PHOTO: STEVE COHEN

Silverton and I love our two-hour stop in Silverton, where I can have lunch, shop, and enjoy the special history of the town."

One perk of the job, Gates said, is a wonderful old home near the Bitteroot Mine, which the owners let train employees use. The house was built in the 1930s, and the owners have retained all the furnishings of the time. "It's gorgeous," Gates said of the house. "It's two stories and it still has books of the '30s and a bedspread of the '30s and it's wonderful. The owners, who live in Denver, let the railroad crew spend the night or picnic there and we love it."

Except for the second floor, which Gates said is reportedly haunted. "I didn't stay up there long enough to find out, though," she said with a laugh.

A guest book allows visitors to share their memories of the house with others. "There are notes from the 1930s," Gates marveled, "nd the telegraph phone is still there, too."

Gates said she hopes everybody who visits the Four Corners, and those fortunate enough to live here, will make plans to ride the Durango & Silverton Narrow Gauge train. "This is a beautiful area with a rich history," Gates said. "When you ride the train, you step out of today's world and step back into a time when poor men became rich when they discovered silver and gold."

Today's passengers may not find gold and silver in the mines that dot the landscape along the train route, but they will find a wealth of beauty in the mountains, the meadows, and the wildlife that make the ride to Silverton a bounty of memories.

riders. A run, a swim, and more are included in this great event. (A hint from the Insider—this weekend is not the time to attempt to drive from Durango to Silverton, as the roads are closed for the race.)

La Plata County Fair
2500 Main, Durango
(970) 247–4355

County fairs bring out the best in people—and one of the best times you'll have all summer. A livestock show and auction, barbecue dinner, dances, tractor pulls, flower and vegetable show, and stiff competition amongst bakers, jelly makers, quilters, photographers, and wood workers combine to make the La Plata County Fair an event to remember. The fair is usually held the first of August.

Western Movie Festival
Sheraton Tamarron Resort
40292 U.S. Hwy. 550, Durango
(970) 259–6145

Movie stars, cowboys, and just us regular folk join in the Western Movie Festival held each September. The festival is a celebration of Western films and includes entertainment, a dinner with stars from the old Westerns, and a marketplace. Camera crews and reporters love this festival as much as Insiders do, and many of the Hollywood movie stars enjoy mingling with enthusiastic fans.

Music in the Mountains
Purgatory Ski Resort
1 Skier Place, Purgatory
(970) 385–6820
www.misicinthemountains.com

This three-week classical series is usually held in mid-July, and features musicians from major symphony orchestras and chamber music programs. Music in the Mountains is a classical music lovers dream! It's hosted at Purgatory Ski Resort. Call for a schedule.

Four Corners Iron Horse Motorcycle Rally
Ignacio
(888) 284–9212
www.fourcornersrally.com

This motorcycle rally gains momentum and attendance each year. The Four Corners Iron Horse Motorcycle Rally offers bikers bull riding, bands, 24-hour entertainment, biker field events, arm wrestling contests, tours of the Four Corners, and a tattoo row. It's held each year during Labor Day weekend. If you're a motorcycle enthusiast, you'll want to make this rally a "must do" on your trip through the Four Corners.

Arts

Music

Fort Lewis College Community Concert Hall
Fort Lewis College, Room 1000, Durango
(970) 247–7657

Fort Lewis takes seriously its mission to provide its students and the community of Durango with wonderful fine arts. Musicians of all genre perform in the Concert Hall. The Dirty Dozen Brass Band play wonderful jazz; Spyro Gyra offers a contemporary jazz sound; and the San Juan Symphony is a group of professional musicians from northern New Mexico and southern Colorado. They all join the Fort Lewis College bands and choirs to offer a variety of music sure to please almost everyone. Call the college for information on what will be available when you make your trip to the Four Corners.

Museums

Animas Museum
31st St. and W. 2nd Ave., Durango
(970) 259–2402

Exhibits on the history of the Durango area and the Indian cultures are spotlighted at the Animas Museum. The Animas Museum is Durango's only history museum, and its exhibits offer wonderful glimpses into the lives of miners, railroaders, merchants, ranchers, and outlaws. The museum board of directors strives to collect, preserve, and interpret the history of the area to visitors, while highlighting its great culture. A handcrafted saddle, porcelain Victorian dolls, and beautiful Native American arts and crafts are displayed in this museum, which is worth a stop when you visit the Four Corners. The museum also includes a nice gift shop.

Children's Museum of Durango
802 E. 2nd Ave., Durango
(970) 259–9234

Kids will love this museum for its hands-on exhibits for youngsters 2 to 11 years old. Exhibits include Seeds, Shovels and Sun; A Garden's Life, which attempts to help youngsters learn the science of gardening as well as the joy of it. Planning a garden, planting it, and growing and harvesting herbs, flowers, and vegetables are activities children participate in. Other exhibits include Robotics, where children build and expand their own robot; the Watershed, where they learn about erosion and deposition, build a dam and use a hand pump to get water; and a wood shop, where children use hammers, drills, saws and sandpaper, under the careful supervision of adults, to create something special.

Durango & Silverton Narrow Gauge Railroad Museum
479 Main Ave., Durango
(970) 247–2733

If you're not a railroad enthusiast when you arrive in Durango and see the train, you will be after you visit this museum and ride the D&SNG. The museum is a wonderful trip down memory lane, with its locomotives, lamps, locks, photos, art, library, and view of a roundhouse. This museum is a must see when you visit Durango.

Grand Motorcar and Piano Collection
586 Animas View Dr., Durango
(970) 247–1250

One Insider discovered this wonderful museum just before he moved from the Four Corners and has returned several times to visit it. For classic and antique car buffs, this will keep you enthralled for hours. If you're of the "they don't make 'em like they used to" car enthusiast, this museum alone will make your visit to the Four Corners worthwhile. There are also two incredibly beautiful unique grand pianos on display. Don't miss it.

Live Theatre

Diamond Circle Melodrama
Strater Hotel, 699 Main Ave., Durango
(970) 247–3400

For a great time, you must take in the melodrama at the Diamond Circle. You never know who's having more fun, however—the cast or the audience. This will most certainly be a highlight to your trip to the Four Corners, and your children will love it! Call for schedules and events.

Galleries

Toh-Atin Gallery
145 W. 9th St., Durango
(800) 525–0384

The Toh-Atin has a reputation among Insiders of offering quality Native American, Southwestern, and Western art. The gallery also specializes in Navajo rugs, and has a wonderful array of them.

New West Galleries
747 W. Main, Durango
(970) 259–5777

New West Galleries also has wonderful Southwestern and contemporary art for you to enjoy and purchase. Southwest gifts and jewelry are also available. This is a gallery you won't want to miss.

Voyager Productions—The Durango Gallery
123 W. 9th St., Durango
(970) 385-7496

If you enjoy contemporary nature photography, you'll love the beautiful photographs of the desert and the mountains of the Southwest. For those who think great art is only created on canvas, this gallery will change your mind.

Cortez Cultural Center
25 N. Market St., Cortez
(970) 565-1151

The Cortez Cultural Center offers Cortez residents and visitors alike the opportunity to enjoy wonderful events. Art and photography exhibits, interpretive exhibits in the museum, a gift shop, an anthropological research library, an authentic Navajo hogan, Native American dances, and the Community School of the Arts, are all part of this active community cultural center.

Galloping Goose Historical Society of Dolores Inc.
421 Railroad Ave., Dolores
(970) 882-7082

The Galloping Goose is a wonderful piece of history in the center of Dolores, where the railroad once chugged through the town. Here, you'll discover the history of this lovely little town and appreciate those who have worked so hard to keep that history alive.

Mancos Visitor Center and Pioneer Museum
400 N. Main, Mancos
(970) 533-7434

The center and museum offer a look back at the little town of Mancos, giving visitors a peek at the Old West. The visitor center and museum pay homage to the early pioneers of Mancos. Friendly folks will answer any questions you may have about the community and will gladly tell you the best places to shop and eat while you're here. Although, be forewarned that this community is tightly knit and believes every business is the best. The locals enjoy their Western heritage and love to play the part. You won't find any rhinestone cowboys or cowgirls here, but you'll find friendly people who love to share the history and uniqueness of the place they call home. A nice gift shop is also available.

Ute Tribes

History

They can lay claim to being the oldest continuous residents of Colorado, and they have a history that is as colorful as the state they call home. The Ute Indians were nomadic and lived primarily by hunting big game and gathering grasses, berries, and fruit in the mountainous areas of Colorado and parts of what is now Utah. The Utes were small family units in the beginning, and were associated in a loose confederation of seven bands—the Mouache, the Capote, the Weeminuche, the Uncompahgre, the Parlanuc, the Yampa, and the Uintah Utes.

The Southern Utes first encountered Anglo-Americans in 1806, when Lt. Zebulon Pike entered the San Luis Valley of Colorado. The Utes had been friendly with Mexican farmers, but in the 1830s, the farmers attempted to settle on Ute land. Angry, the Utes joined forces with their neighbors, the Navajos, and raided Mexican farms and settlements. In 1849, the Utes signed a peace treaty with the U. S. government that created boundaries between the two nations. When the gold rush to the San Juan Mountains began in the 1860s, the Utes were persuaded to give up all rights to the mountains, in spite of the fact that the land represented one-fourth of their reservation. This created the loss of their summer lands and deer harvest.

The Hunter Act of 1895 allowed for the remainder of Ute territory to be allotted. The Weeminuche Ute band refused to go along with the allotment plan and moved to the western end of the reservation around Mesa Verde and Sleeping Ute Mountain. The Weeminuche are now called the Ute Mountain Ute Indian Tribe, with headquarters in Towaoc, Colorado. In 1906, The U.S. government traded about 50,000 acres of the Ute Mountain Ute Reservation to establish Mesa Verde National Park. The Ute Mountain Utes received land near the Utah border, including most of the land around Sleeping Ute Mountain, in exchange for the park land. The legend of the Sleeping Ute is that he was a great warrior god who fought against all evil ones. When he was wounded in battle, he lie on his back and fell asleep. His blood turned to water and his blankets changed from green in the summer to white in the winter. Even in slumber, legend has it, Sleeping Ute continues to care for his people, inspire hope, and remain a spiritual focus for the Utes.

In 1937, about half of the original reservation was returned to the tribe—land that was rich with energy, which has provided the Southern Utes with a great source of income. The tribe owns and operates Mouache-Capote fencing, an oil field, a road development company, and the municipal water, sewer and irrigation-system.

Insiders' Tip

The Ute Mountain Ute Reservation covers 553,008 acres, with the land held in trust by the U.S. government. The Southern Ute Reservation includes more than 750,000 acres.

Insiders' Tip

The Ute Mountain Utes' resources include a casino, RV park, an archaeological park, and a pottery factory. Income from oil and gas wells also contributes to the tribe's economy. The tribe employs some 600 people in its enterprises, with about 400 more people employed by the tribal government.

The Ute Mountain Utes and the Southern Utes have casinos, which contribute greatly to the economy of both tribes. In 1992, the Ute Mountain Utes opened the Ute Mountain Casino, and in 1993, the Southern Utes opened the Sky Ute Casino. Both casinos hire members of the tribe and both casinos draw tourists, as well as regulars from southern Colorado and northern New Mexico. In addition to the casino, the Southern Utes have Sky Ute Events Center, which offers horse shows and other related activities. Several pow wows and the Ute Fair are also held there.

The Southern Utes and the Ute Mountain Utes enjoy a modern lifestyle and do much of their shopping in Cortez, Ignacio, Durango, and Farmington. Their children attend public schools and both tribes work diligently to instill in their youngsters the importance of their tribe, family, cultures, and traditions.

Hotels and Motels

Price Code

The price code is based on the cost of a standard room for two adults for one night.

$ . . . .$0–$30
$$ . . . .$31–$70
$$$ . . . .$71–$100

The Southern Ute and Ute Mountain Ute tribes have motels on their reservations, and there are accommodations in nearby communities. The two motels I highlight here are on the reservations and both are very nice and pleasant places to stay. Major credit cards are accepted, hotels are wheelchair accessible, but pets are not allowed.

Sleeping Ute Retreat $$
3108 U.S. Hwy. 160, South Cortez, CO
(877) 460–1260

The Sleeping Ute Retreat is a bed and breakfast with wonderful amenities and beautiful surroundings. There are two rooms, an apartment, and traditional hogans. The bedrooms are furnished with Native American accents and have private baths. Breakfast is healthy and served continental style. The Navajo Room has a double bed and French doors that open to a small deck with a wonderful view of the La Plata Mountains. The Catwalk Room has a queen size bed and a view of the

mountains. These rooms are priced from $69 to $129. The apartment is 1,200 square feet and can accommodate up to seven people. It has a full kitchen, a queen size bed, a day bed in the bedroom, and two double futons in the living room. The apartment is priced from $89 to $129. There are two hogans available for those with an adventurous spirit. Hogans have dirt floors and no indoor plumbing, but porta-potties are close by. A solar shower will refresh you and cooking is over the campfire. The larger hogan has a double-single bunk bed (double on the bottom, single on top) and a double futon. It rents for $30 for up to four people, with a $5 fee for each additional person. The smaller hogan sleeps two on cots and is $15 per night. The 30 acres of the Sleeping Ute Retreat include a stocked trout pond, which is fun for the kids as well as a more experienced angler. There is plenty of land to hike and explore and the hosts encourage visitors to do so. The Sleeping Ute Retreat offers a smoke-free environment.

The Sky Ute Lodge $$
14826 CO Hwy. 172, North Ignacio, CO
(800) 876–7017

The lodge is adjacent to the Sky Ute Casino and is a nice place to stay while you tour the Southern Ute Reservation or enjoy the games and slot machines in the casino. The rooms are spacious, and non-smoking rooms are available. A whirlpool and swimming pool are located just outside the hotel, a snack bar is available in the casino, and a restaurant is in the hotel area. The Sky Ute is in the little town of Ignacio, and while it isn't a large community, services are available.

Campgrounds

Each reservation has its own campground and they are clean and comfortable. The Ute Mountain Utes and the Sky Utes are proud of their campgrounds and they take great care of them so visitors will return.

You will find other campgrounds and RV parks along the way, and you're encouraged to try them, too.

Ute Mountain Casino RV Park and Campground
3 Weeminuche Dr., Towaoc, CO
(800) 889–5072

This campground is right next to the casino and is very nice. Restrooms and showers are provided and laundry facilities are available. There's a playground and game room for the kids, and a sauna, indoor pool, and wading pool for the family. There are 84 spaces for your RV or tent, or you can stay in one of the campground's tepees. Cost of camping here is $14 for a full hookup.

Lake Capote Campground
Located at the junction of U.S. Hwy.160 and CO Hwy. 151, Chimney Rock, CO
(970) 883–5359

This campground is located next to Lake Capote on the Southern Ute Reservation and is a lovely spot to camp. Camping sites are surrounded by trees, and the fishing in the lake will provide dinner for the campfire. The campground is open from mid-April through Labor Day. Because it's a popular spot to camp for locals and tourists, campsites fill up quickly, so arrive early for the best site selection. As this book went to print, this campground was closed for renovation, but it's a great spot, so call to see if they've re-opened.

Restaurants

Price Code

The price code is based on the cost of two entrees, and does not include appetizers, desserts, or alcoholic beverages.

$ . . . . .less than $15
$$ . . . .$16–$50
$$$ . . . . .more than $50

Both Ute Mountain Casino and Sky Ute Casino have restaurants, which serve basic, but good, food. Native Americans are fond of fast food and simple menus, and that's what you'll find at these restaurants. Buffets are popular with Native Americans, and are offered at the restaurants as well.

Kuchu's $$
Ute Mountain Casino
3 Weeminuche Dr., Towoac, CO
(800) 258–8007

Kuchu's offers breakfast, lunch, and dinner, with a varied menu that should please just about everybody. Steaks, seafood, and Mexican food are offered, and a seafood buffet is a Friday night standard. No liquor is served at the restaurant or on the reservation.

Pino Nuche Buffet $$
Sky Ute Casino
14826 CO Hwy. 172, North Ignacio, CO
(800) 876-7017

This restaurant offers only a buffet, which includes traditional Southwestern offerings as well as other dishes that change daily. The food is good and hearty and you're not apt to leave hungry. Liquor is served in the restaurant, but not in the casino. The casino's Rolling Thunder Café, located just off the casino floor, offers sandwiches and hamburgers.

Trading Posts

There are no trading posts on either the Ute or the Southern Ute reservations because of the close proximity to local towns, where trading posts find a wider customer base. You will find Native Americans selling beautiful arts, crafts, and jewelry along the reservation highways, however, and you're encouraged to stop and browse. Many of the finest works of Native American art are discovered at roadside vendors.

Arts

As with most Native Americans, traditional dances play a major role in the arts and culture of the Ute Mountain Utes and the Southern Utes. The Utes speak a Shoshonean language, which is part of the Uto-Aztecean language family, but has become distinctly their own.

The annual Ute Bear Dance is held in June and honors the grizzly bear, and was created to teach the Ute strength, wisdom, and survival, and resistance of the mischief of Coyote. The dance is performed to awaken the bear, which will lead the people to gather roots, nuts, and berries. During this four-day festival women select partners, which usually leads to a courtship and marriage. Visitors may watch the dance and cameras are allowed, but out of respect for the Utes, please ask their permission before taking photographs.

The Ute Sundance is held once a year and is a quest for the spiritual power between the Sundancer and the Great Spirit. The dancer must be commanded, often in a dream, to take part in this ceremony, which bonds the Utes. The dance begins with a four-day

Southern Ute Indian dancers. PHOTO: KRISTEN HARTZELL

fast from both food and all liquids. The dancer is traditionally male. While the Sundancer takes part in the ceremony as an individual, he also is a member of a family. The family pitches their teepee or shade lodge in designated locations around the periphery of the Sundance grounds. The Sundancer comes forth as their representative, and they support him both spiritually and physically in singing, in drumming, or simply in silent participation. The presence of the family is critical and gives the Sundancer strength and sustenance as he undergoes his quest. The family's presence is also crucial in reminding the dancer that although he is there on his own and the "medicine power" if gained will be his to use, the power is actually not his at all, but comes from the ultimate source (The Great Spirit), and is given to him for a purpose to be used in the service of his family and community.

In addition to the dances, the Ute Mountain Utes and the Southern Utes take part in two major powwows each year. The summer powwow is usually held around July 4th, and the other at Thanksgiving. The powwows welcome back the Utes to celebrate and dance together as a family and to celebrate life. They are an important part of the arts and culture of the Ute tribe.

The Utes also enjoy and support other arts, and you'll find these attractions will certainly be highlights of your trip to the Ute reservations and your tour of the Four Corners.

The Cortez Center
25 N. Market St., Cortez, CO
(970) 565–1151

The Cortez Center serves as a museum and orientation facility for those who want to participate in archaeological and Native American cultural experiences. The center, through a partnership with the University of Colorado, offers interpretive exhibits on the Basketmaker and Pueblo periods of the Anasazi civilization. Displays from the Ute Mountain Ute Tribe and a variety of traveling exhibits are featured in the center throughout the year. During the summer months, demonstrations of native crafts and lifestyles are offered. The Octubre Fiesta, held in the fall, celebrates the ethnic populations of the area, with art shows and Native American cultural events as the highlight. There is always something of interest going on at the Cortez Center and visitors are encouraged to stop and check it out.

Southern Ute Indian Cultural Center
14826 CO Hwy. 172, North Ignacio, CO
(970) 563–9583

The Southern Ute Indian Cultural Center offers a glimpse into the history of the Ute people. The Circle of Life, a permanent exhibit in the center, tells the story of the Ute people during the seasons. A collection of beautiful beadwork is on display, and the museum store offers equally magnificent beadwork for sale. An example of the powwow outfits worn by the Utes is on display, as is a collection of historical Ute tools. A life size display offers an explanation of the meaning and importance of the Bear Dance. This is a wonderful collection of the art and history of the Ute Tribe and should be included in your travel plans, especially if you're making a stop at the Sky Ute Casino and Lodge, which are next door to the center.

Ute Mountain Tribal Park
Junction of U.S. Hwy. 160 and
U.S. Hwy. 666, Towaoc, CO
(800) 847–5485

Visitors to the Ute Mountain Tribal Park have the opportunity to explore and discover wonderful cliff dwellings and kivas, and to learn a special Native American interpretation of the culturally diverse homelands of the Ute Mountain Ute Tribe. Tree House is a cliff dwelling that was built around 1140 A.D. and was occupied for 15 to 20 years. Each dwelling was rebuilt and occupied for about one full generation, then was abandoned, never to be used again. The kiva was once covered by roofs and accessible only by ladder. It displays a beautiful painting around the interior wall. Pottery making is often demonstrated at the park, and visitors may see Ute Mountain Utes create incredible art that reflects the land and their heritage.

Ute Mountain Indian Pottery
Junction of U.S. Hwy. 160 and
U.S. Hwy. 666, Towaoc, CO
(800) 896–8548

To encourage the talents of tribal artists, the Ute Mountain Utes formed a pottery factory in 1973. It employs about 30 tribal members who participate in all phases of production and management of the pottery. The pottery is poured by hand into ceramic molds, then is turned and cleaned. Artists create their own designs and sign each piece. The pottery is of museum quality, but many visitors purchase it to use every day. Whether you opt to use the pottery or simply display it, you'll have a wonderful memento of your trip to the Ute Mountain Ute Reservation.

Healthcare

The Ute Mountain Utes and the Southern Utes are provided healthcare by the Indian Health Services, an agency within the U.S. Department of Health and Human Services. The IHS provides federal health services to American Indians and Alaska Natives. As the principal healthcare provider and health advocate for Native Americans, the IHS strives to ensure the availability and accessibility of comprehensive, culturally acceptable personal and public health services to Native Americans and Alaskan native people.

Insiders' Tip
More than half of the U.S. Native American population live off the reservation, but most return home regularly to participate in family and tribal life, and to retire.

The Southern Colorado Ute Service Unit (SCUSU) provides ambulatory care services through two health centers, one at Towaoc and one at Ignacio, and a field health station in White Mesa, Utah. Care includes medical, nursing, dental, optometry, nutrition, health education, community health nursing, mental health, social services, substance abuse, and environmental health services. General clinics are provided to educate and inform Ute Mountain Utes and Southern Utes on well-child, chronic diseases, allergies, women's health issues, and podiatry. A pharmacy, a laboratory, and radiology services are provided at each of the centers. Additional healthcare services, including in-patient and specialty care, can be arranged through contacts with a variety of healthcare providers in the local area.

The Towaoc Community Mental Health Program provides general counseling for relationships, nutrition, and domestic violence. There is no charge to use the program and patients must be a Native American living on or near the Ute Mountain Ute Reservation.

The Ute Mountain Ute Tribe and the Southern Ute Tribe realize the importance of providing quality healthcare to their people, and tribal leaders strive to make healthcare services available and accessible.

Education

Youngsters from the Ute Mountain Ute Tribe and the Southern Ute Tribe attend public schools in Cortez and Ignacio, respectively. While tribal leaders believe students receive quality education from those schools, they are also concerned about young tribe members continuing their education in the traditions, cultures, and issues of their own tribes.

The Ute Mountain Utes are working in cooperation with the local school district, the Crow Canyon Archaeological Center, and other local leaders to establish a Youth Opportunity Program. The idea behind the program is to create a one-stop center to serve the youth of the Ute Mountain Ute Tribe by guiding them back into the classroom or into jobs, or offering suggestions and opportunities for future careers. The goals of the program are to include more job training and placement, tutoring, career and skill assessment, cultural awareness, physical fitness and health, mentoring programs, and work experience.

The program also seeks to encourage young people to learn skills that will help them in government, natural resource management, agriculture, law enforcement, construction, planning, retail, archaeology, arts and culture, and education on the reservation. While tribal leaders are committed to helping their young people learn new skills and continue their education, they are also concerned about having them return to the reservation to share what they have learned. Going off the reservation for technical training or to college is good, leaders recognize, but there must be jobs for them on the reservation if the young people are expected to return.

Members of the Southern Ute Tribe have established a school for their children who are ages 3 through 9. Tribal leaders structured their own curriculum and hired as many Native American teachers as possible to teach at the Southern Ute Indian Academy. Students are divided into age groups instead of class, and are taught by the Montessori method, which encourages self-exploration. Students also learn the Southern Ute culture and traditions, which tribal leaders believe will make them appreciate and embrace their rich history.

Students at Ignacio High School, which is located on the Southern Ute Reservation, include members of three ethnic groups—Native American, Anglo, and Latino. Students are taught to appreciate their own ethnic background while learning about the backgrounds of their fellow students. The school also allows students entering the 11th grade the option of developing a plan that includes dual credit and college credit classes for their remaining two years in high school and one additional year. By the end of their senior year, the students will complete all, except one, high school graduation requirement, which allows the students to attend high school one more year. That extra year allows the students to continue taking dual credit classes and to complete both high school graduation and associate requirements. Students who participate in the optional year graduate from high school with an associate of arts or associate of science degree at no cost.

Leaders of the Ute Mountain Ute Tribe and the Southern Ute Tribe want their young people to be educated members of their tribe, with an appreciation and respect for their culture while being role models for the next generation.

Utah

Hotels and
Motels
Bed and
Breakfasts
Campgrounds
and RV Sites
Restaurants
Shopping
Kidstuff
Recreation
Attractions
Arts

First-time visitors to the southeastern part of Utah are often struck with the beauty of the area. The ever-changing colors of the desert stretch to meet the green of the mountains. The rich red of the sandstone that creates some of the most beautiful natural wonders of the world reaches up to a sky that's bluer than blue and a sun that's brighter than yellow. You'll enjoy the Utah portion of your trip to the Four Corners and, after meeting the wonderful people who live there and marveling over the great beauty of the area, you may just decide your next trip will be to visit the state. You will be warmly welcomed.

Utah was the 45th state, celebrating its statehood on January 4, 1896. The name of the state, Utah, is a Ute Indian word meaning "home on mountain top." With 84,916 square miles of land in the state, the federal government owns an incredible 65 percent of it.

Utah's first known residents were the ancient Pueblo people, also known as the Anasazi Indians. The Ute Tribe and the Navajo Indians roamed the region, and many of them still call Utah home.

Utah's most famous residents, however, are members of the Church of Jesus Christ of Latter-day Saints (Mormons). The pioneers, let by Brigham Young, were the first non-Indians to settle permanently in the valley, which later became Salt Lake City, the capital of Utah. The pioneers fell in love with the beauty of the area, and quickly began planting and growing crops. In 1848, more emigrants arrived in the valley, but a late frost, drought, and a plaque of crickets nearly destroyed the harvest. Help came in the form of flocks of seagulls, however, which consumed the crickets and enough of the crop was saved to help the settlers survive the bitter winter. In gratitude, the seagull was later named the state bird.

Also in 1848, Mexico gave the area to the United States and, in 1850, the "State of Deseret" became the Utah Territory. Deseret means "honeybee," a symbol of industriousness. The beehive is Utah's state symbol.

As you travel throughout southeastern Utah, you will find countless photo opportunities, more than enough things for your family to do and enjoy, and that wonderful, laid-back lifestyle that typifies the Four Corners. You will visit with residents who have called Utah home for a long time, and with visitors from across the world who have come to take advantage of the beauty of the area and its people. Insiders encourage you not to rush the Utah portion of your trip through the Four Corners. For it will be the minutes you spend talking to a Utah native that you will realize that the beauty of this area is only enhanced by the hospitality and generosity of those who call it home.

Insiders' Tip

Utah's culture emphasizes a family and community lifestyle. Thirty-five states have higher violent crime rates than Utah.

Hotels and Motels

Price Code

The price code is based on the cost of a standard room for two adults for one night.

$ . . . . .0–$30
$$ . . . .$31–$50
$$$ . . . .$51–$70
$$$$ . . . .$71 and up

Most of the major hotels and motels have facilities in southeastern Utah, and I certainly encourage you to stay at them if they meet your needs. There are other hotels and motels along your tour of the Four Corners that may offer a taste of the neighborhood and might be worth a look, or a stay. All places accept major credit cards unless otherwise noted, and all establishments are wheelchair accessible unless stated otherwise. All facilities have smoking and non-smoking rooms and pets are welcome unless noted. Always call for information and reservations and for exact rates. Wherever you stay, Insiders' want you to enjoy your accommodations and the hospitality of the Four Corners. You'll see most accommodations are in Moab, which is the largest town in southeastern Utah.

Big Horn Lodge $$$$
550 S. Main, Moab
(800) 325–6171

If you're looking for rustic, but not discomfort, you'll enjoy the surroundings at Big Horn Lodge. Lodge-style rooms complete with log furniture offer rustic ambiance and the opportunity to put your feet up without fear of marring the tables! The staff at Big Horn realizes the value of a bike to the mountain biker, and allows bikes to be kept in the rooms. A bike workstation with a stand and wash area is also offered. Big Horn specializes in package deals, so you may include rafting, four-wheeling, horseback riding, rock climbing, or just sightseeing tours during your stay. Big Horn not only loves pets, but has rooms just for them. Call for availability. A family restaurant is on the premises. Refrigerators and that all-important coffee pot are included in the rooms.

Nicholas Lane Lodging $$$
50 E. Center St., Moab
(800) 505–5343

Nicholas Lane isn't just another motel—in fact, it's NOT a motel. These one-bedroom condominiums are perfect for those looking for something a little more than another motel room. Condos have fully equipped kitchenettes with coffee, double and queen size beds, telephones, cable TV, laundry facilities, patios with barbecues, and a hot tub. These condominiums are just right if you plan to stay in the Utah portion of the Four Corners for more than a few days. The residential atmosphere of the neighborhood will make you feel at home. Please call for reservations.

Recapture Lodge $$$
250 Main St., Bluff
(435) 672–2281

In the tiny town of Bluff (population about 300) and tucked in the trees and 300-foot cliffs along the San Juan River is Recapture Lodge, a motel that strives to make you think you are home without the responsibilities. With free interpretive slide shows, an outdoor pool and hot tub, laundry facilities, some kitchen units (be sure to request a kitchen unit when you call for reservations; the limited number go quickly during the busy tourist season), and approximately 100 acres of space bordering the river, you'll find much to do during your stay at Recapture Lodge. The lodge also provides tables, grills, and loaner utensils if you decide to take a picnic to those beautiful bluffs and enjoy the sunset. The staff is familiar with many outfitters and tour guides and will help you schedule outdoor excitement. During the tourist season, Recapture Lodge also offers a light, self-service breakfast in the lobby. Get to know the people of Bluff, explore the town and the attractions nearby, and enjoy your stay at Recapture Lodge.

The Virginian Motel $$$$
70 E. 2nd South, Moab
(800) 261–2063

A pretty little motel just off Main Street, the Virginian Motel is a pleasant place to hang your hat while touring the Utah portion of the Four Corners. With fully equipped kitchenettes, complete with refrigerator and stove, you will certainly be able to make yourself at home at the Virginian. There is a modest additional $5 charge for kitchenettes. The motel also offers a back yard with picnic tables and a barbecue if you'd like to grill a steak or hamburger, and a golf practice net for those who want to keep it under par during their stay. The Virginian is adjacent to Moab's nature walkway. Get out and enjoy a leisurely walk after dinner or

before breakfast to witness the incredible sunrises noted in this part of Utah. If you've brought your bicycle along, the Virginian has a secure and locked storage unit for it. Call for reservations and exact rates.

Bed and Breakfasts

Price Code

The price code is based on the cost of a standard room for two adults for one night.

$ . . . . less than $30
$$ . . . . $31–$50
$$$ . . . . $51 and up

Southeastern Utah has a wide variety of bed and breakfasts you and your family may enjoy. Each of them is distinctive and worthy of your attention. Many of them are historic homes, opened up by their owners to allow visitors to truly enjoy the history of the Four Corners. The ones I've listed are but a sampling. Major credit cards are accepted, unless otherwise noted.

Cali Cochitta Bed & Breakfast $$$$
110 S. 200 East, Moab
(888) 429–8112

Cali Cochitta, the "House of Dreams," is a late-1800s Victorian home, restored and renovated to its classic original style. Cali Cochitta has three large guest rooms, one suite, and a cottage. Each room has a private bath and queen size beds. The suite includes a queen size and double bed, with two rooms connected by an open doorway. The cottage is adjacent to the main house and has two bedrooms, each with a twin bed and bath. Cali Cochitta hosts are culinary artists as well as gardening enthusiasts, which combine to ensure a wonderful breakfast for guests. You may choose from a light, more continental breakfast to a hot breakfast entree. If you'd like a boxed lunch to take with you the next day, or an intimate dinner to celebrate a wonderful vacation, Cali Cochitta hosts will make sure your needs are cared for. Your stay at Cali Cochitta may be one of your fondest memories of the Four Corners. Cali Cochitta is a non-smoking bed and breakfast.

Dream Keeper Inn and Retreat $$$$
191 S. 200 East, Moab
(888) 230–3247

While the rooms at Dream Keeper Inn and Retreat are lovely, it just may be the gardens and the beautifully cared for yard that will make you feel at home. A vine covered arbor, big shade trees and lovely flowers invite guests to spend time in the yard of the Dream Keeper. A swimming pool and hot tub add to the easy-going attitude of this most gracious home. Each guest room has a private bath and most open onto the garden, so you can enjoy it whenever you choose. A healthy and hearty breakfast is served in the cheerful dining room or on the patio by the rose garden.

The Mayor's House B&B $$$$
505 E. Rose Tree Lane, Moab
(888) 791–2345

Go ahead, tell your friends you stayed at the Mayor's House while on your trip through the Four Corners. They might be impressed, but they'll be delighted when you tell them this Mayor's House was a lovely bed and breakfast. Built in the 1980s, the Mayor's House may not be as old as some bed and breakfasts, but it is luxurious. After settling in upon your arrival, you may decide a dip in the large heated pool would feel good, or if you've spent the day hiking or bicycling, maybe the hot tub will appeal to you. Before

retiring for the night in one of the Mayor's House nicely appointed rooms, you may want to enjoy a good book in the library, or select a movie to take to your room to view. Whatever you opt to do, the hosts at the Mayor's House will strive to make sure you're comfortable and well cared for during your visit. A healthy breakfast will await you at the breakfast bar. The Mayor's House B&B is a non-smoking facility and pets are not welcome. The hosts of the Mayor's House enjoy having children visit, but ask that they be supervised at all times for the comfort of all their guests.

Rogers House Bed & Breakfast Inn $$$$
412 S. Main St., Blanding
(800) 355–3932

A lovely leaded glass front door beckons visitors to the Rogers House Bed & Breakfast and is just an indication of the charm of this wonderful historic house. The house was built in 1915 by early settlers to the area and was renovated in 1993. Antique furniture, glossy hardwood floors and balustrades provide a comfortable, relaxing atmosphere to all who enter. Visitors just might hear music from the antique mahogany piano as another guest tickles its ivories. On warm evenings, guests gather to share travel information and get to know each other on the large front porch. Smoking is allowed in the yard or on the front porch of the Rogers House and pets are not welcome. Rogers House hosts make sure guests leave their home with a bountiful breakfast, which includes coffee, juice, sweet breads, seasonal fruit, homemade granola and a freshly made entree. When you leave the Rogers House, you will leave with a full tummy, happy memories and, very likely, a yearning to return.

Campgrounds and RV Sites

While southeastern Utah has its share of quality hotels and motels that provide comfort to the tourist, the Utah portion of the Four Corners takes great pride in the campgrounds and RV sites it offers. If you're pulling a complete "home on wheels" or have your tent and bedroll stashed in the trunk of your vehicle, you'll find wonderful outdoor accommodations. Major credit cards are accepted at most campgrounds and RV sites; those that do not accept credit cards will be noted. Children and pets are also welcomed at most places, and if not, that will be noted in the description of them. Facilities that are not wheelchair accessible will also be noted; otherwise, be assured that your comfort has been addressed in the park you select.

Moab has several very nice places to pitch your tent or hook up your RV—you may find it difficult to decide which of them to call your temporary home.

Public campgrounds are available for your camping pleasure. For campgrounds located in national parks, call (435) 259-7164; and for those on BLM land, call (435) 259-6111.

Cadillac Ranch RV Park
U.S. Hwy. 191, Bluff
(800) 672–2262

A relatively new RV park in Bluff, the Cadillac Ranch RV Park offers a quiet place in which to unwind after a busy day sightseeing in the Four Corners. With 17 RV spaces and room for 10 tents, the Cadillac Ranch is the perfect place to base your visit to the Four Corners. If you don't get enough fun during the day, you may rent a paddle boat at the park (the kids will love that!), fish in a private pond, arrange for a horseback ride, or bask in the solitude of the area. Fees vary with the activity, so ask for rates when you check in. Pets are welcome at the Cadillac Ranch, but must be kept on leashes. Showers are available. The park is open March through November and reservations are encouraged. Rates are $15 plus tax per night; $85 per week, or $300 per month.

Canyonlands Campground and RV Park
555 S. Main, Moab
(800) 522–6848

The staff of Canyonlands Campground and RV Park is committed to making your stay in the Four Corners memorable. Situated in a lovely area, Canyonlands offers year-round service, shaded and level pull-throughs with cement patios, tent sites with trees and shade huts, restrooms and showers, a swimming pool, picnic tables and grills, cable TV, laundry facilities, a convenience store, an ATM, and jeep and raft trips. The cost of jeep and raft trips will vary, depending on the length of the trip. Check with the camp-

ground staff for more information. Canyonlands is one of those places you think of when you think vacation, and you won't be disappointed with your stay.

Moab Outback Tours and Tipis
P.O. Box 1292, Moab
(435) 259–2667

Maybe, during this Utah portion of your trip to the Four Corners, you're ready for something different. Maybe you want to get out of the tent or RV, but don't really want to stay in a hotel or motel. If that's the case, Moab Outback has the answer and it's one the kids and adults will long remember. Moab Outback Tours and Tipis has more than 20 tepees to accommodate your family or your entire group, if you're traveling together. Your tepee may be set up in an approved BLM campground, or at another location, if permitted. Moab Outback has several sites identified where your tepee may be set up, and the nice folks there will do whatever they can to make sure you're comfortable. Some tepees are already set up, and you're invited to check out those locations to see if one of them will suit you and your family. These tepees are cute and comfortable, and you will not be sorry you made the effort to stay in one. Rates run about $35 a night for a 16-foot tepee, which will sleep four; or about $45 for a 20-foot tepee, which will let six of you slumber peacefully. Tours of the area may also be arranged with Moab Outback, so if you're looking for a unique camping experience, call early for reservations.

Moab Valley RV and Campground
1773 N. U.S. Hwy. 191, Moab
(435) 259–4469

Another great place to stay for campers in the Moab area is the Moab Valley RV and Campground. With full hookups, pull-through sites, grass tent sites, a group grass tent site, and air conditioned cabins, whatever your needs might be, this campground can take care of you. There are 68 pull-through sites with water, electricity, and cable TV hookups. Sites are up to 60 feet long, and have a nice sized grass area, picnic table, charcoal barbecue, and lovely trees to shade your activities. While animals are welcome, there is a two dog maximum per site in this area. There is also an area with 22 back-in sites, which have water and electricity. Maximum length of RV is 26 feet, and no pets are allowed in this area. Tent sites have picnic tables and barbecues, and only charcoal and gas stoves are permitted. Pets are not allowed in tent sites. Rates are based on one- and two-person occupancy and extra people five years and older are an additional $5. Smaller tents cost $16 and the larger tents go for $20 per night

Small cabins will sleep up to four people and the larger cabin will sleep up to six people. Cabins are non-smoking and pets are not allowed. The campground has two restrooms with private shower stalls. A large laundry facility will keep your family clean as well as happy for a nominal cost. This is a peaceful and comfortable campground and will provide you and your family with pleasant surroundings. Moab Valley RV and Campground is open from March through October.

Pack Creek Campground and RV Park
1520 Murphy Lane #6, Moab
(435) 259–2982

Pack Creek Campground is an off-highway campground, but is less than 15 minutes from the center of Moab. Pack Creek is proud of its family ownership and strives to meet the needs of your family. Laundry facilities, restrooms and showers, and a playground for the children are just some of the amenities at Park Creek. Tent sites, sites for RV's up to 55 feet, and camper sites especially for pop-up campers and tent trailers are all available. If you're traveling in a group, Pack Creek offers group sites, which can accommodate up to 200 people. Utilities are also available. With beautiful cottonwood trees to shade you, a quiet stream to soothe you and the La Sal Mountains to inspire you, this campground hopes to make your visit to the Four Corners memorable. A full hookup is $20 per night; $17.50 for electricity and water. Tents are $15 per night.

Riverside Oasis Campground and RV Park
1861 N. U.S. Hwy. 191, Moab
(877) 285–7757

Riverside Oasis Campground and RV Park is another park that strives to give you the necessities of home while you enjoy camping life. Riverside offers 23 pull-through RV sites that can handle an RV of up to 60 feet long, and provides hookups for water, sewer and electric, as well as cable TV. Grass, shade trees, barbecue grills, and picnic tables add to make your stay here as good as it gets. Grass tent sites can handle large and small groups and picnic tables and barbecues are available for your convenience. Please note, however, that Riverside allows only charcoal and gas stoves. Once you've got your tent pitched or your RV hooked up, you'll want to check out the other amenities Riverside offers—a general store that has great souvenirs; 24-hour security, hot showers, restrooms, RV supplies, telephone and e-mail service, laundry facilities and, if you're tired of the RV or the tent, a two-bedroom furnished apartment. Riverside's hosts will also arrange tours for you and encourage you to enjoy the natural beauty of the area. Tent sites are $15 per night for the first one to two people, and $3 per night for each additional guest older than eight years old. Groups must have 20 people to qualify for the $5 per person per night rate. RV rates are $20 plus tax per night for the first one to two people, and $3 per night for each additional guest older than eight years old. Campers who need 50 amp electrical services are charged an additional $2 per night.

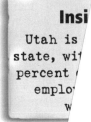

Restaurants

Price code

The price code is based on the cost of two entrees, but does not include appetizers, dessert, or alcoholic beverages.

$ . . . .$15–$24
$$ . . . .$25–$34
$$$ . . . .$35–$49
$$$$ . . . .$50 and up

The southeastern portion of Utah is remote, with few large communities to serve the tourist. You won't find as many restaurants here as in other parts of the Four Corners, but the ones you find will offer cuisine you'll enjoy. The restaurants I've listed are just a few of the ones you'll discover as you travel the Utah portion of your trip through the Four Corners. You may find new eating establishments as your travel and I encourage you to stop and enjoy. More and more fine chefs and great cooks are moving to the Four Corners area to enjoy the view and lifestyle and offer new and varied menus. Most of the restaurants I've listed are in Moab because it's the largest city in this part of the Four Corners.

All major credit cards are accepted unless otherwise noted and all restaurants are wheelchair accessible unless stated otherwise.

Bar-M Chuckwagon $$$
U.S. Hwy. 191, Moab
(800) 214–2085

Located four miles north of the Arches National Park entrance, the Bar-M Chuckwagon is worth the drive for a fun evening for the whole family. Gunfights, games, a Western village, gift shop, saloon, and other great activities will entertain the kids before dinner, and the folklore, great humor, and audience participation will delight them after they've enjoyed a cowboy dinner. Sliced roast beef, barbecue chicken, baked potato, Bar-M baked beans, cinnamon applesauce, buttermilk biscuits, old-fashioned cake, cowboy coffee, iced tea, and lemonade will tempt the palate of almost everyone.

Dinner and show tickets may be picked up at Doc's Medicine Wagon at 6 P.M. The gunfights start at 7 P.M. and supper is served up promptly at 7:30 P.M. This is a great way for the kids to expend some energy and for the family to enjoy a wonderful evening together. Reservations are strongly suggested.

Fat City Smokehouse $
36 S. 100 West, Moab
(435) 259–4302

The wonderful aroma of smokehouse cooking will lure you to the Fat City Smokehouse, where you'll find some of the best ribs anywhere. The Smokehouse isn't a large restaurant, but it is busy with locals and tourists who follow their noses

ttle eatery. The Smoke-
ks up box lunches for those
if you're planning an all day
might want to stop and pick up
before you head out. You're only
em will be waiting until lunch time
at.

The Sunset Grill $$$
900 N. U.S. Hwy. 191, Moab
(435) 259–7146

The Sunset Grill is located in the historic home of Charles A. Steen, a prospector who became a millionaire when he discovered the world's richest uranium deposit in the early 1950s. Steen loved company and every day at 5 P.M. opened his home to visitors. That custom continues today, as guests arrive to enjoy dining by candlelight while watching the sunset. The Sunset Grill doesn't focus on a fancy menu, but creates dishes many of us are familiar with. The chef adds his special touch to make those dishes memorable and delicious. Meats and seafood are hand cut in the kitchen of the Sunset Grill and fresh ingredients are brought in daily. T-bone steaks, filet mignon, prime rib, Colorado lamb, Idaho trout, and honey pecan chicken are included on the menu, as is Cajun shrimp fettuccini that is as good as it gets. The Sunset Grill prepares meals to order and will be happy to prepare your meal to meet special dietary needs. Youngsters are offered a special children's menu, and the staff of the Sunset Grill enjoys kids and are happy to see them. Reservations are suggested.

Cottonwood Steakhouse $
Main and 4th West St., Bluff
(435) 672–2282

An Old West atmosphere will greet you as you enter the Cottonwood Steakhouse, and you may want to enjoy your dinner outside under the old cottonwood tree. This is a quaint steakhouse that offers top-notch steaks, ribs, chicken, and specials. Meals are prepared outside on the grill—even the Western grilled potatoes. The owners keep the menu simple so they can treat their customers as guests, and make sure each dinner is properly prepared and served. Children's plates are available and beer and malt coolers are offered. Reservations are suggested, especially during the tourist season.

Shopping

Because there are no large cities in southeastern Utah, you won't find big shopping malls or retail centers. What you will find, however, are wonderful little shops that will offer unique treasurers to remind you of your visit. Because so many new shops and galleries are opened regularly, the ones I've listed are but a few of the shopping options open to you. I encourage you to visit these shops and any others you find.

Back of Beyond Books
83 N. Main St., Moab
(800) 700–2859

A little, independent bookstore with a big selection of books, Back of Beyond Books is a great place for the book lover. Here, you'll find books on natural history, environmental titles, Southwestern guidebooks and maps, Native American titles and Western history, fiction and nonfiction. If that's not enough, you'll find an assortment of poetry, philosophy, general fiction, current affairs and some really great stuff you just won't find in those big chain bookstores. The store was established in honor of noted author Edward Abbey and named after the hideout of a character in one of Abbey's books, *The Monkey Wrench Gang*. While the store carries many books on the West and natural history, its collection has grown to carry a large selection of children's books and books on Native Americana. Insiders enjoy coming to Back of Beyond Books, but we must warn you—you're likely to spend more time here than you thought, but it will be time well spent.

Mondo Coffees
59 S. Main St., Moab
(435) 259-5551

If you love coffee the way Insiders love coffee, you'll want to stop at Mondos Coffees, smell the brew, and buy the blends. While other, major coffee chains offer quality coffee, there's something about Mondo coffee that's just a little different and just a little more Southwestern with a lot of great flavor. The Mondo Italiano Blend blends four medium dark and dark roasted beans, which offers a slightly tangy, chocolate flavor. The Costa Rican Espresso Roast is medium to dark bodied with a clean, slightly citric flavor that is never bitter. The Colombian Espresso Roast tastes similar to dark chocolate (Yum!) and if you think the flavor of this great coffee is wonderful, you'll find the smell even more intoxicating. Mondo's French Roast is very good, as is the Mondo Agusto Decaf, which you will never guess is decaf. This is a coffee lovers paradise, so if you love your java, make it a point to visit Mondo Coffees.

New Covenant Woodshop
1030 S. Bowling Alley Lane #6, Moab
(800) 599-1718

If you're looking for something uniquely Four Corners for your home, you'll want to stop at New Covenant Woodshop. Aspen, spruce, pine, and fir are gathered from the nearby La Sal Mountains, and shaped into some of the most beautiful custom furniture you'll ever see. Beds, tables, chairs, and more can be yours for the asking, and will be created just for you, just the way you want them. If you've got an idea or a sketch, bring it by and the wood workers at New Covenant will craft it for you. Since your piece may not be ready by the time you head home, New Covenant will ship your new furniture to you.

The Overlook Gallery
83 E. Center St., Moab
(435) 259-3861

The Overlook Gallery is located in one of Moab's oldest structures and offers works of art from some of the area's most talented artists. Visitors to the Overlook Gallery will discover art unique to the area, most of which has been inspired by the incredible beauty of southeastern Utah.

Hozoni Pottery
913 E. Navajo Twins Dr., Bluff
(800) 526-3448

Hozoni is Navajo which means "panoramic beauty," and beauty is exactly what you'll find at this wonderful shop. The Navajo people, their culture, and their land are depicted in much of the pottery here, and you will marvel at the detail and beauty of it. Take a few minutes to stop at Hozoni Pottery, where you'll find wonderful gifts for you and your friends, and will enjoy the atmosphere of this unique shop.

Kennedy Indian Arts
913 E. Navajo Twins Dr., Bluff
(435) 672-2405

The work of the Zuni people is spotlighted at this gallery, which offers everything from jewelry to folk art to Native American fetishes, which are believed to have great magical powers. The Zuni fetishes are as unique as the artists who craft them, and once you purchase a fetish, you may find you'll want more and more. You'll also find beautiful squash blossom necklaces, bracelets and pins, and pottery made by several top Navajo artists. Whether you stop to buy or browse, Kennedy Indian Arts is sure to please your eye and soothe your soul.

Twin Rocks Trading Post
913 E. Navajo Dr., Bluff
(800) 526-3448

For years, Twin Rocks Trading Post has developed a reputation for working with local artists to develop new and unique basketry, rug, and jewelry designs. Because of that relationship, you will find many one-of-a-kind items here that you won't find elsewhere. The staff knows most of the artists and will be happy to share their background with you. Twin Rocks offers jewelry you won't want to ever take off, beautiful baskets, and pottery, as well as Navajo folk art. Whatever you find at Twin Rocks is of the utmost quality and design and you'll find yourself wanting to purchase one of everything. Twin Rocks will ship your items home for you if you don't want to pack them with you—or if you've purchased more than your suitcase can hold.

Kidstuff

Youngsters in southeastern Utah have a wonderful playground to enjoy—the entire outdoors. Surrounded by nature trails, bicycle paths, campgrounds, fishing holes, and the ever-changing attractions at nearby parks and monuments, kids have more than enough to keep them busy. If there is a lack of organized activities in this part of the Four Corners, it is because youngsters here take advantage of the many outdoor activities southeastern Utah offers.

Horseback riding, winter sports, river rafting, and exploring the sites and sounds of the Four Corners are sure to keep youngsters active and happy. Whatever activities your kids like to do, join in the fun—the kids will love it and love you for it.

Most of the visitor centers of national parks and monuments have special activities just for the kids.

At Bryce Canyon National Park, youngsters can join a ranger for games and activities on ecology and the park, and participate in star parties, where they can join an astronomer from Hansen Planetarium and view the sky through telescopes.

Kids who love to fish will find lots of places to reel 'em in here in southeastern Utah. From the small, stocked ponds available at many motels and campgrounds to the Colorado and Green rivers, fishing is good in the Four Corners. Fishing licenses are not required for youngsters younger than 14. Non-resident licenses are $5 for one day and $15 for seven days. There are limits on the number of fish you may take with you, and they vary with each fishing spot. Please check at the nearest ranger station or at the bait shop where you purchase your license for limits.

Bar-M Chuckwagon
N. U.S. Hwy. 191, Moab
(800) 214-2085

The kids are sure to love the Old West fun at the Bar-M Chuckwagon. Gunfights, games, Western village, and the entertainment will keep youngsters enthralled for hours. This is an opportunity for kids to learn to rope, sing a few Western tunes, and pay their respects at Boothill. The $10 admission provides youngsters 4 to 10 great gunfights, a cowboy supper, and a Western stage show. Admission is $20 for adults. The kids will love the entertainment and the menu is kid-friendly.

The Dinosaur Museum
754 S. 200 West, Blanding
(435) 678-3454

This museum is sure to be a kid favorite. For a nominal fee, kids can see displays of dinosaur eggs from around the world and see the skeletons, fossilized skin, and footprints of these huge creatures that roamed this earth long before mankind. The museum is open from 9 A.M. to 5 P.M. April 15 to October 15, and from 8 A.M. to 8 P.M. during June, July, and August. The fee is $1 for youngsters and senior citizens, and $2 for adults.

Hansen Planetarium
Bryce Canyon National Park
P.O. Box 170001, Bryce Canyon
(435) 834-5322

During the Night Skies at Bryce program, kids will learn the stars, planets, and constellations. These are not only educational for kids (don't tell them!), but they're fun as well. Admission is $3.50 for those 21 and younger and $4.50 for adults. The program lasts about an hour. Check with the visitor center for a program schedule. For more information on

the Hansen Plan planetarium in 538-2104.

Recreation

The beautiful rugged country of southeastern Utah lends itself to and Insiders and visitors alike have come to appreciate all this Utah portion of the Four Corners has to offer. With rugged mountains, slickrock, rapidly flowing rivers, bubbling brooks and new places to explore and discover, southeastern Utah is a haven for the outdoor enthusiast. The opportunities provided are just a sampling of all that's offered in this most beautiful area. The skies seem to be bluer, the sun seems to shine brighter, and the outdoors seems to beckon more here, so pack the gear you need for whatever sport you love, and head to the Four Corners. For information on outdoor recreation in southeastern Utah, a good web site is www.moabutah.com.

Fishing

There are many great fishing spots in southeastern Utah and as you travel through this part of the Four Corners, you'll find Insiders who will gladly share their favorite fishin' hole with you. They will encourage you to fish those spots and others you might find along your path, for every serious angler knows that lesser known fishing holes often produce the best fishing and the best fish. If you're looking to catch trout, Huntington Creek in the La Sal Mountains is where you need to head. It's noted as one of the premier fly fishing streams in the state, and whether you catch a few or enough for an old-fashioned-fish fry, you'll love reeling in the trout in this beautiful stream. Joe's Valley on the Ferron/Price Ranger District is a 1,200-acre reservoir which offers fishing and motor boating fun. If you're fishing for catfish, try the Green River and the Colorado River.

Remember that fishing in the national forest requires a valid local license, so visit a bait shop before you put your lure in the stream. One-day resident fishing licenses are $7; non-resident fees are $8. For seven-day licenses, residents will pay $15, while non-residents will pay $21. Always remember there may be limits to the number of fish you can keep, and the type of lure you may use, so always check with the ranger station, visitor center, or bait shop before you wet your line.

Four-wheeling

Moab has become known as a mecca of the four-wheel-drive world, with more than 30 trails to choose from. These trails cover some of the most beautiful, but rugged, country you'll find anywhere. Steep canyon

Insiders' Tip

The average maximum day time temperature for Utah ranges from 37 degrees in January to 93 degrees in July. Because of the state's inland location, Utah's snow is unusually dry, earning it the reputation of being the world's greatest powder.

Moab Off-Roaders

...ils and beautiful country attract thousands of four-wheelers to the
...ach year. Moab is considered by many to be the mecca of the four-
...ve world, and one of the biggest events is held here each Easter weekend.
... Knight, information officer for the Red Rock 4-Wheelers, Inc., said that while
...oad enthusiasts arrive in Moab daily to enjoy the area, the thousands who
...tend the Easter Jeep Safari double the town's normal population.

"We've gotten people from more than 30 states and from six foreign countries
who come to the Easter Safari," Knight said. "Moab's population is between 5,000 to
6,000, and we have about 1,700 vehicles for the Safari. We figure an average of 2.75
people per vehicle, so that pretty much doubles our population for the nine days of
the event."

The Easter Safari offers more than 30 trails for off-roaders to travel, with trails
ranging from easy to almost impossible to navigate, Knight explained. "We have
some trails that are basically two-track roads that are semi-maintained, but are
enough to make people feel like their four-wheeler's been challenged. Our most difficult trail is an uphill climb, punctuated by rocks, ledges and poor traction. We've
got something for everybody, and everybody really enjoys it."

Four-wheeling, Knight said, has grown in popularity over the years. "I guess it
probably all began when the war was over and surplus four-wheel-drive vehicles
became available," Knight said. "And it's just grown since then. Today, we have
Bronco clubs, Hummer clubs, and Land Rover clubs, with people getting together
with other people who own the same type of four-wheel-drive vehicle and going off-
roading."

Many of those who attend the Easter Safari and the Jeep Jamboree at Labor Day
bring vehicles they've all but built from scratch, Knight said. "They strip the vehicle
down and rebuild it, adding taller tires, more ground clearance, lower gears, whatever they can to make it better on the trails," he said, adding that most people love
their four-wheel-drive vehicles and the adventures they have driving them over challenging trails.

"Four-wheeling is a family activity, too," Knight said. "We get a lot of families
who come to the Safari and the Labor Day event. It's become a family outing, where
they can see beautiful country and be challenged by the trails. Our club tries to make
our events fun for the family, and we try very hard to keep it a sober event and
we're pretty successful."

Safety is always a concern for club members when they're working with events.
Countless volunteers work the nine days of the Safari, with one heading up each trail
group, one in the middle, and one at the end. "We use citizens band radios to keep
in touch and we encourage everyone to use their seatbelts and drive safely, without
doing anything dangerous," he said.

Making sure vehicles stay on the trails is another challenge they meet. "We don't
want people driving off the roads and destroying property," Knight said. "Sometimes
it happens, but we're really careful about it."

The club pays almost $40,000 annually in land use fees, some of which is
recouped in fees charged for the events, he added.

While the events attract more people every year, Knight said, the club tries to
keep attendance at a controllable number. "If we get too many people, it can really

Four-wheeling in Moab, Utah. PHOTO: BER KNIGHT

tie up traffic in Moab," he said. "We try to meet at places without a traffic light, so we don't slow up traffic, but we're running out of places to meet. On Saturday of the Safari, we shut down Main Street, but we don't want to do that all the time because it's not fair to the downtown businesses."

Knight said the community enjoys the events, and the economy benefits from it. "But we don't want to get so big the locals leave home to get away from it," Knight said. "We want to make it safe, fun, and a family event for everyone, whether they're from Moab or the Netherlands."

The beautiful country in southeastern Utah and the many off-road trails it offers, lures many people all year long, Knight said. "People come alone, or in groups, and they come to face the challenges of the trails and to see the scenery. It's a great sport and Moab is one of the best places to enjoy it."

Information: Red Rock 4-Wheelers, Inc., P.O. Box 1471, Moab, Utah 84532-1471; (435) 259–7625 between 8:30 A.M. and 10 P.M.

walls and rims, rivers, mountains, forests and deserts, plus the famous Moab "slickrock," offer a variety like you've never seen before. Trails range from easy to next-to-impossible, and four-wheelers from all over the country come to Moab to conquer the trails and claim victory when they do. The annual Easter Jeep Safari is a popular event with four-wheel enthusiasts from throughout the country. For information about the safari, call (435) 259-7625 between 8:30 A.M. and 10 P.M.

Golf

There are only a few golf courses in southeastern Utah, but the ones that are here are courses you'll enjoy playing. With the beautiful days in this part of the Four Corners and the meticulously cared for greens of these courses, Insiders say the only way golf could get any better is if they could birdie every hole.

New golf courses are being developed, so check with the chamber of commerce in the town you're visiting for information on new and established courses.

Moab Golf Course
2705 SE Bench Rd., Moab
(435) 259–6488

This 18-hole course was built in 1986 and is a grass course with water in play. It's open all year and tee times are accepted 30 days in advance. Golf carts are available and a golf pro is on site. Rental clubs are also available. A driving range, putting green, and sand and chipping area are also on site. A beverage cart and snack bar is provided and a bar with beer service only is on the premises. Green fees are $20.

Blue Mountain Meadow
549 S. Main, Monticello
(435) 587—468

Built in 1961, Blue Mountain Meadow is a 9-hole, bent grass course with water in play. It's open from March 1 to November 1 and tee times are accepted one day in advance. Carts and clubs are available to rent. A putting green, sand and chipping area, and a teaching pro are provided. A snack bar and a bar with beer service only are on the premises. Green fees at Blue Mountain are $13.

Horseback Riding

Horseback riding is a given recreational sport for many people who live in the Four Corners, and those in southeastern Utah are no exception. But the people lucky enough to live near the La Sal Mountains can experience many opportunities to mount their horses and head out to where the solitude is loud enough to truly enjoy. Day trips or horse packing expeditions are offered in the La Sals, as well as into Canyonlands National Park. There are beautiful trails on BLM administered land in the area as well, so if you're ready to saddle up and go, you'll find scenes and sites you thought only lived in your dreams. A late afternoon or evening ride, complete with dinner over a campfire and marshmallows toasted for dessert might just be one of the many highlights of your trip to the Four Corners. Please contact public land management agencies for regulations before you ride your horse into the sunset, however. Horses may be ridden on any of the trails in the La Sal Mountains, but the Geyser Pass Trail is especially pretty. The Halfway Stage Station, the site of an old stage stop between Moab and Thompson, is also a beautiful ride, taking you through wonderful red rock canyons. In Canyonlands National Park, horses are allowed on all backcountry roads and in Horseshoe Canyon. Day use permits are required, however, but are free, except in Horse Canyon/Peekaboo and Lavender Canyon in the Needles, where only seven animals per day are allowed and a small fee is charged. Permits for day use are free; however, a $10 permit is required for those planning to spend the night.

In Horseshoe Canyon and other areas of the park, no more than ten animals and ten people are allowed. Contact the reservation office at (435) 259-4351 for information.

Mountain Biking

Mountain bikers appreciate the many opportunities to test their skills in southeastern Utah. There are many primitive trails and abandoned roads that lure bikers to stray from the beaten path and discover the treasures that might lie ahead on a path less traveled. Before you set out on your ride, however, check with a bike shop in the area to determine which areas will be best for you. Always wear safety equipment and carry plenty of water. Since most of the mountain bike paths are remote, it would also be wise to take along a first aid kit, and to travel with someone. Some of the trails you might want to try include Shiprock Bike, a difficult, 9.6-mile trip that will take you about half a day; Hurrah Pass, a trail that's relatively easy, but is 33 miles round trip and should take you all day to complete; Gemini Bridges, a moderately difficult trail that's 13.5 miles long and, again, will take you about a day; and the Monitor/Merrimac, another easy trail that's just over 13 miles long and will take about a half day. These trails are all near Moab. Information on biking is available at all visitor centers of national parks and monuments, so check with the center before you begin your ride.

Utah
and
tif
y
you'r
as
the
and
**pack out everything
you pack in.**

River Running

Those who love the water and the challenges it offers will enjoy the rivers of southeastern Utah. The rivers around Moab and Green River not only offer churning rapids, but beautiful, quiet sections that reflect the sunshine and the smiles of those lucky enough to be floating downstream. While the more adventurous might want to strike out on their own after a visit to the Moab Information Center to get river reports and information, others might want to take one of the many commercial trips offered. Calm water floats can run from one to two days, and a more challenging one will take three to four days. Whitewater rafting is found on the Green River and the Colorado River. The Green River "daily" is a one- to two-day trip north of Green River and will challenge you to seven rapids. On the Colorado River, Westwater Canyon, northeast of Moab, is a one- or two-day whitewater adventure that is popular with Insiders and visitors alike. The river flows through a deep inner gorge of Precambrian black rock, which is backed by incredible 1,000-foot canyon walls. This 17-mile stretch of river is nicknamed the "Little Grand" of the Colorado River and offers 11 whitewater rapids for thrills and chills. In Canyonlands National Park, Cataract Canyon is the most famous Utah stretch of the Colorado River. You can enjoy a trip from one to seven days, and travel 112 miles from Moab to Hite Marina on Lake Powell. This is a trip Insiders know to be almost perfect—the challenge of the 26 rapids, combined with the incredible rock art, cliff dwellings, and the beauty of the area, will lure you back again and again. Permits for rafting may be obtained from the Canyonlands National Park, 2282 S. West Resource Blvd., Moab, Utah 84532. Permits will run between $10 and $25, depending on the area you wish to raft.

Mountains, located within the Manti-La Sal National Forest, offer great winter, snowmobiling, sledding, and snowman-making. If you love winter sports and visiting the Four Corners during the ski season, you might enjoy staying at the La Sal Mountain Hut System. These three rustic cabins, which include cooking and dining facilities, will put winter recreation right out your front door, giving you more time to enjoy that wonderful white stuff. For information on the mountain huts, call (800) 435-3292. For skiers, the La Sal Mountains offer worked trails and backcountry terrain. Be careful as you ski, however, because these same trails are often shared with snowmobilers. Those who choose to ski the backcountry should call (435) 259-SNOW November through April for updated information on weather, road conditions, and avalanche potential. These beautiful mountains are steep and have a higher potential for avalanche than other mountains in Utah, so please make safety your primary concern. Cross-country skiers will find miles of trails and countless backcountry skiing possibilities. The groomed trails pass by several wonderful meadows, and lead to high terrain where experienced backcountry aficionados will find slopes that will certainly add to their skiing experience in the Four Corners. Snowmobiles are allowed on many of the same trails used by skiers. There are many roads which provide long tours for snowmobilers, and Insiders encourage you to explore them to find the ones you like the best. When there isn't a great deal of snow, however, please stay on good snow cover to protect the vegetation in the area. Again, please be careful of avalanches and put safety before excitement. For those whose idea of great winter activities include sledding, snowball fights, and making snowmen, the snow in the La Sal Mountains will provide you with hours of enjoyment. Insiders and Utahans hope you have a good time while in these mountains, but ask that you respect the land and the wildlife by not leaving trash behind or destroying the natural habitat. We want you to return to southeastern Utah and rediscover the many delights you've found this trip. For more information on the La Sal Mountains and the Manti-La Sal National Forest, call the Moab Ranger District at (435) 259-7155.

Attractions

Southeastern Utah has much to offer visitors to the Four Corners. Outdoor enthusiasts have been known to call this area "Heaven on Earth," because of the many activities and attractions provided. The towns located within the Utah portion of the Four Corners are attractions themselves. Bluff, situated between the bluffs of the San Juan River, was the first town in San Juan County, Utah. A pioneer cemetery in the town offers visitors a glimpse of a colorful and historic past, with a wonderful view of the valley below. Blanding can boast of four distinct cultures that have helped create its great history—Ute, Navajo, European pioneers, and the Spanish. Monticello sits at the foot of the Blue Mountains and is the county seat of San Juan County. Agriculture and mining have been the economic base of Monticello since it was founded more than one hundred years ago. Moab's history can be traced back ten thousand years and is visible in the area's many panels of ancient petroglyphs.

The friendly people who live in Bluff, Blanding, Monticello, and Moab enjoy the quality of life the small towns provide, and the outdoor opportunities the area offers. As you travel through the Utah portion of your trip to the Four Corners, you'll understand why the residents of these towns are willing to forgo huge shopping malls, hundreds of restaurants, and the multitude of movie theaters found in larger cities for a more simple life—a life where you can see the sun as it rises over the horizon, hear the eager chirps of a baby robin as it waits for food from its mother, and breathe air that isn't laden with pollutants. You may decide, as these residents have, that life is good in ʃ

Remember these are just a sampling of all southeastern Utah has you travel this area of the Four Corners, you'll find Insiders at your hʲ ground, and at restaurants and service stations who will be happy tʲ spots with you. Take advantage of their information and enjoy your Utah.

Some of the attractions listed below charge admission fees. Plea ter for information before you leave for your destination. All attra chair accessible unless otherwise noted. The first attractions are listed in alphabetical order because they do not all fall within the corridor from Bluff to Moab. The attractions under the Other Attractions section are listed according to town beginning with Bluff, then moving north.

Arches National Park
Visitor Center (near park entrance)
5 miles north of Moab, off U.S. Hwy. 191
(435) 259–8161

Arches National Park contains one of the largest concentrations of natural sandstone arches in the world. The spires, pinnacles, pedestals, and balanced rocks are extraordinary and, with the contrasting colors and textures of the land surrounding them, offer a spectacle you simply cannot describe with words. The beauty of this wonderful park will remain with you forever, and you will treasure the days you spend here. The visitor center, located near the entrance of the park, includes a museum, exhibits, and a bookstore. It is also here that you will find schedules for special events, walks, guided hikes, and evening campfire programs. The 48 miles you will drive on paved roads in Arches National Park will take you through spectacular scenery and to park features, including hiking trails of varying length and difficulty. There are more than 2,000 cataloged arches in the park, ranging in size from a three-foot opening (the minimum considered an arch) to the longest one, Landscape Arch, which measures 306 feet from base to base. Insiders continue to be amazed at the effect erosion and weather have on the arches, and no matter how many times you visit Arches National Park, you will discover a new arch has formed or a favorite one has been destroyed by the effects of time and weather.

While simply marveling at the wonder of the beautiful arches in the park is worthy of your time, most visitors also enjoy the great hiking and biking that's available. It is by getting out of your car and hiking or biking back into the area on designated trails that you will fully comprehend the beauty of the area. Check at the visitor center for hiking and biking trails that appeal to you and discover what Insiders have known for some time— Arches National Park is a treasure and, as such, should be savored, enjoyed, and remembered. Always hike or bike in a group, for your safety, and always wear safety equipment if you're riding your bike. If you're walking, make sure you're wearing good hiking shoes, so blisters don't mar your trip. Stay on the trails and please pack out what you pack in, leaving the area as you found it.

There is but one campground in Arches National Park, Devils Garden Campground. It is first come, first served, and no reservations are taken. Devils Garden Campground is located 18 miles from the park entrance and is open year-round. From mid-March to late October, a small $5 fee is charged, but water is not available; from late October to mid-March, that fee is half. You may pre-register for the 52 campsites at the entrance station, with pre-registration beginning at 7:30 A.M. The campground fills quickly from March to October, usually by 9 A.M., so you must pre-register during those months. Portable water, tables, grills, and pit-style and flush toilets are available in the campground, although water is shut off during the winter months. There are no showers and you must bring your own wood or grills. Wood gathering and [fi]res are prohibited in the park. [Co]untry camping is allowed, but a [...] permit is required and must be [ob]tained at the visitor center when you arrive. Two group campsites are available at Devils Garden for groups of 11 or more people. The Juniper Basin campsite will accommodate up to 55 people; the Canyon Wren campsite up to 35. The group campsite fee is $3 per person per night with a $33 per night minimum. Check with the visitor center for details.

Whether you come to Arches National Park for a day or plan to camp and spend several days exploring the park, you'll be glad you came.

Bryce Canyon National Park
East of Cedar City, 86 miles from Zion National Park
Take Rt. 12 east to the park
(435) 834–5322

The visitor center is one mile inside the park boundary and includes a natural history museum. Bryce Canyon National Park is named for one of a series of horseshoe-shaped amphitheaters carved from the eastern edge of the Paunsaugunt Plateau. Colorful Claron limestones, sandstones, and mudstones have been shaped by natural erosion, creating thousands of mazes, spires, fins, and pinnacles. These are called "hoodoos," and will delight young and old alike.

While you're visiting Bryce Canyon National Park, you may notice the air seems cleaner—for good reason. The area is proud of its air quality, some of the best in the nation. The wonderful clear air and the lack of industry and lights, make it perfect for those who enjoy stargazing.

Bryce Canyon has two campgrounds, North and Sunset, with about 220 sites available on a first-come, first-served basis. There are no hookups and sites are frequently filled by early afternoon during the summer, so make your camping plans accordingly. Camping fees are $10 per night, with a limit of six people, three tents, and two vehicles.

Group camping is available in Sunset Campground; only one site is available, however, and reservations must be made. The North Campground has laundry facilities, showers, and groceries; however at Sunset Campground, plan to go one mile for those services.

Hiking and biking is allowed in the park, but check at the visitor center for information. Pets are not recommended in the park, but if Fido must come, make sure he's on a leash and under control at all times.

Because of the rugged nature of Bryce Canyon, not all areas are wheelchair accessible. You will find accessible campsites and restrooms, but check with the park ranger for information before venturing into the park.

Regular activities and events are planned at Bryce Canyon. Check with the visitor center to see what is available during your trip to this incredibly beautiful part of the Four Corners.

Canyonlands National Park
2282 S. West Resource Blvd., Moab
(435) 259–7164

As mentioned in the Four Corners Attractions chapter, the park is divided into four districts by the Green River and the Colorado River—the Island in the Sky, the Maze, the Needles, and the water ways of the two rivers. The park is an outdoor enthusiasts heaven, but for those physically confined or not in the hiking/biking/rough-road-riding mode, the Island in the Sky offers incredible views from the many overlooks provided on the paved road. For those who choose to hike, you are encouraged to bring the proper footwear, clothing, and supplies for the journey. The nearest outdoors store can be found in Moab. Cyclist will find flat tire kits and the like for their journey also in Moab. Water buffs come equipped with kayaks and canoes because the immediate area does not have a store that supplies those needs. Camping opportunities for the park are mentioned in the Four Corners Attractions chapter.

Turk's Head, Green River. Canyonlands National Park. PHOTO: NATIONAL PARK SERVICE

Natural Bridges National Monument
47 miles southwest of Blanding
(435) 692–1234

Natural Bridges National Monument is blissfully remote. It attracts those truly interested in the innate beauty and history of the area. The Indian cliff dwellings, pictographs, and white sandstone canyons scattered throughout the area are juxtaposed with one of the largest solar power generators in the world, the Photovoltaic Array. The generator was built here in 1997 in an effort against global warming. Some 384 solar panels retain solar energy to provide electricity for the gas pumps at Dangling Rope Marina, where more than 250,000 boaters stop for fuel each year. For information on the hiking trails and camping opportunities, see the Four Corners Attractions chapter.

Rainbow Bridge National Monument
Southwest of Bluff in San Juan County
(520) 608–6404

There is no visitor center at Rainbow Bridge National Monument and the only way to see this most beautiful bridge is by boat. But the opportunity to take to the wonderful waterways of Lake Powell and visit Rainbow Bridge is one you won't want to pass up. If you don't have your own boat, you may rent one, or take a tour boat. The tour boat is fun, but an individual boat allows you to take advantage of the other spectacular offerings of Lake Powell. Tour boat fees vary. Call (520) 645–2741 for rates. For those who would like to rent a boat for their private tour of Rainbow Bridge, rentals are available at the Wahwheap Marina. Boat rentals start at $225 a day.

Rainbow Bridge is the world's largest natural bridge, and has surely inspired

Rainbow Bridge. PHOTO: DOROTHY NOBIS

people throughout the ages. You simply cannot look at this magnificent creation of Mother Nature and not be awed by what she accomplished without the aid of engineers, draftsmen or construction workers.

Insiders ask that visitors remember that Rainbow Bridge continues to be sacred to Native Americans, who come to the area frequently to pray and make offerings, and that you respect the culture and the beliefs of them. Please don't walk up to, or walk under, Rainbow Bridge, instead view the bridge from the viewing area.

You'll want to take photographs of this beautiful bridge, so don't forget your camera. The nearest services are at Dangling Rope Marina, where you may purchase water, gas, and supplies.

Rainbow Bridge may be one of the most photographed bridges in the world, and visitors from all over the world visit the site. Don't miss this attraction when you visit the Four Corners.

Other Attractions

Dinosaur Museum
754 S. 200 West, Blanding
(435) 678–3454

Children of all ages will enjoy the Dinosaur Museum, which offers the complete history of the world of dinosaurs. Skeletons, fossilized skin, eggs, footprints, state-of-the-art graphics, and realistic sculptures present the great dinosaurs that roamed the Four Corners region. Exhibits show dinosaurs from different countries and offer the latest in dinosaur research. This is a wonderful museum and youngsters will certainly proclaim it a highlight of their trip to the Four Corners. The entry fee is $2 for adults, and $1 for children and senior citizens.

Dan O'Laurie Museum
118 E. Center St., Moab
(435) 259–7985

The spectacular landscape of southeastern Utah and the history of the area is

spotlighted at the Dan O'Laurie Museum. A trip to this museum will help you understand the archaeology of the area and how it was formed. Graphic displays show the evolution of a salt valley, the Moab fault, and the stratigraphy of the region. A paleontology exhibit includes dinosaur tracks and a dinosaur femur, sure to delight the kids. Prehistoric tools, textiles, pottery, and jewelry are all displayed, as well as a model pit house and a large burden basket discovered by three teenagers in 1990. Native American women hung a burden basket across their shoulders and used it to carry herbs, berries, and the twigs for firewood they came across during the day. The burden basket was also hung at the door and when visitors arrived, they "deposited" their troubles in the basket, so their visit would be pleasant and without worry. You won't want to miss this introduction to the landscape and the history of the southeastern Utah portion of the Four Corners. Admission is free, and there is no gift shop.

Moab's Skyway and Rim Trail
1800 S. Highland Dr., Moab
(435) 259–7799

For 12 minutes, you will float through the air as you take in spectacular views of Moab, the Colorado River, and Arches National Park. This chairlift ride will give you photo opportunities and views of the area you'd never get in an airplane or by car. This is an attraction the kids will love and you'll enjoy just as much. While photos are best taken during the day, the evening ride will delight you with the lights twinkling throughout Moab and the area. The chairlift is an open car and will hold up to four people. Although kids love it, very young children may not enjoy the ride because it rises 1,000 feet above the town. Tickets, which include sales tax, are $9 for adults, $8 for senior citizens, and $7 for children ages 6 to 12. Youngsters five and younger ride free.

Arts

Much of southeastern Utah's taste for the fine arts is satisfied with the innumerable exhibits and activities at the national parks and monuments in the area. Almost everybody can find an event there that will fill the soul with musical and artistic beauty. (See the end of this chapter for the addresses and contact information for these sites.)

There are several major events of note, however, that attract not just the local Insiders, but visitors from throughout the country. I encourage you to take advantage of all that the national parks and monuments have to offer, as well as the following events, too, if time permits. Since dates and times vary from year to year, call ahead for information.

Canyonlands Film Society
www.moab-utah.com/film

The Canyonland Film Society strives to provide monthly screenings of independently produced films. The film society believes in fostering audience exposure to ideas and perspectives beyond the mainstream, which offers the Moab community the opportunity to enjoy creative, entertaining, and thought provoking films.

Canyonlands Film & Video Festival
59 S. Main St., Suite 214, Moab
Canyonfilm@hotmail.com

The Canyonlands Film & Video Festival began in 1995 and has become an annual event held in November for independent filmmakers from around the world. The festival is primarily sponsored by the Canyonlands Film Society, a non-profit organization that seeks to expand and support the creation and screening of independently produced films. Works presenting thought-provoking material are always given special consideration. The festival screens films in narrative/dramatic features or shorts, dramatic features, dramatic shorts, documentary features, documentary shorts, and Southwestern regional issues. Westerns, experimental, comedy, outdoor adventure, student produced, and animation are also included. The cost to attend the festival is $6. Directors and producers are often present and the film society encourages interaction between those who attend and the professionals from the film industry.

Moab Music Festival
59 S. Main St., Moab
(435) 259-8003

The Moab Music Festival began in 1992 and has become an annual event held in September. The festival is dedicated to providing cultural and educational enrichment through the presentation of fine instrumental and vocal chamber music programs. The festival also holds an educational outreach program for young people from kindergarten through high school. That program brings local students and world-class musicians together to perform at the festival. Tickets for the Moab Music Festival cost about $15.

Contact Utah's national parks and monuments for more art information:

Zion National Park
Springdale
(435) 772–3256
Entrance fees: $20 per vehicle; $10 per pedestrian

Arches National Park
U.S. Hwy. 191, 5 miles north of Moab
(435) 259–8161
Entrance fees: $10 per vehicle

Canyonlands National Park
2282 S. West Resource Blvd., Moab
(435) 719–2313
Entrance fees: $10 per vehicle; $5 for an individual

Arizona

The sixth largest state in the country, Arizona has 114,006 square miles of incredible scenery. Nicknamed the Grand Canyon State, the name Arizona is believed to originate from a Native American word meaning "small spring place." Arizona is on Mountain Standard Time and does not spring forward or fall back to daylight savings time when the rest of the nation does. The largest percentage of land in the state is designated Indian lands.

In the northeast corner of the state, which is the Four Corners portion of Arizona, is Plateau Country, home to the reservations of the Hopi Tribe and the Navajo Nation. When you visit this portion of Arizona, you'll also see the beautiful towering red rock formations of Monument Valley, the tall spires of Canyon de Chelly, the colorful horizons of the Painted Desert, and the wonders of the Petrified Forest. With the rolling landscapes, vistas that seem to go on forever, and canyons so beautiful they defy description, you'll also find land that seems virtually unchanged for thousands of years. The Navajo people, who learned shepherding from the Spanish and who have perfected their artistic skills, are one of the nation's largest tribes. Here, too, are the Hopi, whose reservation on top of three windswept mesas is surrounded by the Navajo Nation. When you visit the villages of the Hopi people, you'll wonder how a civilization could sustain itself in the harsh terrain for hundreds of years.

While the Grand Canyon draws many people to Arizona, there's more to see and do in this, the 48th state of the Union. As you explore northeast Arizona you will find places, sights, and people who will give you a greater appreciation of the state and make you understand why almost five million people call it home.

Hotels and Motels

Price Code

The price code is based on the cost of a standard room for two adults for one night.

$ . . . . .less than $70
$$ . . . .$71–$100
$$$ . . . .$100 and up

From the serene beauty of the desert of northeastern Arizona to the splendor of the mountains of Flagstaff and the incredible canyons of Glen Canyon National Park, visitors to the Four Corners will discover views and sites that will inspire them to return again and again. Since this portion of the Four Corners, like the other three, tends to be sparsely populated, there are few choices of places to stay during your visit. But in the cities of Page, Chinle, Tuba City, Winslow, and Flagstaff, you will find accommodations that will make your stay pleasant and comfortable. Keep in mind, there are other nice places to stay in northeastern Arizona. Most of the major chain hotels and motels have facilities here, and you may opt to stay at one of them. The ones I've included are unique in one way or another, and ones I think will definitely add to the enjoyment of your visit. The accommodations are presented in an order that flows in steps from east to west starting with Kayenta and moving south to finish in Flagstaff.

All facilities are wheelchair accessible and offer smoking and non-smoking rooms unless otherwise stated. Pets and major credit cards are accepted at all facilities unless noted otherwise.

The residents of northeastern Arizona enjoy the company of tourists and you'll find friendly, helpful locals everywhere. They will answer your questions, give you directions, and do what they can to make your trip to their state memorable.

Kayenta

Kayenta enjoys a position as a gateway to Monument Valley and is a major hub on the Navajo Reservation. It is about 20 miles south of the Utah border on U.S. Highway 163, 148 miles northeast of Flagstaff, and about 100 miles west of Shiprock, New Mexico.

Holiday Inn $$
Junction of U.S. Hwy. 160 and
U.S. Hwy. 163
(520) 697–3221

The Holiday Inn at Kayenta is a nice place to call home during your visit to the Arizona portion of the Four Corners. The hotel offers 163 rooms and eight suites, as well as a cocktail lounge and restaurant. An outdoor heated swimming pool is available for guests, and tours to Monument Valley may be arranged. The gift shop offers authentic art and jewelry. The hotel is within one hundred miles of Monument Valley, Canyon de Chelly, and Lake Powell.

Page

The city of Page was originally created as a construction camp for workers on the Glen Canyon Dam. The city has become a tourist destination as visitors from all over the world flock to Glen Canyon National Recreational Area and Lake Powell. The weather in Page is almost as wonderful as the people who reside there. If your trip to the Four Corners includes spending several days at Lake Powell, you'll find accommodations in Page that will make you glad you came and sorry when you have to leave.

Lake Powell Suites $$$
5 minutes north of Wahweap Marina at
Lake Powell
(800) 525–3189

For those who plan to spend some time exploring Lake Powell and the Glen Canyon Dam Recreation Area, the Lake Powell Suites might be the perfect place to stay. Each suite has two queen size beds (a sleeper sofa and a Murphy bed), washer and dryer, complete kitchen with eating and cooking utensils, and a color television. Bed linens, blankets, and towels are also furnished. These suites are very nice and have a private patio where you can grill hamburgers or steaks while gazing at beautiful Lake Powell. If you bring your boat with you, power is provided in the parking lot for your boat battery. Lake Powell Suites is great if you're traveling with a group, enjoying a family reunion, or just want a more private place to stay during the Arizona portion of your trip to the Four Corners.

Red Rock Motel $$
114 8th Ave.
(520) 645–0062

The Red Rock Motel is perfect for those on a budget. Guests get their money's worth, along with hospitality and comfort. All the beds at the Red Rock are queen size and there is a two-bedroom suite that has a living room and a fully furnished kitchen that's perfect for the family. You can prepare dinner for the family in the kitchen or use the barbecue to cook on the grill on your own private patio. If you plan to spend several days in the Page area, check out the Red Rock Motel—you'll be glad you did.

Uncle Bill's Place $$$
117 8th Ave.
(520) 645–1224

Uncle Bill's doesn't have a lot of rooms—just 12. They are divided into apartments, suites, and private rooms with a shared bathroom. Uncle Bill's doesn't invite youngsters younger than eight to stay and it doesn't tolerate loud, noisy people. Pets are not welcome at Uncle Bill's and if you tend to snobbishness or have teens who tend to brood—well, maybe you better find another place to stay. But if you're looking for a really nice place to stay, a place with character and quiet, and people who are genuinely nice, Uncle Bill's is probably where you want to be. Some 90 percent of the guests at Uncle Bill's are European, which will provide you an opportunity to meet and enjoy the company of these visitors to our country. If you're looking for someplace out of the ordinary, someplace where the hosts will know your name and recognize you, and someplace where the gardens are as lovely as the rooms, call Uncle Bill's. Reservations are usually not needed, but are suggested.

Chinle

Chinle is the host city to Canyon de Chelly National Monument, 95 miles from Gallup, New Mexico. It is a thriving city with a population that increases drastically during the tourist season, when visitors from throughout the world make Canyon de Chelly a vacation destination.

Best Western Canyon de Chelly Inn $$$
100 Main St.
(520) 674–5874

The Best Western Canyon de Chelly Inn is just three miles west of Canyon de Chelly National Monument. The hotel has been remodeled and offers great Southwestern-style rooms with one king or two queen size beds. An indoor heated pool is available for guests and a restaurant offers American, Mexican, and Navajo dishes. Coffee makers in each room help those of us who need caffeine to jump-start us in the mornings. The hotel also offers family benefits, which vary, so call for information.

Tuba City

Tuba City is the second largest city in the Navajo Nation and is located 73 miles north of Flagstaff. Tuba City is a pleasant place to stay and its residents offer visitors Native American hospitality and the opportunity to purchase wonderful works of art during their stay.

Tuba City Quality Inn $$
Main St. and Moanave
(800) 228–5151 or (800) 644–8383

The staff at the Quality Inn makes every attempt to ensure the comfort of its guests. Children under the age of 18 stay free and pets are welcome with a $20 refundable deposit. Hearing-impaired television sets are available and a video library offers video rental at a nominal cost. There is a gift shop on the premises, which will delight the shopper and the Hogan Restaurant serves up Mexican and American food seven days a week. The

Quality Inn is within easy driving distance to many area attractions and the staff is always willing to answer questions about the area and all it has to offer.

Winslow

Winslow was made famous by the musical group the Eagles back in the '70s when they sang about "standin' on a corner in Winslow, Arizona." The "Standin' on a Corner" Park is located in historic downtown Winslow and features a life size bronze statue and a two-story mural depicting the story behind the song. Famous Route 66 also runs through Winslow, as does the Burlington Northern Santa Fe Railroad. You may opt to make Winslow your home base as you tour the Arizona portion of the Four Corners.

La Posada Hotel $$
303 E. Second St.
(520) 289–4366

In 1928, noted designer Mary Colter created La Posada, which became one of the finest small hotels in Arizona. La Posada was built in the style of the late 1700s at a rumored cost of $2 million—a lot of money for the time. The beautiful hotel was open from 1930 to 1957, and escaped total destruction many times in later years. Today, the hotel has been restored with painted ceilings, stone floors, faux-adobe walls, and gardens you'll love to linger in. There are only a limited number of rooms available at La Posada, so call early for reservations.

Montezuma Lodge at Mormon Lake $$
HC 31, Mormon Lake
(520) 354–2220

The Mormon Lake complex is in the Coconino National Forest and is easily reached by taking Arizona Highway 87 from Winslow, then taking U.S. Highway 17 south. Montezuma Lodge specifically is nestled in pine and oak trees 25 miles southeast of Flagstaff. The trees offer pleasant shade and privacy to the lodge. The Montezuma Lodge is the perfect place to enjoy the beauty of northeastern Arizona while soaking in the peace and quiet. Fully equipped kitchens allow you to enjoy breakfast while packing a picnic lunch for your sightseeing tour of the Four Corners. The lodge also provides hiking trails, lakes for fishing, and horseback riding, if you still have the energy after a full day taking in major attractions. Pets are not welcome at the lodge because of the wildlife in the immediate area. The Montezuma Lodge staff includes friendly, knowledgeable folks who will be able to offer suggestions as to their favorite restaurants, nightlife haunts, and family activities.

Flagstaff

Flagstaff is located in the Coconino National Forest and is surrounded by pine trees and the San Francisco Peaks. Northern Arizona University is located here and offers residents plays, musicals, and arts events, in addition to the enthusiasm and energy of its students. Many Insiders, when traveling west through Flagstaff, plan to spend the night here, where accommodations are pleasant, dining is superb, and the people go out of their way to make visitors feel comfortable.

Econo Lodge $$
Lucky Lane and Butler Ave.
(888) 349–2523

The Econo Lodge has been recognized for exceptional guest services and hotel cleanliness and for that, the staff and hosts are understandably proud. They make every effort to make sure your visit is enjoyable and you will want to return. The hotel has 68 very nice rooms, including 16 suites that have balconies, ironing boards, coffeemaker, microwave, and refrigerator. A free continental breakfast is offered, and the hotel has an indoor heated pool and spa, laundry facilities, and hot coffee available all the time. The hotel is 90 percent non-smoking, with one floor completely smoke free. Several restaurants are within walking distance of the hotel. The Econo Lodge is cost friendly, family friendly, and just plain friendly.

Hotel Monte Vista $$
100 N. San Francisco St.
(800) 545-3068

In the historic heart of Flagstaff is Hotel Monte Vista, and once you visit this magnificent hotel, you might leave your own heart here. Built in 1926, the hotel offers lush surroundings for locals and international visitors, not to mention the countless celebrities for whom some of the rooms are named. There are 50 rooms and suites on four floors, all with great views of the city. The rooms are comfortable and historical; and if you're lucky enough to get a room named after notable previous guests—Carole Lombard, Humphrey Bogart, Bob Hope, Theodore Roosevelt, Clark Gable, Spencer Tracy, Zane Grey, Jane Russell, or Bing Crosby—you're apt to feel the magic left by them. Not only will

Insiders' Tip

The busy season in the desert communities of Phoenix, Tucson, and Yuma is during the winter; in the high country of Flagstaff, Prescott, and the Grand Canyon, the summer months find most tourists.

you enjoy the Hotel Monte Vista, you'll enjoy the wonderful shopping available in downtown Flagstaff. After your shopping trip, stop for a cocktail at the Hotel Lounge; you're likely to find great entertainment. For those who plan to make the Hotel Monte Vista their home base during their tour of the Four Corners, an onsite laundry makes keeping the family clean easy and economical.

Bed and Breakfasts

Price Code

The price code is based on the cost of a standard room for two adults for one night.

$ . . . . .less than $50
$$ . . . .$51–$100
$$$ . . . .$101 and up

You won't find many bed and breakfasts in northeastern Arizona, but the ones that are here are topnotch, wonderful places to stay while you're visiting the Arizona portion of your trip to the Four Corners. Most of them are in the Flagstaff area, but there is a most unique one in the heart of Monument Valley.

All bed and breakfasts are wheelchair accessible unless stated.

Aspen Inn Bed & Breakfast $$
218 N. Elden, Flagstaff
(888) 999-4110

Built in 1912, Aspen Inn has been restored and offers quaint, comfortable rooms with private baths and a refrigerator with complementary beverages in each room. Guests enjoy the homey atmosphere of Aspen Inn and stay more than once. Well-behaved parents are always welcome with

their children at Aspen Inn, but pets are best left at home. Smoking is allowed in the back. Guests praise the Aspen Inn's sumptuous breakfast and the care and friendship offered by its hosts.

Birch Tree Inn Bed and Breakfast $$$
824 W. Birch Ave., Flagstaff
(888) 774-1042

Built in 1917, the Birch Tree Inn was once

a fraternity house, but the two-story country-Victorian house has been restored to create a comfortable atmosphere for its guests. There are five rooms in the Birch Tree Inn, each with a distinctive personality. A common area offers a collection of heirloom and country style pieces that will make you feel right at home. The hosts of the Birch Tree Inn rise early to prepare a breakfast that warms your heart as well as your tummy. Those with special dietary needs need only to say so when reservations are made, and they will be carefully accommodated. In the late afternoon, snacks and tea are offered. Before you retire for the evening, you may want to enjoy a game of billiards or chess in the game room, relax by the fire in the living room, or soak your tired muscles in the hot tub in the Inn's garden gazebo. The Birch Tree Inn is a non-smoking facility, and isn't suitable for children 12 years old or younger. Pets are not welcome here and wheelchair access is not available.

Country of Many Hogan Traditional Navajo Bed and Breakfast $$$
2.5 miles west of U.S. Hwy. 163 on Nav. Rt. 6450
(888) 291–4397

The Country of Many Hogan isn't your ordinary bed and breakfast. This unique option to a traditional hotel or motel allows guests to say in hogans, which were built by the Bedonie family, your hosts. Several hogans, one-room structures built of sculpted cedar logs, await your arrival. You'll sleep like a baby on sheep skin, and when you awaken, you'll enjoy traditional Navajo foods prepared over a juniper wood fire. A typical breakfast includes corn products, wild flower "Navajo" tea, fresh fruit, and juices. If you'd like something a little heartier for breakfast, it will be prepared for you. When you visit Country of Many Hogans, don't limit yourself to a good night's sleep and a wonderful breakfast. Demonstrations of Navajo arts and crafts are available to you, as is storytelling, although this must be arranged for in advance. Local tours are also available,

as are horseback riding and hiking. A traditional sweat lodge is also on the premises, but it too must be reserved in advance. Country of Many Hogan is within driving distance of Canyon de Chelley, Navajo National Monument, Arches, Mesa Verde, and the Grand Canyon is just 10 miles southwest of Monument Valley Tribal Park Visitors Center. The Country of Many Hogan is a wonderful opportunity to sleep in the same environment many Native Americans prefer to this day, and will create great memories of your trip to the Four Corners.

Fall Inn to Nature Bed & Breakfast $$
8080 N. Colt Dr., Flagstaff
(888) 920–0237

If you're seeking solitude as well as comfort, and want them both in beautiful surroundings, Fall Inn to Nature Bed & Breakfast indulges your desires. A lovely cedar home on 2.5 acres, Fall Inn to Nature offers two very nice rooms with baths. Outside the home are pine trees and a summer and springtime carpet of wildflowers. Fall Inn to Nature also provides personalized tours with an experienced guide to the nearby Grand Canyon, Meteor Crater, Sunset Crater, and downtown Flagstaff. Walking and hiking trails are close by, for those who enjoy a walk before dinner or after breakfast. An outdoor hot tub is also available for guests, who may also choose to gaze into the soft light of the fire in the fireplace before retiring for the night. If you're looking for new friends and extra company while at the Fall Inn to Nature, goats, cats, bunnies, and a dog are ready to make your acquaintance. The Fall Inn to Nature Bed & Breakfast accepts children over five years of age, and designated outdoor areas allow smoking.

The Inn at 410 Bed & Breakfast $$$
410 N. Leroux St., Flagstaff
(800) 774–2008

Nine rooms, with such intriguing names as Sunflower Fields, Canyon Memories, and Monet's Garden, await guests at The

Inn at 410 Bed & Breakfast. A great historic home of Flagstaff has been remodeled many times during the years, and is now a grand bed and breakfast that will greet you like an old friend and treat you like royalty. All of the rooms are lovely, but the Dakota Suite typifies the Old West of Arizona, with weathered barn wood, a queen size long bed, and a separate sitting room with fireplace and a sofa bed that will accommodate up to two children. The Southwest is decorated with local Native American arts and crafts, has a kiva-type fireplace, and a Jacuzzi tub that will soothe the tired muscles of two people. The Inn's gazebo and gardens offer summer guests a tranquil spot to relax after a busy day and enjoy the memories of a wonderful vacation. The Inn requires a two-night minimum stay on weekends from April 1 through October 31; and a three-night minimum stay some holidays. The Inn is a non-smoking facility and well-behaved children are welcome in rooms that will accommodate them. While pets are not allowed, the Inn's hosts will be happy to recommend a local kennel.

The Sled Dog Inn Bed & Breakfast $$$
10155 Mountainaire Rd., Flagstaff
(800) 754–0664

The Sled Dog Inn caters to those who enjoy nature and outdoor sports. You won't find antiques or lace curtains at The Sled Dog Inn, but you'll find decks, a hot tub, sauna, and mountain bikes for your enjoyment. Guided and self-guided outdoor adventures are offered. If you're not an outdoor enthusiast, you'll still enjoy your stay at The Sled Dog Inn. The wind rustles gently through the pine trees, giving you the feel of the great outdoors with all the great comforts of a perfectly appointed bed and breakfast. With ten guest rooms, two living areas and a dining room where breakfast isn't just a meal, but an occasion, guests will enjoy the affability of The Sled Dog Inn's hosts. You'll want to visit the four-legged "hosts" at The Sled Dog Inn—the Siberian huskies that don't bark, but may just offer up a morning "serenade" for you. Children seven years and older are best suited for accommodations at The Sled Dog Inn and pets are not allowed (the huskies don't like the competition).

Campgrounds and RV Sites

Camping in northeastern Arizona is like nowhere else in the world—the sky here is clear and blue, the stars seem to shine brighter, and the sun seems warmer. Sitting around a campfire at night, after roasting hot dogs for dinner and marshmallows for dessert, it's easy to understand why long ago pioneers loved the West and faced countless obstacles to live here.

There are nice campgrounds and RV parks throughout this part of the Four Corners and the ones I list are but a few. You'll find many great places to pitch your tent or park your RV near Flagstaff, but fewer places as you head toward Monument Valley, Canyon de Chelley, and the Grand Canyon. When you're headed to the more primitive sites, remember to take lots of water, food, and other necessities because convenience stores aren't located on every corner. You may not be able to run to the store for forgotten items out in the more isolated parts of northeastern Arizona, but the privilege of breathing clean air, teaching the kids the constellations, and not having to listen to the neighbor's radio may be worth the preparation for your camping trip.

Canyon Gateway RV Park
1060 North Grand Canyon Blvd., Williams
(888) 635–0329

Canyon Gateway RV Park is located near the south entrance of Grand Canyon National Park. This pleasant RV park is near restaurants, shops, a golf course, and the Grand Canyon Railway depot. There are more than 100 RV spaces with full hookups, and 50 AMP service is available at 12 of them. Picnic tables, laundry facilities, restrooms, showers and a pet area will make your stay here enjoyable. Daily rates for full hookups are $20.95 and there is a nominal charge for the laundry facilities.

Meteor Crater RV Park
Located on I-40, Exit 233, between
Winslow and Flagstaff
(800) 478–4002

Meteor Crater has 71 landscaped, pull-through spaces, and includes private individual restroom and shower facilities for its guests. Two wheelchair-accessible restroom/shower facilities are also available. A recreation room and playground will keep youngsters entertained, while Mom and Dad do laundry or shop in the country store. Gas is also available at this RV park. Guests may enjoy hiking Old Route 66, which borders the park, and all guests receive discount coupons to visit Meteor Crater, just five miles up the road. This is a nice RV park, near the Grand Canyon, Petrified Forest, and Flagstaff. A video of the park is available by calling the phone number listed. Prices are $17 to $19 for two people. There is a nominal charge for laundry facilities.

Woody Mountain Campground and RV Park
2727 W. U.S. Hwy. 66 (Exit 191 off I–40), Flagstaff
(800) 732–7986

Nice big pine trees shade the RV park and campground at Woody Mountain and make it a lovely place to spend a few days while visiting the Four Corners. There are 148 sites, which include tent sites and large pull-throughs. The kids will enjoy the playground and outdoor heated pool, while adults might take on a game of horseshoes before turning in for the night. A general store and sandwich shop are available, and if you've brought along a TV and VCR, videos are for rent. Woody Mountain is close to all of Flagstaff's attractions, as well as near the Petrified Forest, Meteor Crater, and Wupatki Indian ruins. Reservations are suggested. Tent spaces rent for $17 a night, while a full hookup is $23. You will pay a small charge if you use the laundry facilities.

Munds Park RV Resort
17550 Munds Ranch Rd., Munds Park
(800) 243–1309

Adjacent to the Coconino National Forest, Munds Park RV Resort has 264 spaces for RVs and campers. Open from April to November, Munds Park is picturesque and a beautiful place to camp for one day or many days. Tall pine trees offer shade in which to cool off after a busy day sightseeing, and the kids will enjoy the playground and game room with a free pool table. Adults will find the lounge with a big screen TV a great place to unwind. A heated pool/spa, restrooms, showers, complete general store, two laundry facilities, and cable television and telephone hookups in the newest section may make you not want to leave this little piece of Four Corners heaven. Full hookups are $23.50 per night, and spots with just water and electricity are $19 per night. There is a small charge for the laundry facilities.

Restaurants

Price Code

The price code is based on the cost of two dinner entrees, but does not include appetizers, desserts, or alcoholic beverages.

$	less than $15
$$	less than $30
$$$	less than $50
$$$$	$50 and up

While Navajo tacos, Mexican food, and South-western dishes remain favorites of the residents of the Four Corners, you'll find menus of every description when you visit. Biscuits and gravy, breakfast burritos, pancakes the size of dinner plates, and huevos rancheros top my breakfast favorites; while any sandwich with green chili, and green chili chicken soup, make for a great lunch. Dinner may be chicken with green chili and cheese, steak with frijoles and rice, or fish with a fruit salsa. We

love our spices in this part of the country and you'll find hot pepper sauce on almost every table in almost every diner you stop. But Italian, French, German, and good ole American food are savored and served up as well. No matter what you're hungry for, you're sure to find it at one of the many wonderful restaurants throughout northeastern Arizona. The restaurants featured in this section are just a taste of what you'll find as you travel the Four Corners. Enjoy these, and remember cooks and chefs here are very proud of their ability to serve a dish that isn't just good, but memorable.

While Flagstaff has the most restaurants to offer, you'll find diners and nice restaurants throughout northeastern Arizona. Many of them are family businesses and menus change with the seasons and the request of local customers. I urge you to try the specialties of those restaurants in addition to your usual comfort food and familiar dishes. For touring the Four Corners means more than enjoying the recreational activities and the attractions, it's all about the wonderful ethnic food you'll find along the way. Fast food places abound in this tourist area, but the places I'm highlighting here offer something special—a dish, dessert, drink, or atmosphere that sets it apart.

Prices at all restaurants may change without notice, so these are approximate prices. Call for specifics when you make reservations. All restaurants offer smoking and non-smoking areas and are wheelchair accessible unless otherwise noted and take major credit cards

Beaver Street Brewery and Whistle Stop Café $$
11 S. Beaver, Flagstaff
(520) 779–0079

This is a place where you can take the kids and they'll enjoy it as much as you do. A comfortable family atmosphere prevails at the Beaver Street Brewery, and you can watch food being prepared in the open kitchen area. The wood fire stove will bake up some of the best pizza you've ever tasted and the kids are sure to love it. Specials are served nightly, with Angus ribeye steaks, seafood, pasta, and regional food prepared just the way you like them. If you haven't gotten enough of the outdoors, you can sit outside in the beer garden, and feast your eyes on the San Francisco Peaks while feasting your stomach on the great food. A unique brass bar highlights the Beaver Street Brewery, and the brewery offers up ales that are exceptionally good.

Busters Restaurant and Bar $$
1800 S. Milton Rd., Flagstaff
(520) 774–5155

Busters has been named Flagstaff's best restaurant for more than five years, and for good reason. The food is wonderful, the menu is varied, the drinks are great, and the staff is attentive and great fun. Fresh fish is flown in daily to Busters, and is prepared with care and skill. Salmon, halibut, swordfish, mahi mahi, and oysters are served up with flair, and the oyster bar will make your mouth water. Angus prime rib and steaks are grilled perfectly and the shrimp, chicken, veal, and pasta dishes are equally good. Busters offers 66 beers, and most of the college students who frequent the bar work hard to try each of the 66, in order to have their name inscribed on the walls. A really good wine list is offered and you'll enjoy your meal in the comfort of pleasant surroundings. The early bird specials offered from 5 to 7 P.M. don't skimp on portions, just price.

Chez Marc Bistro $$$$
503 N. Humphreys St., Flagstaff
520) 774–1343

If you're looking for French food, you'll find some of the best at Chez Marc Bistro. The extensive menu includes fresh fish, a wonderful smoked duck breast salad, roasted quail, and guinea hen breast. The sauces that accompany most dishes are worth the visit themselves, and dessert— well—dessert is a must when you visit Chez Marc. Chocolate mousse cake, crepes simmered in a Citrus Essence, and Lemon Cheesecake Mousseline set over a fresh fruit compote are worth the extra calories. This beautiful French restaurant is a perfect way to end a day of sightseeing, but if you're a cigar lover, you won't want to miss Marc's Cigar Club, located on the second floor of the restaurant. A lounge with sofa, television, and games accompanied by an intimate dining room with tables for two and four, Marc's Cigar Club is a wonderful place to spend some time. Marc's offers a complete cigar menu, which includes some of the best cigars available at decent prices. If you're looking for an alternative to steak and potatoes and want a real dining experience, check out Chez Marc Bistro.

Down Under New Zealand Restaurant
$$$$
6 E. Aspen Ave., Flagstaff
(520) 774–6677

The Down Under is not just another comfortable restaurant with great service—it has great food that you just won't find most places. While many of us may never have the opportunity to visit New Zealand, we can certainly enjoy its culinary delights while visiting Flagstaff. The chef uses only fresh ingredients with creative marinades, dressings, and sauces to compliment his dishes, and only free-range, hormone and steroid free meats are served. Venison, lamb, kangaroo (really very good), and fresh fish top the Down Under menu. There is a lovely patio where you can dine during the warmer months, when the great mountain air of Flagstaff just adds to your enjoyment of dinner, dessert, and fine wines. The wine list is extensive and offers many good New Zealand wines, as well as fine Australian ones. Dessert is almost a must-have here, since Flagstaff has honored the Down Under as having the best dessert in the "Taste of Flagstaff" competition. Because everything is served to order and the chef is a perfectionist, figure two hours from the time you order until you finish your dinner. Because of that, the Down Under probably isn't the best restaurant for tired, restless youngsters. For a truly different dining experience, try the Down Under.

Dam Bar & Grille $$
644 N. Navajo, Page
(520) 645–2161

A pleasant bar and grille with décor influenced by the Glen Canyon Dam, the Dam Bar & Grille is a nice place to eat after a full day at the lake or sightseeing. The menu offers up just about everything a casual diner would want at a reasonable price. However the All You Can Eat Chicken Wings and a bottle of Dom Perignon will set you back $150. Chicken wings are a staple on the appetizer menu of most casual restaurants in the Four Corners, but they're usually washed down with a tasty microbrew instead of the Dom Perignon. Ample portions of salads, seafood, pasta, steaks, and daily specials are prepared with care at the Dam Bar & Grille. The kids will enjoy this comfortable restaurant and the staff always seems genuinely glad to see youngsters.

Downtown Flagstaff. PHOTO: BRIAN WINTER

Shopping

Shopping in northeastern Arizona is an adventure. With few major shopping malls and centers, residents and visitors to this portion of the Four Corners enjoy a more personal association with the vendors and owners of the shops in which they purchase gifts and necessities. As you travel through this part of Arizona, you'll discover roadside vendors, small shops and trading posts, where a variety of wonderful treasurers await your purchase. The places I've highlighted in this section are but a few of the countless unique stores and shops you'll find along the way. I encourage you to stop and support the Native Americans who offer their arts and crafts—the young Native American who sells you that sand painting, jewelry or piece of art just could be the next "discovery" in the field of art.

Downtown Flagstaff is a wonderful place for residents and visitors alike to shop. Boutiques of every description, outdoor gear outfitters, bookstores, and galleries offer unlimited shopping opportunities. Lots of unique restaurants, microbreweries, and coffee houses offer food and drink to guests, but you'll likely have a hard time deciding which ones to patronize. Downtown Flag is full of energy, from the owners and managers of the businesses to the great college students who frequent the shops, restaurants, and pubs. Just to stroll along the streets, to watch and listen to the enthusiasm that permeates the area, is worth a trip. Don't go through Flagstaff without taking in downtown.

The Dam Plaza
644 N. Navajo, Page

Page has one shopping center, although it's a relatively small one. The Dam Plaza has the Dam Bar & Grille, a coffee house, and an outlet. Bean's Gourmet Coffee House is a must stop for coffee lovers. Espresso, cappuccino, and lattes are offered up in great style and with heavenly flavor. You may want to select freshly baked cookies or a croissant to go with your beverage of choice, or have an Italian soda instead. Just the wonderful aroma of Bean's is worth a stop, and the coffee will make you return again and again. The Dam Outlet store offers Levis, Polo jeans, Polo Ralph Lauren, Pulp/Tensel, and other top names at outlet prices.

Van's Trading Company
P.O. Box 7, U.S. Hwy. 160, Tuba City
(800) 798–9849

Van's Trading Company has great Native American arts and crafts for sale. Navajo rugs, Hopi kachinas, jewelry, handmade drums, clothing, and moccasins are included in the bounty you'll find at Van's. For 75 years, Van's has offered quality Native American pieces. An auction of unclaimed pawn and jewelry is held at 3 P.M. on the 15th of every month. Take a moment and stop at Van's, where employees enjoy showing customers all the wonderful things the store offers.

McGee's Indian Art Gallery and Shopping Center
AZ Hwy. 264 in Keams Canyon
North from I-40 via Winslow on
AZ Hwy. 87
(520) 738–2295

McGee's Indian Art Gallery and Shopping Center on the Hopi reservation isn't just another trading post. McGee's Indian Art Gallery buys Hopi crafts and markets them to collectors from around the world. Just minutes from the Navajo reservation, McGee's also has the opportunity to purchase Navajo rugs and jewelry and you'll find the best of the Hopi and Navajo here at the art gallery. Wonderful pieces of art are available at a variety of prices, so you'll have quality and price from which to select your treasures.

Creative Impressions
120 S. Milton Rd., Flagstaff

Flagstaff is on historic U.S. Highway 66, and if you're looking for memorabilia from it, you'll find it at Creative Impressions. In addition to all the great Route 66 merchandise, you'll also find a nice selection of souvenirs from Flagstaff, the Grand Canyon, and the Southwest. Creative Impressions is a fun shop with a helpful staff.

Flagstaff Mall
4650 N. U.S. Hwy. 89, Flagstaff

Flagstaff is the largest retail hub in northeastern Arizona. The Flagstaff Mall is anchored by JC Penney, Sears, and Dillard's. Victoria's Secret, The Gap, Eddie Bauer, and Bath and Body Works also have retail space in the mall. The Flagstaff Mall is a very nice shopping center, and you'll find everything you need for your family.

Kidstuff

There will be ruins to explore, trails to hike and bike, museums to visit and memories to make when youngsters visit Arizona in their tour of the Four Corners. Arizona, like its sister states in the Four Corners, offers youngsters wide open places where imaginations can soar as high as the birds in the sky. There aren't a lot of unusual organized activities for youngsters in most of the areas of northeastern Arizona because of the many opportunities afforded them in the great outdoors. Interstate highways are few, and huge metropolitan areas are almost non-existent. There aren't many concrete jungles; youngsters have acres in which to play baseball, football, soccer and basketball, they can ride their bicycles without having to worry about heavy traffic, and they can dream in places with only the birds and the wildlife as company. As you travel with your youngsters throughout the Four Corners, you're encouraged to not pack every minute with sightseeing and things to do. Let them discover this great place we call the Four Corners, where the stars appear closer, the skies seem bluer, and the clouds seem few and far between. Give them time to do their own exploring, dream about the Native Americans and early pioneers who lived in this part of the Wild West, and learn about the cultures and traditions of a people they may have only read about in books. Give them an opportunity to meet and get to know some of the youngsters who call the Four Corners home. It will be an experience they will never forget and one they will savor forever.

In addition to the hiking and fishing opportunities virtually everywhere in northeastern Arizona, there are other activities the kids are sure to enjoy. The ones I've listed are but a few, but are ones I think the youngsters will particularly like. New recreational activities for youngsters are established regularly, so if you or your kids see something that looks like fun, check it out. Whatever activities your youngsters decide to pursue, try to include yourself in their fun. The kids will enjoy seeing Mom and Dad doing kidstuff, and you just may rediscover the kid in you—and relish the discovery.

Flagstaff

Thorpe Park
245 N. Thorpe Rd.

Thorpe Park has something for the kid in all of us. Playgrounds, trails, tennis courts, basketball courts, ball fields, and a golf course are just some of the things kids can take advantage of while in Flagstaff.

Bushmaster Park
Alta Vista and Lockett Road

This park has footpaths, picnic facilities, playgrounds, basketball and tennis courts, and a BMX park. Both of these parks are clean and well cared for and will give youngsters the opportunity to expend some energy while offering parents a chance to catch their breath and watch the kids have a lot of fun.

Jay Lively Activity Center,
1650 N. Turquoise Drive, Flagstaff

The ice skating rink is open from mid-September through April. Lessons, public skating, figure skating, and hockey are offered. Admission for youngsters younger than 6 Monday through Thursday is $1, and from Friday through Sunday, admission is $1.25. For those aged 7 to 17, Monday through Thursday admission is $2, and $2.50 from Friday through Sunday. Skates may be rented for $1. Ice skating lessons are available on Tuesdays and Thursdays for 25 minutes at a cost of about $25, plus a one-time fee of $4. For kids who love to rollerblade or rollerskate, that season runs from June through the end of August. This is a wonderful center and one the kids are sure to enjoy.

Lake Powell

Kids of all ages will find much to do at Lake Powell. Fishing, swimming, and sunbathing are popular pastimes at Lake Powell, as are taking in the incredible sights at this beautiful spot in the Four Corners. While most vacations mean taking it easy and doing little, we've discovered some activities the kids may enjoy doing while at Lake Powell.

Twin Finn Dive Center
811 Vista Ave., Page
(800) 530–3406

You and the kids may want to take kayaking and diving lessons. Kayaking lessons will run from $60 to $150 per person; and diving lessons range from $45 to $425. Call for the prices and lesson times. Kids may want to learn to snorkel instead of diving, and for under $50, instructors will show them how, all in half a day. A resort diving course for the non-diver and a scuba review for a certified diver needing a refresher are one-day classes offered for under $100. The instructors at Twin Finn are certified and will provide everything

you need to dive and discover the wonderful treasures in Lake Powell.

Lake Powell Marine
84 S. 7th Ave., Page
(520) 645–3114

If diving and kayaking aren't what your youngsters want to do they can try a water trampoline. At Lake Powell Marine, a 20-foot trampoline rents for about $150 a day; a 15-foot one for about $125 a day. These trampolines are similar to the ones found in the back yards of many families. With the water trampoline, however, there's no danger of youngsters falling off and hitting hard ground. The laughter and giggles these trampolines elicit from youngsters is worth the price. The trampoline is presented to you deflated, with detailed instructions for inflation. Two people can set it up in about an hour. That time is likely to seem much longer for the kids, however, as they anxiously await the opportunity to jump, turn somersaults and land in the beautiful water of Lake Powell. The trampolines are bright and colorful. If the kids decide they want a souvenir of Lake Powell, the marine staff will credit a portion of the rental price toward the sale price.

Rod and Paddle Guide Service
PO Box 2987, Page
(520) 608–0632
Rod and Paddle Guide Service provides a kayaking tour flaunting the wonders of Lake Powell that not everyone has the opportunity to witness. A 24-foot sport fishing boat takes you 25 miles up the lake, where you climb onto an kayak for a two- to four-hour paddle into areas not usually seen by the average tourist. You'll be able to swim or snorkel (remember those snorkeling lessons?) away from heavy boat traffic. Rod and Paddle guides are licensed and insured and will do whatever they can to make your kayak adventure a once-in-a-lifetime experience. You can opt for a half-day tour, which will run about $60 per person with a four person minimum; a full-day tour, which is about $85 per person with a four person minimum; or tours that will keep you exploring Lake Powell for several days at a cost of approximately $150 per person, again with a four person minimum. The choice will be yours and the adventure will be priceless.

Recreation

With miles of trails to hike, countless bicycle paths to pedal, mountains of snow to ski, and plenty of fish to catch, outdoor enthusiasts won't have any difficulty finding things to do in northeastern Arizona. The incredible beauty of this part of the Four Corners encourages almost everyone to spend whatever spare time they have outdoors. There is so much to do here, it may be almost impossible for you to try it all if you're on a limited time schedule. Enjoy the recreation that appeals to you most now, and plan to visit the enchanted Four Corners area again to take advantage of the recreational opportunities you missed this time. Those of us fortunate to live here will welcome the chance to have you as a guest again and again. We do ask that you respect the land, the wildlife and the cultures—we want it preserved for generations to come.

Hiking and mountain biking are popular among locals, as well as tourists. As you travel throughout the Four Corners, you'll find bike enthusiasts in local bicycle stores willing to share their favorite trails with you, and hikers in sporting goods stores offering advice on the best trails and the challenges they offer. I encourage you to visit and get to know them, for they will provide the best suggestions so you can fully enjoy your favorite sport while in the

Insiders' Tip

A basic survivor kit for hikers in Arizona should include a whistle or mirror for signaling, waterproof matches or a lighter for building a fire, a space blanket and two large plastic bags which can be used for shelter, a compass and map for navigation, and first-aid supplies. Moleskin for blisters, a knife, snacks, extra clothing, a hat, and a walking stick are also items you may need.

Four Corners. Please respect the land and the environment when you hike or bike and pack out what you pack in. Remember, too, to take enough water with you for the time you plan to be gone, let someone know where you're going and when to expect you back, and wear whatever safety gear is appropriate for your sport.

Fishing is as important to many residents of the Four Corners as breathing, and every angler you meet will have a favorite fishing spot. As you travel through northeastern Arizona, you'll have the opportunity to fish many popular spots and, if you ask local anglers, they may share with you a fishing hole most tourists aren't aware of. We encourage you to ask about good fishing spots when you stop for gas, for meals, or to shop at a local sporting goods store. Arizona anglers are proud of the fishing in their state and are usually willing to tell a new friend where the biggest trout, bass, or crappie can be found, and the best lure to catch them with. Please make sure you have a fishing license before you drop your line in the water, and know what the limits are for the spot you're fishing. Fishing licenses in Arizona are $12.50 for one day and $26 for five days for adults. Those younger than 18 may purchase a combination youth hunting and fishing license for $25.50. Remember, if you plan to fish Lake Powell, you must have a fishing license for the state in which the lake lies. Check with the marina for information and prices.

There are a couple of great and unusual recreational opportunities listed in this section. These are just a few of the fun things you can do outdoors here in northeastern Arizona, so keep you eyes open and your schedule ready for an unexpected sporting opportunity.

Arizona Sunbowl
16 miles north of Flagstaff of U.S. Hwy. 180
(520) 779–1951

Flagstaff is home to the Arizona Snowbowl, which is located in the Coconino National Forest. There are 777 acres of land in the Snowbowl, with 137 of them skiable. Skiers love the Snowbowl because of its 2,300 feet of vertical drop, 32 scenic alpine trails, four lifts and one tow rope, two sports shops, full-service equipment and repair, private, group and children's lessons, and two restaurants and two bars. Not to mention the 260 inches of snow it receives. Snowboarders and skiers alike flock to this ski area as soon as the snow falls. In addition to a terrain park, boarders will find step-in bindings on all rental boards, stone grinding for snowboards, repairs on all makes and models of boards, binding parts, straps, and buckles. For those who want to learn to snowboard, private and group lessons are offered, as well as "Learn to Snowboard" packages. If skiing isn't your thing, or you happen to be traveling through Flagstaff during the warmer months, the Snowbowl has warm weather activities, too.

Hiking trails that provide challenges to both beginners and experienced hikers are found on and around the San Francisco Peaks. Easy hikes along Rocky Ridge Trail, Fat Man's Loop, and Sunset Trail are offered, and vary in distance from 2 to

Cross-country skiing in Flagstaff, Arizona.
PHOTO: S. AITCHISON

4 miles. Moderate hikes are offered on Kachina Trail, Sandy Seep Trail, and Oldham Trail and are from 1.5 miles to 5.5 miles in length. Elden Lookout, Humphreys Trail, and Weatherford Trail are the most difficult and vary in distance from 3 to 8.5 miles. Each trail will take you along beautiful countryside that will add to the enjoyment of your hike.

McDonalds Ranch
(520) 774–4481

McDonalds Ranch, a horseback riding stable and Western adventure operation, is another addition at Snowbowl. Experienced wranglers take guests on a one- or two-hour ride through the Coconino National Forest. Rides begin and end at the corral at the Fort Valley Barn and begin at 9 A.M., with the last ride beginning at 5 P.M. On the first and third Thursdays of each month, visitors can enjoy a hay ride through the woods to a campsite, where a barbecue dinner is served. For groups, parties, or special events, a hay ride and cowboy cookout can be arranged. A one-hour horseback ride costs about $25, with a two-hour ride about $35. Hay rides begin at about $10 each.

Scenic Skyride
(520) 779–1951

During the warmer months in Flagstaff, the Scenic Skyride is offered at the Arizona Snowbowl. Guests can view more than 70 miles of northern Arizona beauty, including the Grand Canyon and downtown Flagstaff. The Skyride will take you 11,500 feet into the Arizona sky, and offers great opportunities for photographs, seeing wildlife, hiking, or just enjoying the ride. A member of the Forest Service is on hand to answer any questions you may have about the area. The Skyride runs from 10 A.M. to 4 P.M. from Memorial Day through Labor Day, and on Fridays, Saturdays, and Sundays through the middle of October. A restaurant is available at the top of the Skyride for those who find their appetites whetted by the mountain air. The Skyride costs about $10 for adults, $7 for seniors 65 to 69, and $5 for children 8 to 12. Seniors 70 years and older ride free, as do children seven years old or younger when accompanied by an adult.

Hummer Affair
530 Humphreys St., Flagstaff
(520) 213–0000

For those seeking the ultimate adventure, look no further than Hummer Affair. A Hummer Affair allows guests to drive a open-top vehicle through attractions like Canyon de Chelly. The vehicles are equipped with a global positioning system, two-way radios, central tire inflation system, a cooler stocked with the guests' beverages of choice, and first aid kits. Most of the tours offer varying degrees of challenge, so the driver and the vehicle are put to the test. The Canyon de Chelly tour offers access to private land not usually available to tourists and provides views not often seen. Navajo guides explain the features and history of the canyon. Tours of Canyon de Chelly are available from May through June and September through October. Tours don't come cheap—count on about $4,000 per person for a four-day tour if you ride in the front seat, and about $2,600 per person for the tour if you're a backseat rider. Guests are treated like royalty for the duration of the tour, however. Safari Suites (very, very nice portable rooms) have electricity, and beds with mattresses, satin sheets, and huge fluffy pillows. Fresh flowers and fresh fruit are placed on the coffee table in your suite, which also includes a fully stocked mini-bar. Breakfast on the tour is more than donuts and coffee. You'll awaken to the wonderful aroma of freshly brewed coffee or tea, and a wonderful a la carte breakfast prepares you for the morning. The four-course lunch is served at a location especially selected for its beauty and ambiance. Dinner, too, is a special occasion. The staff greets you with iced towels to cool you down and hors d'oervres and an open bar to help you relax before dinner. After a quick shower and change of clothes, you'll be served a five-course dinner, which should, along with that great Arizona fresh air, help you sleep like a baby all night long. For those who become so enamored of the Hummer they want more, Hummer Affair offers state-of-the-art off-road courses for training, instruction, and racing. Students will have their own instructor, and will spend 80 percent of their time behind the wheel of the luxury vehicle. The cost is about $2,000 and includes all meals and three nights accommodations. This just could be the perfect gift for someone who has everything, and a wonderful opportunity to see Arizona attractions. For more information, see the Close-up in the Arizona chapter.

Crawley's Monument Tours
(520) 697–3463, (520) 697–3734

In Kayenta, Crawley's Monument Tours is one you won't want to miss. Bill Crawley arrived in Monument Valley some 40 years ago. Seeing and appreciating the beauty of the Valley, Crawley decided to start a tour business. His first tours went out in four-wheel-drive vehicles into what was then an area few had seen or cared about. Crawley quickly learned about his Navajo neighbors and was awed by their works of art and their culture. Since those early days, Crawley has been host to tens of thousands of visitors, and shares with them his love of Monument Valley and the Navajo people. Visitors may take half-day and full-day tours, or a beautiful sunset tour. The Mittens, the Totem Pole, and the Three Sisters are viewed on tours, and Eye of the Sun, Ear of the Wind, and Moccasin Arch are special treats for Crawley's guests. Gone are the four-wheel-drive vehicles—Crawley now uses passenger vans and mini-buses. Navajo guides share their culture and facts about their reservation. Visitors also get to visit a hogan, the traditional Navajo home, and observe rug weaving by Native Americans. Crawley and his staff offer unique tours that visitors will enjoy and remember as a highlight of their trip to the Four Corners.

Attractions

The number of attractions in northeastern Arizona is enough to keep you busy for weeks. For it is here, in this portion of the Four Corners, that you'll find popular Lake Powell and the Glen Canyon National Recreation Area, Canyon de Chelly, and Monument Valley. But these major tourist attractions are just a sample of the many places to see while you visit northeastern Arizona. The ones I spotlight in this section are places you'll want to see and explore. As you travel through this portion of the Four Corners, however, you'll find signs that indicate other points of interest and if you have the time, it's well worth it to visit those places as well. The spotlighted attractions are listed clockwise beginning with Lake Powell. The two attractions in Flagstaff follow the state's attractions. The culture, the history, and the beauty of the Four Corners can't be absorbed and fully appreciated in a limited time. I encourage you to select the spots you want to see most this time, and to come again to visit those attractions you may not have time for now. The fun of a trip to the Four Corners, whether it's your first visit or your tenth, is that the scenery changes from year to year, as Mother Nature and man have an impact on the land. No matter how many times you visit the same attraction, you're apt to discover something you never saw before, or meet someone you missed visiting with the last time, or simply re-discover the beauty of an area that has been home to great Native American warriors, Americans who have found their place in history books, and pioneers who fought against all odds to make this land their home. As you stop to look, learn and absorb, you'll have the opportunity to meet people from all parts of the country who, like you, are interested in the land, the culture, the traditions, and the beauty of this unique

Hummer Affair

A camping trip for most of us means sleeping bags, a tent, cooking over an open fire, and eating on paper plates using plastic utensils. While that's usually great fun and a wonderful way to enjoy the outdoors, the Hummer Affair, 503 North Humphreys Street in Flagstaff, has a unique alternative.

Marc Balocco has had a love affair with the Hummer for many years. A former automobile racer with many years of experience in the hotel/restaurant business, Balocco said he was looking for a new challenge when someone suggested "high-style" camping. "I've spent all my life in the hospitality business, working with big corporations that were looking for a unique way to entertain clients and valued employees," Balocco explained. "I had visited the Four Corners and was totally awed by the beauty here, and thought it would be a great place to start a business."

But it wasn't just any business Balocco started. Balocco decided camping needn't be just "roughing it," but could be an experience similar to visiting a five-star hotel. With several Hummers parked outside his front door, fine linens in his closet, exquisite dinnerware packed and ready to go, and hundreds of miles of natural wonders to explore, Hummer Affair was born.

Clients basically purchase the front seat of the Hummer, Balocco explained, which gives them the opportunity to drive the famous machine. If there are more than two people in the client's party, the backseat of the Hummer is sold, but those people don't drive the vehicle, he said. The party has the option of touring Monument Valley, Moab, or Canyon de Chelley and during the winter months, Balocco takes clients to Baja, California. At least one guide accompanies each tour.

Clients leave the company's headquarters in Flagstaff and head out to the location of their choice. A cooler in the Hummer contains cold drinks for clients to sip while they enjoy the beauty of the area, Balocco said. When it's time for lunch, you won't find Hummer Affair clients eating peanut butter and jelly sandwiches from a brown bag. Lunch includes four courses served from a camp that has been set up with the client's comfort in mind. "We usually offer a cold buffet," Balocco said, "with salmon, chicken, salads, French bread—all prepared with the finest ingredients. Beverages are served, but no wine at lunch because we are driving."

While the good china isn't used for lunch, Balocco said, "nice plasticwear, not the paper kind, but really nice plasticwear, is used. We want to make lunch as nice as possible."

After lunch, the staff cleans up while the tour group continues to its destination. Upon arriving at the campground, clients are presented with iced towels to refresh themselves before they shower, then allowed to change and rest before dinner is served.

If clients linger in their tents before heading to dinner, it's understandable. These tents provide bedrooms that include showers, a bed covered with satin sheets, nightstands, a vanity with mirror, and a conversation area, where wine may be enjoyed by candlelight.

Once clients have showered, changed, and recovered from the day's drive, drinks, French wine, and hors d'oeuvre are served. With "happy hour" over, staff members announce that dinner is served.

Dinner is offered under a star-shaped tent on round tables covered with fine linen tablecloths. Fine crystal holds the French wine, and china and silverware add to the enjoyment of the cuisine, Balocco said.

"Dinner is five courses," he said. "We start with a cold appetizer—maybe smoked salmon or crepes with sour cream and caviar. Then there's the salad, followed by the entree, which may be steak on the grill, stuffed quail, pork tenderloins, lobster tail, or a fresh fish course. Dessert may be a crème Brule, chocolate cake, or a cream puff stuffed with ice cream and topped with a chocolate sauce."

Once clients have savored their dinner, Balocco said after dinner wine and drinks are served. Quality cigars are offered to those who wish to end their day with a good smoke, he added.

After a good night's rest, guests arise to find a full-course breakfast awaiting them, then they continue their journey. Rarely is a client disappointed in this unusual camping adventure, Balocco said. "We have many, many repeat clients," he admitted. "And each year, it seems large companies are using the Hummer Affair as a reward to employees, in addition to entertaining important clients. We have a lot of fun, the service is wonderful, the food divine, and the accommodations are very, very nice."

The emphasis for Hummer Affair isn't just on food, drink, and accommodations, however. Balocco said he has the blessing of many Navajo families, who allow him to take clients across land to points of interest few visitors get to see. "We're allowed to camp at the bottom of cliffs on the land of these wonderful Navajo families," Balocco said. "At night, with the campfire going, the scenery is absolutely incredible and something you don't get to see if you're just driving through the area."

For Balocco, giving clients the opportunity to tour a beautiful area in luxury is a dream come true. "It's like an African safari," he said with a smile. "Except we're not in Africa and we don't see any elephants."

For more information, see the Recreation section of this chapter.

Camping out Hummer Affair style. PHOTO: HUMMER AFFAIR

area. I encourage you to make new friends while you're here. I want you to enjoy this visit and come again. The Four Corners is truly America the Beautiful with traditions and cultures that are as unique as the wonderful people who live here.

Glen Canyon National Recreation Area/Lake Powell
691 Scenic View Dr., Page
(520) 608–6404
www.nps.gov/glca

It was the early 1950s when the Bureau of Reclamation proposed building a dam on the Colorado River at Glen Canyon's southern end. The area was relatively unrecognized, although those who had passed through Glen Canyon were aware of the majestic beauty it offered. Construction of the dam began in 1956 and was completed in 1962. The lake behind the dam, Lake Powell, did not completely fill until 1980. Today, Glen Canyon Dam provides electricity for millions of people, as well as water for irrigation. The water depth drops more than 500 feet at the dam and its crest spans 1,560 feet, rising more than 700 feet above bedrock. There are five rivers that feed into Lake Powell—the Green River from Wyoming, the Colorado River from Colorado, the San Juan River from New Mexico, the Escalante River from Utah, and the Dirty Devil River from Utah. It is the second largest man-made lake in the United States, with 1,960 miles of shoreline and 96 different canyons to explore. Lake Powell provides relaxation and recreation for thousands of people who come from all over the world to bask in the sunshine and beauty of the area. The Glen Canyon National Recreation Area stretches for hundreds of miles and offers boating, fishing, swimming, backcountry hiking, and four-wheel-drive enthusiasts plenty of space to enjoy their sport.

Most visitors begin their tour of Glen Canyon and Lake Powell at Page, which is two miles from the dam and the visitor center. Page is a friendly community and offers stores, motels, restaurants, churches and a hospital. While many people opt to stay in Page, Wahweap Marina, 5.5 miles from the visitor center, includes Wahweap Lodge (520) 645–2433, which is on the shores of the lake and is a pleasant place to stay. In addition, housekeeping units are available at Hite Marina, Hall's Crossing, and Bullfrog Resort and Marina. The units include separate bedrooms, two bathrooms with tub and shower combination, a full kitchen with dishes and utensils for eight people, a microwave, linens, television, and a picnic table and grill. The housekeeping units are comfortable and offer more privacy than the lodge. For those who plan to stay more than a couple of days exploring Lake Powell, a housekeeping unit may be more economical, as well as a lot of fun. For information on housekeeping units, call the visitor center.

Many people opt to take advantage of all Lake Powell's offerings by renting a houseboat and cruising the lake. Houseboats vary in size (from 36 feet to 59 feet), amenities (swim slides to sound systems), and cost (about $1,100 to about $3,000 for three days). All houseboats come with everything you need for your Lake Powell cruise, including life jackets, toilet tissue, and a corkscrew. Be forewarned, however, that reservations must be made well in advance, and flexibility in your vacation plans will help you get the boat you want. Reservations should be made at least one year in advance, and even then, you may expect scheduling challenges. Once you've confirmed your rental, a deposit must be made to secure the houseboat. If you cancel or change your reservation, a portion or all of your deposit may be retained by the rental company. Deposits run from $350 to $600, depending on which houseboat you select. For more information on renting houseboats, call (800) 530–3406. Those who have rented houseboats are enthusiastic about the experience and fun they have on the boats and return again and again for their vacation on beautiful Lake Powell.

Fishing is a popular attraction at Lake

Powell and residents of the Four Corners frequently make the trip to catch stripers, largemouth and smallmouth bass, and crappie. Some anglers fish for walleye, channel catfish, and bluegill sunfish from the waters of Lake Powell. The Colorado squawfish, humpback and bonytail chub, and razorback sucker are endangered species that are also fished from the waters. However, if you catch them, you must release them alive immediately. The penalties for keeping endangered fish are stiff and law enforcement officers enforce those laws vigorously. You must have a valid Utah and/or Arizona fishing license to fish Lake Powell. Licenses may be purchased at all the marinas. Check at the marina before packing your tackle box and fishing pole and heading out. Record-sized fish have been caught at Lake Powell and anglers are always hoping to top those records. Records range from a 5-pound smallmouth bass to a 48-pound striped bass.

Hiking is also popular at Glen Canyon National Recreation Area and the staff at the visitor center will be happy to direct you to the best places to hike and the challenges they offer.

Almost everyone who spends time at Lake Powell visits the Rainbow Bridge National Monument, which is about 50 miles by water from Wahweap, Bullfrog, or Hall's Crossing. This beautiful natural bridge is one of the most photographed bridges in the world. Please stay on the approved paths, however, because Rainbow Bridge remains a scared ground to the Native Americans. (See the Attractions section in the Utah chapter for more information about Rainbow Bridge.)

There is so much to see and do at Lake Powell, you'll want to spend several days. It's almost impossible to accurately describe the area, because the canyons, cliffs, mesas, and water are so beautiful they defy description. Locals who visit Lake Powell regularly always come home with stories of new spots they found, fishing holes they discovered, and a better appreciation of all the Glen Canyon

> ## Insiders' Tip
> While New Mexico, Colorado, and Utah participate in daylight savings time, Arizona has chosen to remain on Mountain Standard Time throughout the year. The Navajo Nation in Arizona, however, observes Daylight Savings Time.

National Recreation Area has to offer.

The visitor center operates from 7 A.M. to 7 P.M. Memorial Day through Labor Day, and from 8 A.M. to 5 P.M. the rest of the year.

**Monument Valley Navajo Tribal Park
East of U.S. Hwy. 163, about 24 miles
north of Kayenta
(801) 737–3287
www.navajonationparks.org**

You may never have visited Monument Valley, but chances are excellent that you've seen it. One of the most photographed areas in the country, Monument Valley has been featured in countless movies and television commercials. The automobile industry likes using the top of Right Mitten for TV ads. Noted Hollywood director John Ford first used Monument Valley in a movie when he directed Stagecoach, starring John Wayne. Other notable movies shot in Monument Valley include *She Wore a Yellow Ribbon* in 1949; *How the West Was Won* in 1962; *Back to the Future I and II* in 1983 and 1991; and *Forrest Gump* in 1993.

Monument Valley may epitomize the Wild West to many, but for those of us who live in the Four Corners, it is more than a great spot to shoot movies and television commercials, it is a place where the beauty of the area seeps deep into the soul. Great formations rise from a flat, sandy desert like hands reaching to the gods. A canvas of color created by the rising and setting of the sun offers different shades and incredible shadows.

Monument Valley lies entirely within the Navajo Indian Reservation on the Arizona/Utah border. The state line passes through many of the landmarks, giving residents of both states bragging rights. There is but one main road, U.S. Highway 163, which links Kayenta with U.S. Highway 191 in Utah. The most photgraphed image of Monument Valley can be seen from the stretch of road that approaches the border of the two states from the north. And while visitors can see a lot of the valley from that road, much of the beauty is hidden behind cliffs.

The view from the visitor center is wonderful, but the valley can be best seen from Valley Drive, a 17-mile dirt road that winds from the visitor center among great towering cliffs and mesas, including the beautiful Totem Pole. Unfortunately, the road isn't a very good one, and four-wheel-drive vehicles are recommended. There are Navajo guides and four-wheel-drive rental outfitters who will gladly take visitors on the tour. You also have the option of touring the valley on horseback.

Youngsters will especially enjoy Monument Valley because of the great rock formations that resemble animals or other images. Kids will get a kick out of the Right Mitten; the Three Sisters, which resemble three nuns dressed in habits; the Hub, which not only looks like the center of a wagon wheel but is also the geographic center of Monument Valley; and

the Totem Pole, a 400-foot high rock formation that looks like a replica of a totem pole. Once you've actually visited Monument Valley, it will be easily recognizable in movies and commercials, but only those who know firsthand how incredibly beautiful the valley is can truly appreciate the magic that surrounds it.

The visitor center provides assistance from 7 A.M. to 8 P.M. May through September, and from 8 A.M. to 5 P.M. October through April.

Canyon de Chelly National Monument
Chinle, AZ
(520) 674–5500
www.nps.gov/cach.

Canyon de Chelly National Monument is 95 miles from Gallup, New Mexico, via U.S. Highway 666, U.S. Highway 191, and Arizona Highway 264. Two scenic routes provide the best and easiest way to see the ruins and the canyons. The South Rim Drive offers the most popular overlooks. A park ranger or guide must accompany you if you decide to travel into the canyon. Be ware, you can only do this on foot.

The hogan on the south side of the visitor center offers a museum, local artist exhibits, and a ranger-staffed information desk. Restrooms are also available at the visitor center, which is open from 8 A.M. to 5 P.M. daily October to April, 8 A.M. to 6 P.M. May to September.

Much more information on Canyon de Chelly can be found within the Four Corners Attractions chapter.

Hubbell Trading Post National Historic Site
0.5 mile west of Ganado on AZ Hwy. 264
(520) 755–3475

Established in the late 1870s, Hubbell Trading Post is the oldest continuously operating trading post in the Navajo Nation. John Lorenzo Hubbell began trading with the Navajos in 1876, after he learned some of the Navajo culture and language. Hubbell and his Navajo neighbors rarely exchanged money for goods; instead, they bartered for the things they needed. The Navajos would bring in blan-

Insiders' Tip

The saguaro cactus bloom, Arizona's state flower, is a large white flower that grows on the ends of the saguaro, which is the largest cactus in the United States. It grows to a height of 50 feet and lives up to 200 years.

kets or jewelry, and Hubbell would give them coffee, flour, sugar, cloth, or other needed items in exchange. Hubbell was well respected and thought of by the Navajo, who believed he treated them fairly, honestly, and in friendship. The National Park Service has exhibits and programs that explain Hubbell's work and how trading posts once linked the Navajo with the outside world. Weavers and silversmiths frequently demonstrate their art in the visitor center and a tour of Hubbell's house is also available. The house has wonderful rugs, paintings, baskets, and other works of art Hubbell collected before he died in 1930. Today, more than 100 years later, the Navajo people bring in rugs and jewelry and the Hopi bring their finest kachinas to the Hubbell Trading Post to sell. This attraction should be a "must see" when you visit the Four Corners—it is a testimony to the wonderful artistic talents of the Native Americans, and of a man's respect and honor of those people.

Homolovi Ruins State Park
5 miles northeast of Winslow on AZ Hwy. 87
(520) 289–4106

Homolovi Ruins is Arizona's first archaeological state park. Located along the Little Colorado River, it includes four major pueblo sites thought to have been occupied between A.D. 1200 and 1425 by ancestors of today's Hopi Indians. More than 340 acres are within the park, and campsites, agricultural features, and pit houses are included. Archaeologists continue to work in the park in June and July and offer special exhibits and programs. The ruined walls and broken pottery scattered throughout the park are testimony to the people who once lived here. This is a wonderful opportunity to see ruins, archaeologists in action, and learn about the people who traveled northeastern Arizona. The visitor center is open from 8 A.M. to 5 P.M. every day except Christmas.

Meteor Crater National Landmark
20 miles west of Winslow, 35 miles east of Flagstaff on I–40
(520) 289–2362
www.meteorcrater.com

The Meteor Crater is sure to excite and thrill the kid in everybody. When a huge iron-nickel meteorite hurled through the atmosphere at about 40,000 miles per hour some 50,000 years ago, it hit the earth in northeastern Arizona with an explosive force that was greater than 20 million tons of TNT. The meteorite is estimated to have been about 150 feet across and weighed several hundred thousand tons. Scientists believe it crashed into the earth in less than a few seconds and left a crater 700 feet deep and over 4,000 feet across. Blocks of limestone, some the size of a small house, were bounced out of the crater, landing on the rim. Today, the crater is 550 feet deep and almost two miles in diameter. In 1902, a Philadelphia mining engineer, Daniel Barringer, became interested in the site as a potential source of mining iron. He visited the crater and firmly believed it had been formed by the impact of a large iron meteorite. In 1903, Barringer formed the Standard Iron Co. He had four placer mining claims filed with the federal government and obtained the patents and ownership of the two square miles containing the crater. The topographical terrain of Meteor Crater resembles that of the Earth's moon and other planets so closely that NASA designated it as one of the official training sites for the Apollo astronauts. Meteor Crater remains the possession of the Barringer family, who lease the crater to Meteor Crater Enterprises, which operates the visitor center at the crater. A Museum of Astrogeology and an Astronaut Hall of Fame are included in the center, which also has a gift shop and snack bar. The museum offers visitors a self-guided tour of exhibits and video presentations that portray how the meteorite impacted the earth and the devastation it created. A 1,406-pound meteorite, the largest one found in

Wupatki National Monument. PHOTO: BILL HUDSON

the area, is also on display. The visitor center is open 365 days a year, from 6 A.M. to 6 P.M. from mid-May to mid-September, and from 8 A.M. to 5 P.M. the rest of the year. This is a wonderful, educational, and fun attraction for the entire family. An admission fee is collected and a RV park is available. The park has 71 pull-through spaces, restroom and shower facilities, recreation room, laundry facilities, a playground, country store, and a gas station. For information on the RV park, call (800) 478–4002.

Petrified Forest National Park
1 Park Rd., Petrified Forest, (Exit 140 at
Holbrook and take U.S. Hwy. 180 to the
park's south entrance)
(520) 524–6228
www.nps.gov/pefo

Fossils of ancient amphibians, reptiles, and early dinosaurs in layers of the Chinle Formation will thrill youngsters and adults alike when they visit the Petrified Forest. While the trees no longer stand in this forest, the petrified logs are beautiful, with incredibly bright colors you don't expect from a tree. In addition to seeing petrified trees and wonderful fossils, petroglyphs and ancient pueblos highlight this unusual national park. Self-guided auto tours, hiking trails, and wilderness backpacking permits are available at the visitor center. A museum, picnic area, gasoline, and a restaurant are all on the park grounds. You'll want to check out Blue Mesa, where erosion gradually exposes petrified logs; Jasper Forest, a large expanse of logs scattered over a wide valley; Crystal Forest, once cluttered with logs which contained clear quartz and purple amethyst crystals that were removed by treasure seekers years ago; and Rainbow Forest, which has the most densely scattered petrified wood. An old hut, Agate House, is nearby, which was constructed entirely of petrified wood by Native Americans back in the 16th century. The Petrified Forest is adjacent to the Painted Desert, a beautiful stretch of land that bursts with purple, red, and gray, creating a scene you'll never forget. The visitor center sits at the north end.

Wupatki National Monument
39 miles north of Flagstaff off
U.S. Hwy. 89
(520) 679-2365
www.nps.gov/wupa.

Wupatki National Monument is the site of many ruins scattered over a large area of desert northeast of Flagstaff. The pueblos all have a similar red color and were built from local Moenkopi sandstone. There are more than 800 identified ruins in Wupatki, but five of the largest ones are close to the main road and viewed by most tourists. The Anasazi and Sinagua Indians lived in the houses during the 12th and 13th centuries. The Wupatki Pueblo is the largest ruin and was once the home of some 300 people. The three-story house sits on the edge of a small plateau and enjoys views of the Painted Desert and the Little Colorado River. A short, paved self-guided trail leads to the house, and a leaflet is available which explains the various points of interest. The Lomaki Pueblo was built on the edge of a small canyon, and has a great view of the San Francisco Mountains. It is accessible by a short trail. Wupatki National Monument is a wonderful opportunity to view several ruins, and you are encouraged to visit it. The visitor center is open daily.

The Arboretum at Flagstaff
4001 S. Woody Mountain Rd., Flagstaff
(520) 774--442
www.thearb.org

Two hundred acres of ponderosa pine trees await visitors to the Arboretum, where you can also experience a wonderful variety of plants native to alpine tundra, coniferous forest, and high desert. Visitors may join a guided tour, borrow an explorer's backpack and take a hike on a nature trail, view threatened native fish, sample plants from one of the largest herb gardens in the Southwest, see how

The Clark Telescope, Lowell Observatory.
PHOTO: LOWELL OBSERVATORY

water is recycled in the Constructed Wetland, and take photographs of the beautiful flowers in the wildflower meadow. The Arboretum is a nature-lover's dream come true. Bring your lunch and sit at a picnic table, surrounded by nature's beauty, while you feed your body and your soul. The Arboretum offers programs for all ages and, in the summer, offers native plants for sale. The beauty of this attraction just can't be overstated. It's open from 9 A.M. to 5 P.M. April 1 through December 15. Call for information about tour schedules.

Lowell Observatory
1400 W. Mars Hill Rd., Flagstaff
(520) 774-3358
www.lowell.edu

The Lowell Observatory was the first astronomical observatory in Arizona. In 1894, Dr. Percival Lowell, a mathematician and amateur astronomer from Massachusetts, was searching for clear skies so he and his fellow astronomers could better see the planets and the stars. He found the perfect place in Flagstaff. Lowell believed there was life on Mars, and he spent much of his time observing the planet. His observations, however, quickly extended to other areas. In 1930, Clyde Tombaugh, an amateur astronomer from Kansas, completed a search begun by Lowell some 25 years earlier, and discovered a planet—later named Pluto—on February 18, 1930. It is the only planet to be discovered from the United States and North America. Today, the Lowell Observatory continues to pursue the study of astronomy and offers visitors the opportunity to explore the modern visitor center and participate in hands-on exhibits. Lowell's century-old Clark Telescope is housed in a historic wooden dome, where night-sky viewing is enjoyed most of the year. Hours are varied at the observatory, so call for information. There is a small admission fee.

Arts

With Northern Arizona University in Flagstaff, residents are blessed with great fine art, and they are enthusiastic about taking advantage of it. But it's not just those who live in Flagstaff who find and participate in the arts. Throughout northeastern Arizona, you'll find people enthralled at concerts, tapping their feet at musicals, and enjoying hours at museums. During your visit to northeastern Arizona and the Four Corners, you may want to take in some of the many art forms that the locals appreciate and support on a regular basis.

The places listed here are but a sampling of the great art available in Arizona. As you travel through northeastern Arizona, you'll discover other museums, events, and galleries you'll want to visit. If you happen to come across another event during your tour of the Four Corners, I encourage you to take advantage of it. With the tremendous history of the Four Corners, new facilities and art attractions are established regularly, which makes a visit to this beautiful part of the country an on-going adventure.

The Artists Gallery
17 N. San Francisco St., Flagstaff
(520) 773–0958

This contemporary fine art and craft cooperative tucked in historic downtown Flagstaff features the work of more than 40 local artists. The history of this area alone is worth a trip to this unique gallery.

Beasley Gallery
Northern Arizona University,
S. San Francisco St., Flagstaff
(520) 523–3471

The Performing and Fine Arts Building of the NAU campus houses the gallery, which highlights the works of NAU students. The gallery includes juried and fine arts exhibits.

Flagstaff Symphony Orchestra
113A E. Aspen Ave., Flagstaff
(520) 774–5107

The Flagstaff Symphony Orchestra has entertained residents of Flagstaff and the surrounding areas for more than 50 years. From September through April, the 75 members of the orchestra fill the Ardrey Auditorium with strains that lift the heart and the soul. Call for schedule information. Don't miss an opportunity to hear this great symphony orchestra.

The Museum Club
3404 E. U.S. Hwy. 66, Flagstaff
(520) 526–9434

The Museum Club plays host to rising country music stars as well as ghosts of days gone by. The Southwest's largest cabin was built in 1931 as a home for Native American artifacts and a collection of genetically unique animals carefully preserved. In later years, it became a nightclub called the Zoo, where musicians trav-

The Museum of Northern Arizona. PHOTO: GENE BALZER

eling across the country on Route 66 stopped to entertain. The Zoo continues to offer great music at the Museum Club and is proud to say it's "Biker Friendly." On Fridays and Saturdays, the Zoo offers an after-hours party, which showcases new country, alternative, and rap music. The Museum Club also offers the Friendly Cab, which provides a free ride home for any customer who needs one.

The Museum of Northern Arizona
3101 N. Fort Valley Rd., Flagstaff
(520) 779–1527

This museum finds people of all ages and interests meeting to celebrate the art and cultures of the Hopi, Navajo, Pai, Zuni, and prehistoric people. Visitors will enjoy exhibits on dinosaurs, geology, fossils, native plants, and animals. In addition, the museum offers Ventures Programs, which provide participants the opportunity to enjoy excursions, expeditions, and field seminars. In conjunction with Northern Arizona University Personal and Professional Development Programs, venture groups are small and allow maxi-mum interaction between participants and trip leaders. Program fees include round-trip transportation from Flagstaff, unless otherwise stated, food, community cooking gear, water, entrance fees, permits, cooks, and guides. Ventures are very popular and waiting lists are not uncommon. The museum also has Discovery Programs, in which participants discover the beauty of the arts, sciences, cultures, and history of the Colorado Plateau. Programs are provided for young learners, for learners of all ages, and for the more adventurous learner.

Old Main Art Gallery
Knoles Dr. and McMullen Circle, Flagstaff
(520) 523–3471

This unique gallery can be found in the Old Main Building on the north side of the NAU campus. It has exhibits of paintings, sculpture, ceramics, prints, and jewelry by local, regional, and national artists. Lectures by guest artists, demonstrations, and workshops are held often at the gallery.

Riordan Mansion State Historic Park
409 Riordan Rd., Flagstaff
(520) 779–4395

Riordan Mansion isn't what you usually think of as a state historic park. Built in 1904 as a duplex, the Riordan Mansion has 40 rooms, more than 13,000 square feet of living area, and servants' quarters. The mansion was actually two adjoining mansions and provides insights into the life of a wealthy frontier family in the early 1900s. Handcrafted furniture and period antiques decorate the mansion. During the holidays, the Riordan Mansion is decorated in turn-of-the-century style with wreaths, garlands, greenery, and a huge fir tree decorated with old-fashioned ornaments. Guided tours of the mansion provide a peek into the past and present Christmas traditions of this most beautiful home. Guided tours of the mansion are provided year-round and reservations are strongly recommended. For information on its Halloween tour see the October listing in the Annual Events chapter.

John Wesley Powell Memorial Museum
#6 N. Lake Powell Blvd., Page
(520) 645–9496

John Wesley Powell, an 1800s soldier, inspired this museum. He braved the uncharted waters of the Colorado River and confirmed his belief that a canyon—one he named the Glen Canyon—existed along that river. The museum, which is open from 9 A.M. to 5 P.M. Monday through Friday, offers sketches, photographs, and memorabilia of Powell's voyage along the Colorado River, as well as a wonderful collection of Native American and pioneer artifacts. Additional exhibits focus on the geology of the canyons cut by the Colorado and the history and development of Page. The museum's visitor center provides information on river and lake trips, scenic flights, ground tours, and powerboat and houseboat rentals. A nominal admission fee of $1 per person and $.50 for children in grades kindergarten through eighth (children younger than 6 are admitted free) is definitely worth the price to see the efforts of this courageous pioneer who played a big part in the history of the area.

Hopi Indian Reservation

History

In 1882, four years after the federal government began ceding land to the Navajo Nation, the government also recognized the Hopi Tribe's age-old land rights and began setting aside land for them. About 10,000 Hopi now live on a 1,542,306-acre reservation that is completely surrounded by the Navajo Nation. Government officials have re-drawn the reservation boundaries of the Navajo and Hopi many times, but never to the complete satisfaction of either tribe. In 1978, congressional and court decisions settled a major land dispute between the two tribes in favor of the Hopi, who regained part of the territory previously designated for joint use, but settled largely by Navajo. The Hopi rejoiced over this victory, which they felt was long overdue.

The Hopi Tribe's teachings relate stories of a great flood and other events dating to ancient times, which makes the Hopi one of the oldest living cultures in documented history. The Hopi exist in accord with nature, not against it, and adapt to the climate, plants, and animals of the land. They use "dry farming" instead of plowing their fields, using windbreakers at selected intervals of their fields to retain the moisture, snow, and soil. The Hopi raise corn, beans, squash, melons, and other crops that to others appear inadequate for farming. The dry, arid soil on the Hopi land doesn't look like it would allow anything to grow. The Hopi, by using the "dry farming" method, have adapted the soil to make it produce the crops they need in order to survive. Dry framing depends completely on natural precipitation—the winter snow and the monsoon rains that come in the summer. The perennial springs allow terrace irrigation, which helps keep moisture in the ground and the crops flourishing.

The Hopi Tribal Council makes laws for the tribe (between 10,000 and 12,000 members) and sets policy to oversee tribal business. There are about ten villages and every one has an autonomous government. The Hopi live in pueblos built at both the base and the top of three mesas, which dominate the landscape. First Mesa has three villages on top of the mesa—Tewa, Sichomovi, and Walpi—while a fourth one, Polacca, sits at its base. Walpi is considered to be the most spectacular of the Hopi villages, with old stone houses that appear to cling mightily to the cliffs and overlook a landscape that has changed little in many centuries. Second Mesa's top villages are Shungopavi, Sipaulovi, and Mishongnovi. It is from Shungopavi that most of the religious and ceremonial activities originate. Sipaulaovi is known as the last village established after the Pueblo Revolt in the 17th century, which kept the Hopi free from Spanish domain. The Third Mesa has the villages of Kykotsmovi, Old Oraibi (the oldest continuously inhabited village in North America), Bacavi, and Hotevilla. While much of Old Oraibi lies in ruins, the village remains an important part of modern Hopi life. In 1900, it ranked as one of the largest Hopi settlements with more than 800 residents, but because of disagreements within the village, many of its people left, and moved to surrounding villages.

The Hopi people are recognized as great artisans. First Mesa is known for pottery;

Second Mesa for coiled basketry; and Third Mesa for wicker basketry, weaving, kachina carving, and silversmithing.

As you visit with the Hopi people, you will find them to be deeply religious and to live in peace and good will. While they are talented artists, the Hopi are private people, but they welcome visitors to their land, and even into their homes. All villages, however, strictly prohibit photographing, sketching, and recording, which they consider very disturbing. Visit with the Hopi, learn from them, and purchase the many beautiful works of art they produce. But above all, respect their heritage, their traditions, and their customs. You will be richly rewarded when you do. Visitors to the villages in the past have not always been respectful of the Hopi ceremonies, their traditions, and their land. The Hopi people are proud of who they are and of their great heritage and have always considered it a privilege of a visitor to be part of their lives. When they believed that privilege was being abused, they decided to prohibit any unauthorized recording of any activity in their villages.

Traditions

Religion is a vital part of the Hopi culture. There is an elaborate, nearly year-round schedule of dances in the village plazas and kivas. Kivas are an underground chamber in the pueblos the Hopis use as a place to talk and hold religious ceremonies. These chambers have been used for approximately 1,000 years. Some dances, including those in the kivas, are closed to outsiders, but others may be open to the public. Nearly all Hopi dances are offered as prayers for rain and fertile crops. The elaborate masks, ankle bells, drums, and chanting all invite the attention of the kachinas, supernatural spirits, who bring rain. As you watch these dances, you may see young boys who are learning the ritual. If you are fortunate to see these dances, you are encouraged to remember these are religious services, and you should treat them as such. Don't ask questions, be quiet, and keep out of the way of the performers. Hopi dances most often are held on the weekends. If you'd like to watch one, call the Hopi Cultural Center at (520) 734-2401 for information.

The Hopi base their existence on faith and believe this is the fourth creation of life. The three preceding lives ended in destruction. Conflict, which is not part of the Hopi way, caused the destruction when humanity forgot or denied the plan of the Creator. The faithful have always been protected in order to reach the next world. The Second World's faithful were protected underground with the ant people and the kivas of today represent those anthills.

There are four worlds in the creation story of the Hopi, each associated with a definite direction, color, mineral, bird, and plant. The First World, Endless Space, was a pure and happy universe that contained the First People, but it was destroyed by fire. Dark Midnight was the Second World and was destroyed by ice and cold. The Chosen People survived by hiding in an anthill, then climbing a ladder into the Third World. Floods destroyed the Third World, but Spider Woman saved these ancestors by hiding them in reeds and floating them to dry land in the Fourth World. The Fourth World, the World Complete, has Masau'u, the Fire God, as a caretaker. Unlike the first three worlds which were blocked by ice and water and the Hopi were well cared for, the Fourth World is harsh, with marshes, violent weather, mountains, and deserts. Some Hopi now believe they are about to enter the Fifth World.

Peace is a priority of the Hopi way. The daily life of the Hopi people is centered around their belief of helping others improve their lives. There are 12 clan groups and each has its own ceremonies and sacred fetishes. Men are the religious leaders, but children inherit the clan of their mother. While the men own the livestock and the fruit trees, it is the women who own the land—even the land under those fruit trees. Kivas, used mostly by the men, are the center of the Hopi religious life. Stone walls line the underground chambers of the kiva, and a hole (sipapu) in the floor symbolizes the exit from the ant people's domain.

The Hopi put great importance on religion because it is the connection of a solid community, and a child's instruction in the Hopi religion begins early. Most religious ceremonies relate to rain (Katsinas) or kachinas. There are about 350 kachinas, the gathering spirits that come down from their world at the winter solstice and remain with the Hopi until the summer solstice.

Visitors will notice that the Hopi wear bangs. They use their bangs to recognize the True White Brother and as a sign for him to recognize them.

When you visit the Hopi Reservation, you will see many wonderful ceremonies. Please be respectful of the ceremonies and of the Hopi people. Their spirituality is deeply ingrained into their daily life and things that might seem ordinary to a visitor may have deep significance to the Hopi. Don't touch objects or things unless you're invited to, don't intrude into ceremonies that are not open to the public, and remember, you are a guest of the Hopi people. They will invite you to return if you are a good guest.

Hotels and Motels

You won't have trouble deciding where to stay when you visit the Hopi Reservation— there is but one motel. It is a pleasant place to stay while you're here, but because it's the only one and is very busy, it is wise to make reservations at last three weeks in advance of your arrival.

You may decide to stay in one of the surrounding cities of Tuba City, Winslow, or Flagstaff, which are about 50 to 100 miles away. Check the Arizona portion of this guide for information about Arizona lodging.

The Hopi Cultural Center Motel

**Located on top of the Second Mesa, Second Mesa, AZ
(520) 734–2401**

The Hopi Cultural Center Motel has 33 rooms, a restaurant, museum, and a camping area. Summer rates (March 15 through October 15) are $90 for one person and $5 for each additional person. Children 12 years and younger stay free if they're accompanied by their parents. The rooms are pleasant and the motel will be a great place from which to base your tour of the Hopi Reservation.

Campgrounds

The campground at the Hopi Cultural Center is also the only one in the area. Campsites are free, but are primitive with no hookups available. There are rest areas for day-time use along Arizona Highway 264, but overnight camping is discouraged.

Restaurants

There are several restaurants on the Hopi Reservation, most of them moderately priced. You'll find basic menus in all of the restaurants since the Hopi people enjoy American and Mexican dishes, as well as fast food. The Hopi Cultural Center Restaurant has several Indian specialties, which are very good. While you enjoy those dishes however, the Hopi family sitting at the next table will likely be enjoying hamburgers and French fries! Several families in each of the villages on the reservation serve traditional food from their homes, so watch for their signs if you're interested in real Hopi home cooking. Alcohol is not sold or permitted on the reservation, so be sure to leave those spirits at home.

Trading Posts

While you will find few, if any, trading posts on the Hopi Reservation, you will find countless villagers who sell beautiful works of art from their homes. Often, families will post signs indicating they sell pottery, kachina dolls, or other creative art, and those are open invitations for visitors to stop, browse, and buy.

If you're invited into the home of a Hopi, remember you are a guest and should respect their traditions and beliefs. That means taking no photographs, videos, or recordings of anything without prior consent. You are asked not to take notes or sketch while in their homes.

You will find wicker and twill basketry on Third Mesa; silver overlay jewelry and coiled basketry on Second Mesa, and polychrome pottery on First Mesa. The Hopi take great pride in their craftsmanship and it is the lucky visitor who buys directly from the artist. By being in their homes, surrounded by the things they love, you can truly appreciate the effort and care that goes into the art the Hopi create. The items you buy will likely have special meaning for you, since you have met the artist, shared their friendship, and purchased one of their treasures!

Arts

The ceremonies and native dances of the Hopi people are an art form not often seen off the reservation. With colorful costumes and mystical music, you will be mesmerized by the beauty of these events. Some ceremonies have been placed off limits because of previous visitors' lack of respect. Insiders request that you remember these are important religious rituals and you are a guest of the Hopi people. Before you attend a ceremony or dance, check to make sure visitors are welcome. Dances take place in plazas on most weekends. For information, call the Hopi Tribe's Cultural Preservation Office at (520) 734–2244.

Hopi Cultural Center
Located on the west side of Second Mesa
Second Mesa, AZ
(520) 734–2401

It proclaims itself as being "At the Center of the Universe," and it may just be correct. Both the Hopi people and visitors enjoy this pueblo-style museum/motel/restaurant/gift shop. The museum displays exhibits of Hopi culture and crafts, complete with historic photographs. It's open all year long, with extended hours from late March through late October. There is a small admission fee. You will enjoy your tour of the museum and will be glad you took the time to visit.

Hopi Arts and Crafts, just a short walk across the camping area at the Cultural Center, has a nice selection of traditional art. Hopi silversmiths are often at work here, giving you the opportunity to ask questions, admire their crafts and purchase some as souvenirs.

Hopi Market
AZ Hwy. 264, M.P. 386
Second Mesa, AZ
(520) 737–9434

Hopi Market is located on the Hopi Reservation and has contracts with many of the local artists to display and sell their art. The works of art available here are wonderful, with many of them likely not to be found elsewhere. From the unique crafts to ceremonial textiles, you will enjoy all that's offered at this great market. Unique crafts include rattles, flat doll holders, and leather pouches. Piki Bread, made from fine corn pudding baked over a hot stone, is also offered here. Piki Bread is considered low-calorie and is a taste you've never experienced. Ceremonial textile weavers, slowly decreasing on the Hopi Reservation, are primarily men. Most of them have learned their skills through trial and error, and this art is one of the least known skills taught to others. There are more than 15 ceremonial textiles woven, with many of them imitated by non-Hopis. An imitation is recognizable because it is easily spotted when worn. While the majority of material used in ceremonial textiles today is store bought, in the older days, strings made for weaving were strung from cotton that was grown locally. Examples of this great art are ready for your viewing and purchasing at Hopi Market, and it's almost assured you'll have a hard time selecting just one because of the incredible beauty and art work offered. Coil plaques and baskets are made on Second Mesa villages, where women have been making them and teaching the art to their daughters. The designs are primarily of kachinas, animals, corn, rain clouds, flowers, and other designs that are important to the Hopi. These plaques and baskets, too, will astound the visitor with their intricate beauty. A visit to the Hopi Market should be on your list of "must-dos" while you're on the Hopi Reservation.

McGee's Indian Art Gallery
AZ Hwy. 264, Keams Canyon, AZ
(520) 738–2295

McGee's Indian Art Gallery, originally a trading post, is located in Keams Canyon, within the Hopi Reservation. The Santa Fe Railroad reached Holbrook, Arizona, in 1881, which slightly improved the transportation of supplies to Keams Canyon, approximately 60 miles north from Holbrook. Roads were not paved in the area until the 1940s. In 1906, the trading post was sold to Lorenzo Hubbell. Several owners followed until it was purchased by the McGee family in 1937. Because of its location on the Hopi Reservation, McGee's Indian Art Gallery is noted for buying Hopi crafts and merchandising them to collectors throughout the world. The artwork offered at McGee's is magnificent and a stop here is well worth your time.

Healthcare

Because the Hopi Reservation is inside the Navajo Reservation, healthcare for them comes largely from the Navajo Area Indian Health Services Office, which is headquartered in Window Rock, Arizona. IHS oversees numerous health clinics, centers, and hospitals, and extends its services to include the Navajo, Hopi, and Zuni people. The Indian Health Service is an agency within the United States Department of Health and Human Services. The provision of health services to members of federally recognized tribes grew out of the special government to government relationship between the federal government and Native American tribes. The IHS is the principal healthcare provider and health advocate for Native Americans, and its goal is to assure that comprehensive, culturally acceptable personal and public health services to the approximately 1.5 million Native Americans and Alaskan native people.

There are six hospitals, seven health centers, and 12 health stations available by the IHS to the Hopi people for healthcare. Health centers operate full-time clinics and some provide emergency services. Some smaller communities have health stations that are open only on a part-time basis.

In addition to the IHS facilities, the Tuba City Indian Medical Center is a 65-bed regional hospital with an adjacent outpatient clinic that also serves the needs of the Hopi. The Hopi Health Care Center is a new facility located in Phoenix, and represents a major partnership effort between the Hopi Tribe and the Indian Health Service. The Hopi Tribe is the first in the IHS Phoenix area to build a facility under the Indian Self-Determination and Education Assistance Act. The new facility has a health care program for a projected 70,000 outpatient visits annually. There is also an infirmary with six inpatient beds, a 24-hour emergency room, and a birthing center.

While modern healthcare facilities may be available to the Hopi, many of them are reluctant to take advantage of them. Medicine men continue to play an important role in Hopi healthcare, and healthcare professionals face a constant challenge of trying to provide modern medicine to a people who still believe in the healing powers of the medicine man. It is only by understanding the Hopi people and gently and carefully guiding them into modern treatment that today's healthcare professional can have an impact on the healthcare needs of the Hopi.

Education

Prior to 1980, all schools on the Hopi Reservation were Bureau of Indian Affairs day schools. Hopi communities were involved in the schools only through an advisory board and only allowed to give advice, but not be involved in the decision making process. In 1981, Congress passed the Indian self-determination law, which allowed the Native American communities to take an active role in the operation of their local schools.

Today the education of Hopi children is supported by everyone. Parents encourage their children to complete high school and to go on to college. But while education has been accepted, it has unfortunately removed many Hopi young people away from their traditional ways.

Before the construction of schools on the reservation, many Native American children attended schools off the reservation. Many of the schools were boarding schools, and the students were often forbidden to speak their native language. Since the language has no written form and was traditionally taught by the grandmother, it was difficult to include it as part of a school's curriculum.

With the completion of schools on the Hopi Reservation, children may now attend classes while remaining at home. While they're learning traditional school courses, they still have the advantage of being tutored at home by parents and grandparents who teach the traditions and language of their people.

Today, there are six elementary schools, one high school, and one elementary boarding school on the Hopi Reservation. In each of the schools, a school board has been elected, which mandates policy and acts like any other school board across the country. Students are able to attend school and continue to participate in traditional ceremonies and carry on tribal responsibilities, a blessing to the entire Hopi tribe.

Hopi Junior/Senior High School is located behind the police station on U.S. Highway 264 and serves about 600 students in grades 7–12. The school is part of Northern Arizona Universities Distance Learning Program, which provides the school with a link to the internet. Each classroom at Hopi High has at least one computer with internet connectivity and the computer is used for reporting daily attendance, scheduling of students, progress reports to parents, athletic eligibility, and other management of the school.

Northern Arizona University also has a program in conjunction with the Hopi Tribe to encourage Hopi students at NAU to become teachers and to return to the Hopi Reservation to teach. It is hoped that by having Hopi people teach Hopi students, the wonderful traditions and heritage of the Hopi people will be carried on to future generations.

Many Hopi young people who go off the reservation to attend colleges and universities elsewhere cannot find jobs on the reservation when they've completed their education and are forced to go elsewhere to work and live. That, too, is a concern to the Hopi people, who are proud of the advanced degrees many of their young people have earned, but are saddened that the Hopi people do not benefit from it because jobs are simply not available. In addition, the growing number of young people who leave the reservation, never to return, is a loss of family the Hopi people struggle to cope with.

Navajo Indian Reservation

History

They are a proud people. The Dineh, or "The People" as they call themselves, came to the Southwest from the north around the 15th century. Many believe that the Navajo originally were of only four clans—today there are more than 60.

The early days of the Navajo in American history were difficult. When settlers began moving into northern Arizona where the Navajos were calling home, unrest between the two segments began almost immediately. Raids between the Navajo and the settlers were frequent when the U.S. government stepped in, hoping to end the death and destruction the two factions were creating. Negotiations for a peace treaty were attempted, but were never signed. In 1851, about 30 miles southeast of Canyon de Chelly, Fort Defiance was built. Land that had been used by the Navajo for grazing their sheep was taken over by the soldiers for their horses. The Navajo were outraged and made repeated attacks on the fort. In 1860, about 1,000 Navajo warriors again attacked Fort Defiance, and it was finally abandoned. The Navajos may have won that battle, but they did not win the war. A revenge campaign against them began, and Navajo crops were burned and destroyed, livestock was killed or taken, and the Navajo faced yet another battle—the battle of survival.

A peace agreement was eventually signed in 1861, which included a promise from the U.S. government of rations for the Navajo. The supplies were distributed later that year, and a celebration was held, which included horse racing and betting. In the last race, an army rider who had been accused of cheating was declared the winner, and a fight broke out. The troops retreated to the fort, where a commander ordered them to open fire. More than 30 Navajo were killed, many of them women and children. The celebration was over, and a new era of discontent began.

In 1863, Kit Carson and his troops stormed the land of Canyon de Chelly and rounded up the Navajo people. After burning their homes, their crops and their livestock, the troops forced the Navajo to march to Fort Sumner. The grueling 300-mile march, called "the Long Walk" by the Navajo, was difficult and tormenting for these Native Americans. About eight thousand men, women, and children began the walk, and about 200 of them died along the way due to starvation and cruel treatment. Once they arrived at Fort Sumner, the Navajo men were forced to work, but were given no wood for fires. The land wasn't fertile and corn couldn't be raised for food. Without the warmth of a fire during the cold, wet winter months, and without adequate food to sustain them, many of the Navajo people died.

Finally, in 1868, a treaty was signed, which returned 3.5-million acres of land to the Navajos, which included their old home country. A strong, quiet people, the Navajo once again began the process of rebuilding—their homes, their land, and their culture. Today, centuries after the Long Walk, the Navajos still remember the injustices and the devastation it created, but have joined hands with their white neighbors to work together to create an environment that respects the cultures, the traditions, and the visions of each other.

Traditions

The Navajo people cling to their traditions, even as many of them participate in the world outside the reservation. Traditional clothing is worn by many of them regularly, in addition to the usual blue jeans and Western shirts favored by residents of the Four Corners. It is, however, mostly the older Navajo women who still wear the traditional pleated velvet or cotton skirt, matching long-sleeved blouse, knee-high moccasins, and elaborate jewelry. Men of all ages wear the traditional velveteen shirt and Native American jewelry. The Navajo people believe before an individual receives help from the Great Spirit, he must wear appropriate clothing to be recognized. While many of the older women on the reservation continue to care for the home, weave rugs, and attend to the sheep, the younger generation of women seeks careers, usually off the reservation. But the belief that the family is the strength of the Navajo people is shared by almost every Navajo, and family ties remain strong, no matter how far family members may live from each other.

Hotels and Motels

Price Code

The price code is based on the cost of a standard room for two adults for one night.

$ . . . .$50-$70
$$ . . . .$71-$100
$$$ . . . . . . .more than $100

There are many nice places to stay on the Navajo Reservation. As you travel throughout the reservation, you'll find smaller hotels and motels that will provide you with pleasant accommodations and great service. The ones I highlight in this section are suggestions for you as you tour the Navajo Reservation and meet the wonderful people who live there. All hotels and motels accept major credit cards unless otherwise noted and all establishments are wheelchair accessible unless otherwise stated.

Your tour of the Four Corners and the Navajo Reservation will take you to places you will never forget and you will meet and visit with people you will always remember. Wherever you go, you'll find nice accommodations and friendly people who will do whatever they can to make your stay pleasant.

Goulding's Lodge **$$**
P.O. Box 1, Monument Valley, AZ
(435) 727-3231
gouldings@gouldings.com

Located in beautiful Monument Valley, Goulding's Lodge is a lovely hotel that offers 62 rooms with great views of the valley. Each room has a private balcony, and John Wayne and other Western movies are available to use in the VCR. A coffeemaker is included in each room, for those who

need a caffeine jolt to wake up, and a nice heated indoor pool will help you relax after a busy day sightseeing. This is a popular place to stay and the hosts make every effort to make your stay pleasant.

Best Western Canyon de Chelly Inn **$$$**
P.O. Box 295, Chinle, AZ
(800) 327-0354
www.canyondechelly.com

This Best Western Inn is located in the

heart of Canyon de Chelly and is the perfect place to base your tour of the Navajo Reservation. Rooms are pleasant and offer the usual amenities. A full-service restaurant, gift shop, and an indoor pool are available. This is another nice place to stay and you'll be treated well.

Cameron Trading Post Hotel   **$$**
P.O. Box 339, Cameron, AZ
(800) 338–7385
www.camerontradingpost.com

The rooms at the Cameron Trading Post Hotel have views towards the Little Colorado River, beautiful gardens, and incredible sunsets. If you're looking for more than just another hotel room, you'll find it here. Colorful flowers will lure you outside to walk along the path they border and you'll be tempted to stop, smell the flowers, and breathe in the view—do it. The rooms are most pleasant and the hotel offers suites that will make you want to stay even longer. Luxury suites start at $149 and include a queen size bed, hideaway bed, and a separate living area.

Thunderbird Lodge   **$$**
P.O. Box 548, Chinle, AZ
(800) 679–2473

Another quality hotel in Canyon de Chelly, the Thunderbird Lodge offers 72 rooms that are decorated with Navajo art and rustic furniture. The lodge itself looks like an ancient pueblo and is as pretty as it is pleasant. Cottonwood trees planted by the Civilian Conservation Corps back in the 1930s offer shade to the tired traveler. This is a great place to stay in a great place to visit.

Campgrounds

Campgrounds on the Navajo Reservation are few, and your best camping bets are in national parks or monuments. I've spotlighted campgrounds in this section because of their close proximity to some attractions or because they are unique in some way. I encourage you to look for new campgrounds that spring up on the reservation regularly and try them, if they fit your camping needs.

Mitten View Campground
Monument Valley
(435) 727–3353 or (435) 727–3287

Mitten View Campground is located near the visitor center at Monument Valley and provides 99 sites. Campsites include a table, grill, and trash barrel; and during the summer, restrooms, coin-operated showers, and a dump station. The campground is open year-round on a first-come, first-serve basis. Reservations are accepted for group sites. This is a pretty campground and is perfect for your visit to Monument Valley.

Goulding's Monument Valley
Campground
1 mile west of Goulding's Lodge
at U.S. Hwy. 163
(800) 727–3235 or (800) 874–0902

This campground is in a beautiful canyon setting and the location alone is worth establishing camp. The campground has tent and RV hookups and guests may enjoy an indoor pool, laundry facilities, showers, and a convenience store/gift shop. The campground is open from the middle of March through the middle of October.

Insiders' Tip

The Navajo Nation hosts more Native American rodeos than any other tribe in the United States and Canada combined. Even during the winter months, Navajos continue jackpot team roping and bull riding competitions.

Restaurants

Insiders' Tip

Mutton stew is a popular dish on the Navajo Reservation. Made with lamb, the stew is served often, and is usually accompanied by fry bread.

The Navajo people are especially fond of fast food, so those franchises abound on the reservation. Other family owned restaurants open and close on a regular basis, so you may want to enjoy dinner at the hotel or motel you're staying at, or in the larger cities that surround the Navajo Reservation. You'll also find plenty of roadside food vendors who sell mutton stew, fry bread, and Navajo tacos. Try these if you like, but be aware these vendors are likely not certified by the state and may not abide by the strict cleanliness rules state guidelines require restaurants.

Trading Posts

The trading posts on the Navajo Reservation are reason enough to visit the Four Corners. Each of them is unique and offers its own showcase of great Navajo art. The owners of trading posts are often more than just business people to the Navajo people—they become trusted friends. The Navajos trust the trading post owners to give them a fair market price for their art, and the owners are committed to provide that, as well as share the wonderful art with visitors from throughout the world.

Hubbell Trading Post
P.O. Box 150, Ganado, AZ
(888) 325–7847

The oldest continuously operated trading post in the United States, the Hubbell Trading Post has become as much a part of the Navajo Reservation as the art it sells. John Lorenzo Hubbell established the trading post in 1876 and it still sells groceries and dry goods today. It also offers a bookstore, exhibits, and rug-weaving demonstrations. A National Historic Site, Hubbell Trading Post also offers a self-guided tour of the grounds and a ranger-guided tour of the original Hubbell home. This beautiful trading post should be a "must see" for every visitor to the Navajo Reservation.

Two Grey Hills Trading Post
Tohatchi, NM
(505) 789–3270

The Two Grey Hills Trading Post is out of the way and off the beaten path, but one worth taking the time and trouble to visit. From Shiprock, travel 29.7 miles south on U.S. Highway 666 to milepost 59.3, and turn right toward Toadlena on Navajo Highway 19, which is a blacktop road. After seven miles, you'll pass a housing project on the right, and you'll turn left through a cattle guard onto new blacktop. Go three more miles, pass the chapter house and buildings on the right, and you'll see the rear of the trading post on top of the hill. Continue across the wash, through another cattle guard, then take a left turn onto the old road to Newcomb and another left turn into the parking lot. There are signs, and locals along the road will provide directions should you get lost or disoriented. Two Grey Hills is more than a century old and one of the few historic posts on the Navajo Reservation. The store is constructed of stone and adobe and is the original structure, although it has been updated slightly throughout the years. You won't find checkouts that scan here or the bright lights usually associated with today's modern stores. What you will find, however, are helpful people and caring owners who strive to give the Navajos not only a place to showcase their beautiful rugs and other works of art, but to make sure they receive a fair price for their handiwork.

Two Grey Hills Trading Post. PHOTO: DOROTHY NOBIS

Two Grey Hills doesn't cater to the tourist but instead to the people it serves. Each artist is known by name and many of them come from families who have done business with the store for generations. This is a wonderful peek into the past. The beautiful art and rugs provide pleasure for those who buy them as well as the Navajo people who create them. Two Grey Hills rugs have become treasured pieces of art through the years. The designs, usually created in shades of brown, and black and white, are some of the best of the Navajo people. See the Close-up of Two Grey Hills Trading Post in the New Mexico chapter for more information.

Cameron Trading Post Gallery
P.O. Box 339, Cameron, AZ
(800) 338–7385

Located 54 miles north of Flagstaff, Cameron Trading Post was established in 1916 and is one of the last authentic trading posts. It manages to blend modern commerce with the traditional Native American trading customs and is popular with Navajo artists and tourists alike. The trading post houses a large collection of Native American arts and crafts, but continues to provide sacks of flour and sugar, skeins of native wool, and cooking utensils to its Native American customers. Cameron Trading Post offers baskets, beadwork, and pottery carefully created by Native Americans. This is a wonderful place to spend time (count on at least an hour) and purchase great works of art.

Oljato Trading Post
P.O. Box 360416, Monument Valley, UT
(435) 727–3210

The stone building that houses the Oljato Trading Post has done so since 1921 and has changed little over the years. Pots and pans, corn grinders, ash shovels, canned goods, household items, and more are offered in the store, which is frequented by the Native Americans who live nearby. In an adjacent room, a wonderful collection of Navajo artifacts and crafts are on display, as well as books on Navajo culture and history. Stepping into Oljato Trading Post is like stepping back in time, and you'll enjoy your visit as well as the opportunity to see things as they used to be.

Arts

There are many wonderful attractions and fine arts available on the Navajo Reservation. As with much of the Four Corners, if we were to highlight each of them, you would not be able to carry this travel guide with you. We have selected several to share with you, with the hope that as you travel throughout the Navajo Reservation, you'll take the time to visit museums, galleries, and attractions we have not included here, but which deserve your time and attention. Enjoy each of them, for they portray not just the artistic talents of the Navajo people, but their hearts and souls as well.

Window Rock Tribal Park and Veteran's Memorial
P.O. Box 430, Window Rock, AZ
(520) 871–6413

A graceful red stone arch is a highlight of this small park and it is beautiful indeed. The Navajo Nation headquarters and other government offices were built close to this park because of the rock formation. The Veteran's Memorial stands in tribute to the many Navajos who served in the U.S. military. Many of them have been recognized for their contribution as Code Talkers in World War II. As Code Talkers, they used their native language to create a code that was never broken by the enemy. Historians today credit the Code Talkers for helping win the war. In addition to the great arch and the memorial, the park also has other symbolic structures, including a circular path that outlines the four cardinal directions; 16 angled steel pillars with the names of war veterans; and a healing sanctuary that is used for reflection and solitude. This is a lovely park that shouldn't be missed during your tour of the Navajo Reservation.

Navajo Museum Library and Visitor Center
P.O. Box 9000, Window Rock, AZ
(520) 871–6675

This modern museum is dedicated to the preservation and interpretation of the history of the Navajo Nation. Native displays, a book and gift shop, snack bar, auditorium, outdoor amphitheater, information kiosk, library, and authentic Navajo hogan are highlights of the museum. You'll find wonderful Native American music to purchase in the gift shop. The music is beautiful and you may listen before you select your purchases.

Michaels Historical Museum
P.O. Box 680, St. Michaels, AZ
(520) 871–4171

A simple subdivided stone building, this museum offers a unique insight into the Navajo culture of the early 20th century. St. Michaels Mission of Franciscan Friars enjoyed a great influence on the Navajos with their religions and educational teachings. The Mission remains an important role in the life of the Navajo. Be sure to see *Big Eyes*, a book of photos taken between 1902 and 1908 by Simeon Schwemberger, a friar. The negatives are glass-plate and are incredible.

Dine College Hatathli Center
Tsaile, AZ
(520) 724–6887

The Ned Hatathli Museum and Gallery is housed in Dine College, a six-story hogan-shaped center. Exhibits of Native American culture and sales of authentic Navajo arts and crafts, silverwork, rugs, wool, baskets, and pottery are available. A permanent collection of textiles, baskets, pottery, jewelry, beaded items, leather goods, glassware, paintings, photographs, and printed material are on display. The museum also has several beautiful colored murals, which depict Navajo life. This is a wonderful museum and worth a visit.

Navajo Nation Museum, Library and Visitor Center
Intersection of U.S. Hwy 264 and Post Office Loop Rd., Window Rock, AZ
(520) 871–7941
The Navajo Nation created an educational resource with its museum, library, and visitor center, and it is justifiably proud of the facility. The educational exhibits and programs are meant to bridge the past, present, and future of the Navajo, and the wonderful Navajo collections include the Jack Snow Collection, historic photographs dating from 1930 to 1970. The Navajo Nation Library and Research Collection are also here, and you'll find them all to be most interesting and informative.

As you travel throughout the Navajo Reservation, you may come upon powwows, traditional dancing, and Native American artists at work. Take advantage of as many of these events as you can, for they will provide an insight into the Navajo people you won't find elsewhere. Be sure to ask for permission before taking part or witnessing any event, however, for many of them are sacred.

Healthcare

The Indian Health Service (IHS) is an agency within the U.S. Department of Health and Human Services responsible for providing federal health services to Native Americans and Alaska natives. The government and the Native American tribes recognized the need of such services. The IHS is the principal healthcare provider and health advocate for the Native American and strives to offer comprehensive, culturally acceptable personal and public healthcare.

The Navajo Area IHS office is located in Window Rock, Arizona, and provides healthcare to more than 200,000 members of the Navajo Nation. Care is provided through inpatient, outpatient, contract, and community health programs that are centered around six hospitals, seven health centers, and 12 health stations. School clinics and Navajo tribal health programs also provide healthcare to the Navajos. The six hospitals range in size from the 39 beds in Crownpoint to 112 at the Gallup Indian Medical Center in Gallup. The tribe provides a major portion of the healthcare of the Navajos.

Providing healthcare to the Navajo isn't always easy, however. Cross cultural medicine can be challenging to healthcare professionals, who must treat their Native American patients with care, understanding, and respect of the Navajo traditions and cultures. Navajo concepts of being, health, disease, and the environment are deeply intertwined with the Navajo religion. Healthcare professionals must respect the traditional Navajo healers and work with them to care for the patient. Therapy needed by the patient may be delayed so a traditional healer can be consulted and family decisions regarding healthcare are common. Surgery, in particular, is considered by

Insiders' Tip
The Navajo people use humor to ease difficult and frustrating circumstances and they place a high regard for laughter. The strong emphasis and value the Navajos place on humor is evidenced in the First Laugh Rite, which is celebrated when a Navajo child laughs out loud for the first time.

Insiders' Tip

The Navajo Nation Fair, held in early September each year, attracts visitors from around the world and is touted as the "World's Largest American Indian Fair." The fair is held in Window Rock, Arizona, capital of the Navajo Nation, and is a five-day event.

the family, who may not understand the need for immediate treatment, but must gather and weigh their options with the patient.

Navajos are becoming increasingly aware of the need for professional healthcare outside the reservation. An inner struggle can occur, however, when the suggested healthcare is not in harmony with that of the traditional Navajo healers. By respecting their beliefs, taking time to get to know their Navajo patients, and by establishing a mutual confidence between healthcare provider and patient, today's healthcare professionals can help the Navajo live longer, fuller lives.

Education

Most Navajo children today attend school with their Anglo friends and neighbors. In years past, many children on the reservation were forced to attend a boarding school off the reservation for their education. Increased awareness of the need for schools on the reservation has made it possible for children to attend school, while remaining at home, where they receive instruction on their native traditions, cultures, and teachings. Bus rides for Navajo students may be long, however, as many of them live in remote areas of the reservation, alongside roads that are sometimes difficult to travel. The Navajos are willing to allow their children to make the trip to school, knowing that education is critical to the Navajo Nation and to its preservation and success.

Some students, however, wish to attend Navajo Prepatory School in Farmington, New Mexico. Attendance at the school is limited, and students are screened carefully before being admitted. A minimum of a 2.5 grade point average from the student's previous school is required, as is a strong performance on the school's admission test. Three teacher recommendations must accompany the application and a member of the school staff interviews prospective students before final admission decisions are made. The mission of Navajo Preparatory School is to educate talented and motivated college-bound Navajo youths and encourage them to continue their education and become leaders in their communities. The school offers an academic program that's based on a strong foundation of Navajo philosophy, which is supported by a residential environment that encourages individuality and independence. The school also promotes the preservation of the Navajo language, traditions, cultures, values, and heritage.

Dine College was established in 1968 as the first tribally controlled college in the United States. Under the direction of an eight-member Board of Regents, Dine College strives to serve the residents of the Navajo Nation. College facilities include community campuses in Chinle, Window Rock, Ganado, Kayenta, and Tuba City, Arizona; and in Crownpoint, New Mexico. The college is fully accredited by the North Central Association of Colleges and Schools. Students may earn an associate of arts degree, an associate of science degree, an associate of applied science degree, and a baccalaureate degree in Dine Teacher Education Program. Baccalaureate graduates are encouraged to return to the reservation to teach. The college has 59 full-time faculty members, with 10 percent of them having doctorate degrees and 70 percent with masters. The faculty to student ratio at the college is about 16 students to each faculty member. Dine College, too, strives to promote and preserve the Navajo language and culture, while preparing students for careers that will bring them back to the reservation to work.

Relocation

The wide open spaces, the casual and informal way of life, and the warm, friendly people of the Four Corners have caused many visitors to become residents of this wonderful part of the United States. The percentage of "natives" to the area dwindles each year, as transplants embrace this part of the country and choose to call it home. These new residents are welcomed and quickly become neighbors and friends. In the following sections, you'll discover some of the reasons people are moving to the Four Corners. If you need more information than is provided in these pages, please contact the following chambers of commerce, who will be delighted to make sure you have the resources you need to make your move.

Farmington (NM) Chamber of Commerce
(800) 325–0279
www.chamber.farmington.nm.us

Durango (CO) Area Chamber Resort Association
(800) 525–8855
www.durango.org

Moab (UT) Economic Development Office
(800) 625–6622
www.discovermoab.com

Flagstaff (AZ) Chamber of Commerce
(520) 779–1209
www.flagstaffarizona.org

New Mexico

Real Estate

In spite of the acres and acres of undeveloped land in northwestern New Mexico, not a great deal of it is available for sale. The Bureau of Land Management and the Navajo Nation own most of the undeveloped land, and it takes time, dedication, and a concerted effort to encourage them to sell. The upside to that, however, is that many homes are on land adjacent to those areas, making them prime property. Having a beautiful, undeveloped area next door is a piece of heaven most people dream of, and it can be found in northwestern New Mexico. You'll find real estate of every description here, from beautiful, spacious homes in town to manufactured homes on acres within the county. You're encouraged to meet with a real estate professional, who will guide you to the real estate you're looking for when you relocate in this part of the Four Corners.

Education

New Mexico's state government has always placed a priority on education and spends its tax dollars accordingly. San Juan College is a community college that is one of the best in the state. San Juan County is very proud of this institution of higher learning, which boasts one of the lowest tuition rates in the country. Home schooling has gained increasing popularity in northwestern New Mexico, and there is a large support group of home schoolers who work together to exchange ideas and provide a social and educational atmosphere for their children.

Healthcare

This part of the Four Corners is equally proud of the quality of healthcare it provides. San Juan Regional Medical Center is the primary healthcare provider, and offers one of the top-rated cancer centers in the country. The hospital's emergency room, childbirth center, and intensive care units have all been recently remodeled and equipped with state-of-the-art equipment. The Air Care program of the facility transports patients from remote areas to healthcare facilities throughout the Four Corners when accidents occur, and flies patients to other facilities when the need arises. San Juan Regional makes every effort to recruit quality physicians and medical technicians to the area. If you decide to make northwestern New Mexico your home, you'll find healthcare professionals dedicated to serving the community.

Spiritual Guidance

Northwestern New Mexico enjoys a varied community of spiritual guidance. There is no dominant religious group here, and all of the churches work together for the good of the area. There is a small, but active, Jewish community that includes southwestern Colorado, and the Religious Society of Friends Quakers also has a presence in this part of the Four Corners.

No matter what your religious affiliation is, you'll find warm, wonderful people in all of the churches to welcome you and make you feel at home.

Retirement

Northwestern New Mexico is attempting to attract retirees to this beautiful area to join those who have already discovered that this is a great place to enjoy life. Senior centers are busy places, with seniors gathering to play cards, do physical exercises, shoot a little pool, sing a few songs, take arts and crafts classes, or simply to savor a good cup of coffee and friendship.

The seniors who live here are a happy and energetic lot and are almost always looking for new ways to contribute to the community. Many of them volunteer at San Juan Regional Medical Center, as tutors in the public school system, at area libraries and museums, for Meals on Wheels, the Red Cross, and in their churches. Those looking for volunteer opportunities won't have to look long when they come to northwestern New Mexico.

There are about 50 senior citizens who participate in the Hillbilly Band, a lively group of musicians who play most unusual "instruments." A washboard, spoons, tambourines, and several saws are included with the piano and banjos members play. A senior must be at least 55 years old before they may participate in the Hillbilly Band, and the oldest member is a sprightly 88 years old. The Hillbilly Band practices each week and performs free of charge at many area events. An attraction at the San Juan County Fair for many years, the band always draws a large and appreciative crowd. Two of the members are known locally as the Blister Sisters, and do mean hula dances and can dance the Charleston like nobody around.

While there are no retirement communities in the area, The Bridge Assisted Living, 1091 West Murray Drive, Farmington, (505) 324–6200, offers housing for those who need help with dressing, grooming, bathing, and other day-to-day activities that can become difficult with age. The Four Corners Good Samaritan Center, 500 Care Lane, Aztec, (505) 334–9445, offers apartments to seniors who don't need constant medical attention, but do require some healthcare supervision. There are several quality nursing homes in the area as well.

If you're looking for a place to retire, but don't want the crowds that accompany many of the popular retirement communities, the Four Corners may be just what you're looking for. With mild temperatures, great quality of life, and moderate cost of living, northwestern New Mexico is a great place to call home.

Nursing Homes

Farmington:
Gingerich Home for the Elderly, (505) 632-1234
Life Care Center of Farmington, (505) 326-1600
My Brother's Keeper, (505) 326-7580
San Juan Manor, (505) 325-2910
Aztec:
Crane's Roost, (505) 334-1211
Four Corners Good Samaritan Center, (505) 334-9445
Bloomfield:
Horizon Health Care, (505) 324-6200

Senior Organizations' Information

- AARP, (505) 334-1871
- Arthritis Foundation, New Mexico Chapter, (505) 265-1545
- Disabled American Veterans No. 9, (505) 632-8157
- Meals on Wheels, (505) 327-5962
- Northwest New Mexico Seniors, (505) 326-7462
- Retired Federal Employees, (505) 334-3398
- Totah Senior Citizens Club, (505) 599-1380

Colorado

Real Estate

Because it's a college town and a tourist attraction, rentals in Durango are sought after and claimed by students and those who arrive in the community for seasonal work. There are about 9,000 rental units in La Plata County, which includes apartments, condominiums, and single-family homes. The average monthly rental for a studio or one bedroom apartment is about $450, while a single-family home will rent for an average of $1,000 each month. The cost of purchasing a home in the Durango area has increased at a steady rate in recent years. The average rural home in La Plata County is about $210,000.

Rentals in the Cortez area are also scarce, especially single family housing. Rent for a single-family house will run about $450 to $600, while the average apartment will rent between $450 and $550, depending on size and whether or not utilities are included.

There are several good property management groups in the area that will help you find rental property. A.R.E. M. Property, (970) 247-8299; Cascade Village Management, (970) 259-3500; and Coldwell Banker Property, (970) 259-2891, are all professional and concerned managers and will do what they can to help you in your search for a rental unit.

Buying real estate in Durango can be a challenge as well. Real estate in town is limited because of the hills east and west of the area. Ranches and mountain properties are the primary real estate in those areas. Many of the homes for sale in downtown Durango are well-maintained older homes. That care and historical design may cost you. They are beautiful, however, and most of them are well worth the sale price. New subdivisions are developed on a regular basis, and if you're looking for a new home, be sure to check them out.

There are many qualified real estate companies in Durango, and you will find agents at all of them helpful, knowledgeable, and professional. A list of realtors is available at www.durango.org/rp/realtors.html and you're encouraged to access the web site for additional information. Coldwell Banker-Heritage House, is the number five Coldwell Banker affiliate in all of Colorado. The company is open seven days a week for your convenience, and has more than 40 agents on staff to help.

Home prices in Montezuma County, where Cortez is located, range from $50,000 to more than $200,000. The average price of a home in Montezuma County has increased in recent years, as it has in most of the country. While there are many comfortable homes on the market in town, real estate agents say most people relocating to the area are looking for several acres, where they can have livestock and enjoy the comfort and beauty of being outside of the city limits.

While many of the newer subdivisions in the Durango area have special restrictions, there are few rules in Montezuma County, except for electrical and septic/sewage concerns. If you own 35 acres of land or more in Colorado, you can drill a water well for household water. Before you drill, however, you must remember that the quality of well water in southwest Colorado may not be suitable for drinking. A mining, and oil and gas region for years, locals know that good water may not be all they find when they drill a well.

There are many qualified real estate agents in the Cortez area, and you're encouraged to seek them out when you decide to relocate or retire to southwestern Colorado. Jill Battle of GMAC Preferred Property, 1004 East Main, Cortez, (800) 515-1251, lives in Mancos, Colorado, and will be happy to help you with your real estate needs.

Southwestern Colorado is a beautiful place to live. The only thing that rivals the great scenery is the great people. This part of the Four Corners is a wonderful place to call home, and should you decide to move here, you'll be a welcome member of the neighborhood.

Heartwood Cohousing
Southwestern Colorado
Mynders Glover
(970) 884-7455

Heartwood Cohousing is located on 250 acres of forests, meadows and irrigated pastures, just a few minutes away from Bayfield and about 20 minutes from Durango. Cohousing came onto the real estate scene in the 1970s to help revive communities in neighborhoods. People who live in Heartwood Cohousing each own a private, self-sufficient home on a private lot, and share a common house, greenhouse, workshop, and open space for socializing, gardening, and play. The land for Heartwood was purchased in 1998 and clients have been building homes since 1999. The design plan of Heartwood is to create a balance of private and common spaces, offer homes that are of healthy and earth-friendly construction, have a cluster of about 24 homes which are surrounded by 250 acres of nature, and provide roads and parking at the perimeter, and to make neighborhoods safe for children and available for neighborhood get-togethers. All of the homes in Heartwood are passive solar and energy efficient. The production homes offered for sale are constructed with at least 80 percent of the lumber coming from sustainable harvested forests. Most of the custom homes are constructed using alternative technologies, including using straw clay and straw bale.

Those who have homes in Heartwood enjoy monthly potluck dinners, business meetings, and the Heartwood Cohousing Cyber Chat. There may be rental opportunities in Heartwood and homes for resale. This is an interesting concept that appeals to many, but there are a limited number of sites and homes available. Call for more information.

Education

As in most of the public school systems in the Four Corners, the Durango and Montezuma County school districts provide an excellent education for area students. Administrators are not only concerned about teaching students the basics of education, but offering classes and technology that will aid young people as they head into vocational schools, colleges, and universities.

The educational opportunities in southwestern Colorado are many and I highlight some of them here.

Those seeking to further their education in the Four Corners are fortunate to have a number of colleges and schools from which to chose. Age is never a factor for students attending schools here, and all schools take pride in the age span of their students, recognizing the benefits from a variety of life experiences.

Colorado Timberline Academy
35554 U.S. Hwy. 550, Durango
(970) 247–5898

Colorado Timberline Academy was founded in 1975. Three teachers believed that a small community centered on learning and work, and situated in a beautiful mountain setting, would provide an opportunity for students to grow. A Board of Trustees guides the Academy governed by a director and faculty. The board includes parents, alumni, and faculty, and encourages participation by business people.

Colorado Timberline Academy requires students reach eight basic academic goals and focus on two of them. The eight goals are in the areas of mathematics, English, history, science, arts, psychology and philosophy, language, and computers. To graduate, a student must pass certain tests, write certain papers, and accomplish certain tasks to show they are proficient at the levels of each of the eight goals. The curriculum is designed to be the equivalent of a four-year high school program, but because students work at differing rates, some students graduate in fewer than four years. Although credits are not required for graduation, the Academy keeps records of transferable credits so students who wish to transfer to other schools will have the proper number of credits. The Academy also uses a block scheduling system that divides the academic year into seven 4- or 5-week blocks. The student registers for three academic classes during the block, and classes meet for 1-hour each day. The Academy emphasizes the sports most appropriate to mountain towns—soccer, mountain biking, kayaking, and rock climbing, plus softball in warm weather, and skiing and snowboarding during the winter months. Applicants to the Academy are required to submit an application form, transcripts of previous grades, and four letters of recommendation from teachers, friends and employers. In addition, the applicant must visit the campus for a personal interview. The student body is limited, so students interested in this innovative approach to learning should apply early.

Fort Lewis College
1000 Rim Dr., Durango
(970) 247–7010

Fort Lewis College, "Colorado's Campus in the Sky," is one of the most beautiful campuses in the country because of the La Plata Mountains that stand guard over it and the lovely mesa it stands upon. Fort Lewis is a four-year public liberal arts college with 24 degree programs in arts and sciences, education, and business administration. Almost 5,000 students call this campus home during the year, and provide an energy and enthusiasm to the town that is unmatched. Most of the students come from out of town for their college education, with students from New Mexico, Arizona, California, Oklahoma, Texas, and Illinois topping the out-of-state list.

Many of those students come to Fort Lewis because of the quality of education it offers, just as many come because of the recreational opportunities. But it's not just the student body that enjoys the mountains and the outdoors. The faculty uses the surrounding mountains and deserts for many of their research courses and labs. The area communities, government agencies, tourist resorts, and businesses also contribute by providing learning opportunities for students.

With a variety of degrees offered at Fort Lewis, it is the faculty that gives the college its high standing in the world of academia. More than 91 percent of the faculty have doctorate degrees or the highest degree attainable in their field.

Fort Lewis College administrators recognize the importance of being involved in the community and as such, offer or co-sponsor several programs that aid in the economic and educational development of the region. The John F. Reed Library is open to the public and has some 170,000 volumes and a computer library with access to 3,000 libraries and 21 million books. The Center of Southwest Studies serves as a research center, museum and archive, and is located on the third floor of the library. It has one of the most extensive collections on Native American history in the western United States.

The Office of Continuing Education offers a variety of on and off campus courses of interest to the public; and the Small Business Development Center provides consulting and educational services to small businesses for start-up and expansion.

Fort Lewis College isn't simply a hallowed hall of higher education, it is a good neighbor and friend to everyone who lives in the Four Corners.

Pueblo Community College Southwest Center
710 Camino del Rio, Durango
(970) 247–2929
33057 U.S. Hwy. 160, Cortez
(970) 565–8440

Pueblo Community College Southwest Center is a fully accredited two-year college and provides a quality education for its students at affordable costs. The college offers a variety of classes and students may earn associate of arts degrees, associate of science degrees, associate of applied science degrees and two-year degrees in areas such as criminal justice, nursing, early childhood education, electronics technology, accounting, information processing, and travel and tourism. It is also developing a two-year associate of general studies degree in agri-business. Students may enroll for a full-load with all classes scheduled after 5 P.M. All Colorado residents who have completed 12 credit hours with a grade of C or better at a community college are eligible to enroll at any of the state's four-year colleges or universities, and the Pueblo Community College Southwest Center strives to help its students achieve that goal.

San Juan Basin Vocational Technical School
33057 U.S. Hwy. 160, Cortez
(970) 565–8547

The San Juan Basin Area Vo-Tech School is an accredited school that can tailor programs to fit the needs of a specific business or industry through a state funded customized job training program. Courses are available in accounting, clerk typing, computer information processing, licensed practical nursing, and refrigeration, heating and air conditioning maintenance, all of which are nine-month programs. Auto mechanics, diesel mechanics, electronic technology, heavy equipment, industrial mechanics, media communications, and welding programs are offered in a ten-month program; and heavy equipment maintenance, and electronic technology will take a student 20 months to complete. More than 3,000 students take advantage of the part-time and full-time programs and the school is highly regarded by businesses and industry for the educational benefits it offers.

Healthcare

Southwestern Colorado is fortunate to have two quality hospitals that provide quality healthcare to its citizens. Traditional healthcare is the norm in this part of the country, although there appears to be a movement to provide some holistic care as well.

Healthcare is vital to every community and healthcare professionals in southwestern Colorado are dedicated to provide the best care possible to their patients and to those who travel throughout the Four Corners.

Mercy Medical Center
375 E. Park Ave., Durango
(800) 345–2516

Mercy Medical Center was founded in 1882 by the Sisters of Mercy in the Americas and is dedicated to providing modern technology, uncompromising quality, and care. It is one of the country's largest, nonprofit, mission-based, Catholic healthcare management corporations.

Along with its other healthcare departments in the hospital, Mercy offers a Sleep Laboratory, which provides a wide range of diagnostic services in the field of sleep disorders medicine. The laboratory primarily focuses on sleep-related breathing disorders, and is headed by two board certified pulmonologists with additional training in sleep disorders. The lab uses sophisticated testing equipment and skilled technologists who have extensive experience conducting and analyzing sleep tests. The staff coordinates testing, reporting, and follow-up activities with referring clinics. Information on the sleep lab may be obtained by calling (970) 382-1393 from 8 A.M. to 4 P.M. Monday through Friday.

The Mercy Physical Therapy and Sports Institute is located in the Riverside Medical Building on the first floor of Mercy Medical Center and focuses on general orthopedic and sports injuries. The Mercy Back and Neck Rehabilitation located on the first floor of the main hospital, across from mammography, focuses on back, neck, and spine rehabilitation.

Mercy Medical Center also has a clinic at Purgatory Ski Resort. The clinic is open throughout the ski season and has one medical doctor or mid-level provider, one registered nurse, and one radiology technician on duty. It is a four-bed urgent care unit located on the first floor of Eagle's Nest, behind Farquart's Restaurant. It has x-ray capabilities, trauma and cardiac stabilization for transport, care for general illnesses and minor injuries, and a limited pharmacy for patient prescription.

Mercy Community Health Clinic
3801 Main Ave., Durango
(970) 385–5385

The Community Health Clinic was established by Mercy Medical Center in 1993 to provide healthcare to La Plata County residents who don't have access to healthcare elsewhere, who are uninsured, and who fall within the clinic's economic guidelines. The Mercy Health Foundation with community-wide donations and in-kind contributions supports the clinic financially. The clinic sees patients by appointment only, and patients are billed on a sliding scale, based on income. The clinic is staffed by a physician's assistant and a nurse practitioner, supervised by a physician.

Durango-Animas Family Medicine
375 E. Park Ave., Suite 103, Durango
(970) 247–2611

Durango-Animas Family Medicine specializes in family medicine and has 12 physicians and two family nurse practitioners on staff. All phases of healthcare are provided at Family Medicine, and include both inpatient and outpatient medicine. The physicians and staff put an emphasis on preventive medicine and long-term continuity of care.

Southwest Memorial Hospital
1311 N. Mildred Rd., Cortez
(970) 565-6666

Southwest Memorial Hospital opened in May of 1948, after the local Lions Club raised money to build a new healthcare facility. The hospital was dedicated as a memorial to the veterans of Montezuma and Dolores counties who were killed in World War II. By 1977, the needs of the community had outgrown the facility and a new hospital was built on land that had been previously donated. The hospital today is a recognized leader in healthcare and the residents of Cortez continue to be proud of the facility and its staff.

The hospital offers several programs that are of special benefit to the community. Lamaze classes are offered to prospective mothers and their partners. The class guides mothers-to-be in planning for the birth of their baby, and the physical changes they can expect in their own bodies and in their baby when it arrives. The class also offers advice and counsel on diet, and focuses on the care and feeding of the newborn baby. Prenatal classes are also offered, which include a tour of the hospital and the opportunity to meet the healthcare professionals who will care for mothers and their babies. This class, too, encourages good health habits during and after pregnancy, as well as for the baby. Assistance in all aspects of getting ready for the birth and the days following the birth are provided for mothers-to-be and their families.

Outpatient cardiovascular wellness is also provided at Southwest Memorial. A Phase II cardiac rehab is beneficial for people who have suffered a heart attack or have undergone angioplasty, stint replacement, or coronary artery bypass surgery. Phase III and IV cardiac rehab is available for those who want to lose weight, lower their blood pressure, and increase cardiovascular fitness and strength to avoid future health problems. Information on cardiac rehab may be obtained by calling (970) 564-2293.

A home health program is offered by Southwest Memorial during those times when a patient or the family are unable to meet all the necessary healthcare needs. Services provided include nursing care, assessment of condition, dressing changes, wound care, patient education, medication administration, therapy, counseling, personal care, and medical equipment and supplies. The home healthcare staff is committed to patient care, and is especially attentive to a patient's personal preferences and needs. For more information, call (970) 565-1457.

Spiritual Guidance

Residents of southwestern Colorado have a vast number of churches in which to worship. There is no primary denomination here, but many religious affiliations. No matter what your personal faith, you're sure to find a congregation that shares it with you in this part of the Four Corners. Most major daily newspapers have a religion section, which usually runs on Fridays. That section highlights religious events, new pastors, and news of churches in the community.

Retirement

With winters that tend to be cold and tourists who flock to the area, southwestern Colorado isn't a likely retirement area. While there are beautiful areas to live and enjoy the great quality of life, retirees haven't yet discovered this part of the Four Corners. There are senior centers in Cortez, Dolores, and Mancos, with area seniors sharing meals, entertainment, and a social atmosphere. Visiting any one of the centers will find seniors playing cards and other games, and sharing local news and maybe even some gossip.

There are several assisted living homes in the area, and all of them are staffed with people who have a genuine love of senior citizens and a desire to make life better for them.

There are many volunteer opportunities for seniors who wish to donate their time to help others. The school system, area churches, and healthcare facilities are always grateful for seniors who will share their life experiences and talents.

Sunshine Gardens West Assisted Living
25 Sunshine Ct., Cortez
(970) 385–4090

There are accommodations for 12 independent living residents at this lovely home. Sunshine Gardens strives to make life pleasant and comfortable for its residents, as well as provides healthcare as needed. The facility is located in Cortez and near the Durango city limits, which offers a variety of shops and stores in which to browse and buy.

Vista Mesa Assisted Living Residence
1206 N. Mildred, Cortez
(970) 564–1888

Vista Mesa offers residents a variety of things to do in beautiful surroundings. Three meals are served each day in two bright and sunny dining rooms; and great rooms with fireplaces, vaulted ceilings, and wonderful views provide residents a lovely place to visit, read, or simply reflect. There is a private reading library, an activity room that has something for almost everyone, and a full-service beauty salon. Laundry facilities are available and a housekeeping staff makes sure things are clean and cared for.

Madison House Assisted Living
120 S. Madison, Cortez
(970) 565–2047

Another lovely assisted living facility, Madison House serves up home cooked meals that will make your mouth water. Housekeeping, laundry and linen services are offered, and there is a 24-hour personal care service and medication administration on site. The staff at Madison House makes sure there are many social activities to keep clients happy and healthy, and the barber and beauty salon makes sure they all look as good as they feel.

Senior Organizations'

Information

· AARP, (970) 565–1068
· Area Agency on Aging, (970) 259–1967
· Senior Citizen Center/Nutrition Out reach, (970) 565–4166
· Meals on Wheels, (970) 565–8131

Utah

Real Estate

Rental units in southeastern Utah won't be easy to come by. Most people who move here buy homes. Duplexes, apartment complexes, and some houses are available to rent, with costs varying greatly. If you're hoping to rent before you buy, check with a real estate agent, who will be happy to help you find something suitable.

In Moab, there are about 40,000 homes, with the average price of a home about $120,000. Builders in Moab don't skimp on lot size, and you'll have a nice piece of property to landscape as you see fit. Wide streets add to the ambiance of this community, and if you decide to make Moab your permanent home, you'll find great friends and neighbors.

There are several new town home developments available in Moab, with prices ranging from about $156,000 to $200,000. Moab Realty, with offices at 550 North Main in Moab, handles some of them and the staff will be most happy to show these units. Call them at (800) 897-7325.

In San Juan County real estate is less expensive. The average home in Blanding is about $50,000, with rent averaging about $325 a month. While you won't find a lot of homes for sale, there are several professional real estate companies who will be happy to help you. Canyon Country Realty, (801) 587-2146; Coldwell Banker, (801) 587-2585; and Lex Realty, (801) 587-2424, are in Monticello; while Neighborhood Realty, (801) 678-2850, is in Blanding. All of these agencies are staffed with agents who will go out of their way to help you find your new home—whether you rent or buy.

Education

A look at a map of southeastern Utah shows lots of wide open spaces and few interstates, but that doesn't mean education is lacking in this part of the Four Corners. While students may travel a bit further to school, the quality in the classroom matches that of many larger school systems. For these students, studying the history of the pioneers who moved west across America has special meaning, and the places those pioneers traveled and triumphed over is right outside their classroom windows.

Public schools educate most of the students in southeastern Utah, although home schooling is increasing in popularity here, as it is throughout much of the nation.

Utah Christian Home School Association
P.O. Box 3942, Salt Lake City
(801) 296-7198
utch@utch.org

The Utah Christian Home School Association provides support, education, and fellowship for Christian families who educate their children at home. The association provides field trips, workshops, support group meetings, high school graduation ceremonies, an annual convention, a resource library, an annual used book sale, and a monthly newsletter. The association also notifies members of pending litigation that might affect those who home school. More parents are turning to home schooling as an alternative to sending their children to public and private schools, and the support and resources offered by the Utah Christian Home School Association are a positive step in making sure parents and students benefit from that decision.

College of Eastern Utah-San Juan Campus
639 W. 100, South Blanding
435) 678-2220

The San Juan Campus was established in 1976 by a group of citizens who were committed to making higher education more accessible to area residents. In 1977, the Utah State Board of Regents recog-

nized the San Juan Campus as an administrative unit of the College of Eastern Utah, and in 1981, the campus was included in the college's accreditation. The College of Eastern Utah recognizes the uniqueness of this part of the Four Corners and makes special efforts to reach non-traditional and minority students through special courses, programs, counseling and advisement. The San Juan Campus offers a two-year program, with earned credits available for transfer to other colleges and universities throughout the United States.

Utah State University
500 South 700, West Blanding
(801) 678-2072

Utah State University offers upper division courses in seven bachelor's degrees and five master's degree programs. The university offers distance education programs, which allow students to earn college credits while working full time. A recent survey of off-campus graduates showed that 96 percent of those who responded to the survey were employed full time and received a promotion, made a career change, or enjoyed better working conditions because they received a degree from USU. With many residents of southeastern Utah unable to leave home for college because of job or family obligations, distance education programs have proven to be a blessing to them, and most colleges and universities are making those programs available to them.

Healthcare

In spite of the lack of a large city in southeastern Utah, the residents have several fine healthcare facilities. The physicians and medical professionals who staff these facilities enjoy the quality of life this part of the Four Corners offers and like the personal attention they can give patients, which is not always possible in a larger metropolitan area.

Healthcare is a priority for the people of southeastern Utah, and elected officials work with medical professionals and the public to make sure those needs are met.

Allen Memorial Hospital
719 W. 400 N., Moab
(435) 259–7191

Allen Memorial Hospital is a not-for-profit hospital that is the center for specialized medical care with four family practice physicians and two mid-level providers. There are 36 additional staff members who assist with the healthcare needs of patients. Allen Memorial Hospital has 38 beds, and includes a care center wing, which has 17 beds. A new emergency room and birthing room were recently added to the hospital, and future additions will include a long-term care wing, expanded acute care services, and a new medial office building. Allen Memorial Hospital takes pride in the quality of medical care it provides its patients, and the administration and staff work closely together for the good of the community.

Four Corners Community Health Center Inc.
198 E. Center St., Moab
(435) 259–6131

The Four Corners Community Health Center is a comprehensive center for mental health and substance abuse treatment for children, youth, and adults. A staff of highly trained professionals, including social workers, marriage and family therapists, professional counselors, addictions specialists, psychologists, nurses, and psychiatrists, provide quality care for the people of Grand County. Four Corners works with other community agencies to provide improved services for children, youth, and their families. Services include outpatient psychotherapy, groups for survivors of sexual abuse, classes for parents of defiant children, 24-hour crisis availability, out reach, domestic violence treatment, and classes for DUI offenders.

San Juan Hospital
364 W. 100 N., Monticello
(810) 587–2116

San Juan Health Services operates the San Juan Hospital, a 24-bed acute care facility. The hospital is fully equipped and is staffed by four family practice physicians, one general surgeon, one nurse practitioner, and five physician's assistants. Medical staff consulting physicians hold periodic clinics in allergy/asthma, cardiology, dermatology, ophthalmology, orthopedics, and podiatry. A laboratory, radiology, ultrasound, mammography, treadmill, EKG, and physical therapy are also provided. A cardiac care room is also maintained at the hospital. San Juan Health Services also provides an emergency room and birthing center in Blanding; a mobile clinic van, which travels to remote areas of the county providing mammograms and other screenings; the Montezuma Creek Clinic, with services that include a laboratory, radiology, ultrasound, and a dental clinic; the Monument Valley Health Center, which also includes a laboratory, radiology, ultrasound, and a dental clinic; and an ambulance service that operates from Monticello, Blanding, Montezuma Creek, Bluff, Mexican Hat, and Monument Valley. A long-term and nursing home facility is located in Blanding, and provides quality geriatric care to residents.

Spiritual Guidance

Utah is the home of the Church of Jesus Christ of Latter-day Saints (Mormons), and as such, that is the primary religion of the area. There are more than ten million Mormons in the world, and many of them call Utah home. For those who live in Utah, whether they belong to the Mormon Church or not, Mormonism is a unique heritage which has shaped the past and continues to impact the future of Utah. Approximately 70 percent of Utah residents are members of the LDS church.

There are many historic sites and buildings that are important to Mormons throughout the state, but only members of the Mormon Church are allowed in the buildings. Tourists are invited into the visitor center that is usually located next door.

Other religions also thrive in southeastern Utah, however. In fact, the city of Moab has more denominations per capita than any other city in the state. As you travel throughout this part of the Four Corners, and if you're thinking about making southeastern Utah your home, you'll find congregations in your religious affiliation that will welcome you.

4Wheelers4Christ
P.O. Box 44, Castaic, CA
(661) 257–2166
www.4Wheelers4Christ.org

Because four-wheeling is so popular in this part of the Four Corners, 4Wheelers4Christ offers four-wheelers the opportunity to worship together. The organization assists members in offering fellowship services at events, and provides an online magazine that also offers support and spiritual encouragement. Memberships are available for individuals and families, as well as businesses and clubs.

Retirement

While southeastern Utah isn't known as a retirement mecca, there are opportunities for seniors. With mild weather, friendly people, and a landscape that defies description, you may find that retiring to this part of the Four Corners is the best decision you ever made.

The San Juan County Area Agency on Aging provides many services for senior citizens, including home health care, homemaker and chore services, legal counseling, information and referral, senior advocacy, escort, shopping, and outreach.

All senior centers in southeastern Utah provide a variety of special and recreational events, including games, arts and crafts, blood pressure screening, short and overnight trips, and movies. Transportation is provided for all senior activities.

Senior Centers

Monticello Senior Center
80 N. Main St.
(801) 587–2401

Blanding Senior Center
177 E. 200 North
(801) 678–2427

Bluff Senior Center
Bluff Community Center
(801) 672–2390

Meals are served at each center and home meals are delivered. Transportation is provided for seniors to attend center activities, and for medical visits, shopping, sightseeing, and community events. Recreation is available at the centers, and counseling, education, health screening, and some legal assistance is also provided. You'll find lots to do at each of the senior centers throughout southeastern Utah, and volunteer opportunities arise daily, so be sure to check with the senior center director, who will be happy to help you.

Retirement communities and nursing homes planned for in the future for this part of the Four Corners and if you're interested in retiring here, call the Moab Area Economic Development at (435) 259-1348 for information.

Senior Organizations' Information:

· American Association of Retired Per sons, (800) 424-3410
· Area on Aging, (435) 637-5444

· Counsel of Aging, (435) 259-6623
· Meals on Wheels, (435) 259-6623
· Retired Seniors Volunteer Program, (435) 259-9162
· Utah Veterans, (800) 827-1000

Arizona

Real Estate

Arizona is noted for its wonderful weather and its incredible natural beauty, and real estate is at a premium in much of the northeastern portion of the state. Much of this land, too, belongs to the Native Americans, making it difficult to purchase. If you choose to live in the Flagstaff area, you'll find homes in every price range and a qualified real estate agent will direct you to the ones most suited for your needs. In other areas of this portion of the Four Corners, you may find a more limited market, but quality real estate is available, so check with your agent and seek out the area of this beautiful state you want to call home.

Most people consider Flagstaff when they decide to relocate to northeastern Arizona, and for good reason. While smaller communities such as Tuba City, Kayenta, and Winslow have some rentals and homes for sale, Flagstaff has a larger market to select from, with the amenities many people prefer. The smaller communities do offer a quieter life, and enough shopping and services that make them attractive places to live. Prices are comparatively lower in smaller, more remote communities, and if you're looking for the quality of life a small town offers, I encourage you to check out those areas.

There are many rental units available in Flagstaff, but the more than 20,000 students who attend Northern Arizona University and Coconino Community College snatch them up quickly. Prices of those rentals vary greatly. For a complete list of available rental units, log on to www.flagrealestate.com.

For those who want to buy a home in Flagstaff, you'll find more than 20 real estate agents and brokers willing to help you. You'll find homes in every price range, and new subdivisions are being developed everywhere. Homes in downtown Flagstaff are coveted, and tend to be expensive. Many of the homes, however, date back to the turn of the century, and some have been passed down through generations. Some of the finest homes are sold before they ever get on the open market. Many of these beautiful old homes have been converted to commercial use, and a buyer should be knowledgeable about zoning. Prices in the greater area have ranged from $100,000 to more than $300,000.

Munds Park is located about 17 miles south of Flagstaff off I-17. The more than 3,200 properties enjoy mature trees, and some canyons and meadows. Munds Park is primarily a second home community with facilities that include golf, swimming, tennis, a clubhouse, and restaurant. Mobile and manufactured homes share the area with simple cabins and luxury homes. Prices in this area run from about $75,000 to more than $300,000. Some lots remain for sale, with price tags from $35,000 to more than $100,000.

No matter what kind of home you're looking for, or what you plan to pay, you'll find something you're sure to enjoy in Flagstaff and the surrounding areas. There are many qualified real estate agents and agencies that will help you in your search for a new home. Real estate agencies are listed on the web site of www.flagrealestate.com and you're encouraged to check them out. Many of them provide online home searches, complete with photographs and particulars. Those who already live in this special part of the Four Corners will welcome you as neighbors and will be glad to call you friends.

Education

Arizonians pride themselves on their educational system, and rightfully so. Northern Arizona University not only provides a quality education to its students, but is active in the communities in which it has branches. Community courses are offered and the university offers many events that appeal to almost everyone. State government emphasizes education, and works to attract some of the best educators in the country.

Along with fine institutions of higher education, the state also has quality public school systems. The Flagstaff Unified School District strives to provide students with the basic skills needed to rank in the top one-third of Arizona schools in scholastic achievement (reading, writing, and math). The Tuba City Unified School District also strives to provide the best education possible for its student body, the majority are Navajo or Hopi. Charter schools, private schools, and home schooling continue to draw students away from public schools, and gives residents choices on how their children are educated.

Northern Arizona University
NAU Box 4082, Flagstaff
(520) 523–9011

Northern Arizona University is one of Arizona's three state universities, with students from every state in the Union and from 60 countries. With more than 120 undergraduate programs available, as well as graduate and doctoral programs, the university attracts some of the brightest students. A wide range of degrees are available at NAU, including business, arts and sciences, physical therapy, and forestry. The campus of NAU covers 730 acres in the heart of town, and is a lovely campus that is reminiscent of the ivory-covered university towers of days gone by.

In addition to providing comprehensive academic programs for students, NAU's broader mission includes promoting the value of cultural diversity, providing educational opportunities to the non-metropolitan areas of Arizona, and offering a variety of public service programs. The administration of the university maintains that valuing cultural diversity is crucial to a well-rounded education, and the university exercises leadership in multicultural appreciation by recruiting under-represented and ethnic students, faculty, staff, and administrators by providing multicultural activities and programs. NAU offers programs that assist Native American and Hispanic students in their desire to further their education.

The university also provides teacher education throughout the state, by offering extensive state wide instruction through interactive television programming, continuing education classes, state wide academic offices, and an academic center in Yuma. NAU offers a variety of services to the citizens of Arizona, including serving as a fine arts center for the region and assisting with rural education and economic development, particularly with Native American nations.

A visit to Northern Arizona University to see the campus, enjoy the facilities, and visit with the students will leave visitors with the sense of compassion, enthusiasm, and a yearning to learn, which symbolizes this university and its impact on the town of Flagstaff.

Coconino Community College
3000 N. 4th St., Flagstaff
(520) 527–222

Coconino Community College was founded in 1991 and is the fastest growing college in Arizona. It serves a culturally diverse population, and is spread over about 18,600 square miles and includes portions of five Native American tribal reservations—Havasupai, Hopi, Hualapai, Kaibab-Paiute, and Navajo. The college has two campuses, one in Flagstaff and the other in Page, and offers classes at extension sites throughout the county. Coconino Community College provides two-year associate degrees, which can be transferred to a university or can help students enter the business world. The college also offers a Continuing Education Program, which offers credit-free courses and workshops throughout the year. Tuition and fees at Coconino Community College are among the lowest in the nation, and financial assistance is provided to students through federal, state, and institutional programs and scholarships. The average age of a student at CCC is 29, and the college is proud of those students who return to school and the success they achieve.

Healthcare

Many of the healthcare providers in northeastern Arizona are on the reservations, and I have covered those facilities in separate sections of this book. In Flagstaff, however, residents of this portion of the Four Corners will find an abundance of qualified healthcare providers. I highlight some of them here, and encourage you to seek out others you may hear of during your visit to northeastern Arizona.

In addition to traditional healthcare, alternative healthcare is offered in northeastern Arizona. I provide information on several of them but encourage those who are interested in alternative healthcare to seek out other professionals in the field as well.

Northern Arizona Healthcare
1200 N. Beaver St., Flagstaff
(520) 779–3366

Northern Arizona Healthcare is the umbrella organization that includes Flagstaff Medical Center and Northern Arizona Homecare. Northern Arizona Healthcare is a not-for-profit organization that is dedicated to providing quality healthcare services to the people in this portion of the Four Corners. Flagstaff Medical Center offers a wide range of services but has some outstanding services I highlight for you here.

The Children's Health Center offers specialty pediatric outpatient clinics for children with disabilities or chronic illnesses. Children's Rehabilitation Services, the Newborn Development Follow-up Clinic, and Safe Child, a sexual abuse examination/interview clinic, are some of the special programs the center provides. The Safe Child clinic conducts forensic interviews and medical exams on children who are potential sexual abuse victims. The Newborn Developmental Follow-up Clinic provides multi-disciplinary evaluations and referrals for children under the age of three when there is a concern of developmental delay. The Flagstaff Medical Center believes every child deserves quality medical care and the staff works tirelessly to provide it. Childbirth and parenting classes are also offered at the center.

The Cancer Center of Northern Arizona offers not just treatment for the cancer patient, but support and care for the patient's family. The staff of the Cancer Center believes that a healing environment is critical to the treatment process of the patient and work together to create that kind of environment. The experienced staff of the Cancer Center includes a radiation oncologist, physicist, radiation therapists, dosimetrist (a technician who reads a device that measures and records the amount of radiation absorbed by the patient), registered nurse, social worker, and a dietitian. Individual and family counseling and support groups are offered to the patient's family. Circle of Friends is a program that connects patients with experienced survivors who act as a resource and give comfort, and who provide lots of support during the treatment process.

Concentra Medical Center
120 W. Fine Ave., Flagstaff
(520) 773–9695

Concentra Medical is staffed and equipped to provide professional medical care for acute illness and injury for the family. Medical services include minor office surgery, physicals, occupational medicine, sport-related injuries, X-ray, physical therapy, and pathology. A physician is available during clinic hours. The center sees all patients (including residents who have a primary care physician, but are unable to see him) and travelers who seek medical attention. A report on the traveler's treatment will be provided to his primary care physician, if requested. Appointments are not necessary at the center, but prepare for an extended wait if it happens to be cold and flu season. Patients are seen as quickly as possible, with the severity of a patient's condition to determine priority. Payment is expected at the time of service, and the center takes major credit cards. Most insurance is accepted, but be prepared to present your insurance card for verification.

Naturopathic Medical Center
809 N. Humphreys, Flagstaff
(520) 774–1770

Naturopathic physicians believe that nature acts powerfully through healing mechanisms in the body and mind to maintain and restore health. These physicians work to restore and support those inherent healing systems when they have broken down using methods, medicines, and techniques that are in harmony with natural processes. Naturopathic physicians prefer non-invasive treatments, which minimize the risks of harmful side effects. They are trained to know which patients they can treat safely and which ones they need to refer to other healthcare professionals. The center offers women's healthcare, which includes gynecologic exams and pap smears, treatment of menstrual and hormonal disorders, infections, menopause, osteoporosis, and diaphragm and cervical cap fittings. Children's healthcare is provided for well baby/child visits, acute and recurrent infections, digestive problems, skin disorders, and asthma. Prostate health and cardiovascular health are men's health issues the center treats. The physicians at the Naturopathic Health Center offer free 15-minute consultations, which introduce and explain naturopathic healthcare approaches. If you're looking for an alternative to traditional medical healthcare and procedures, visit the Naturopathic Health Center. The staff is friendly and helpful and will do their best to answer all your questions.

Womancare Midwifery Center, L.L.C.
220 W. Birch, Flagstaff
(520) 779–6064

Licensed midwives are trained professionals who are regulated by the Arizona Department of Health Services. Midwives are trained to offer care and support to a woman and her newborn during the normal childbearing process. The Womancare Midwifery Center staff believes birth is a normal healthy experience and every woman has the right to safe, satisfying healthcare. They believe every family has the right to participate in decisions regarding pregnancy and birth, and that childbearing should be a family centered experience. The staff is experienced and dedicated to making the birth of a child joyous and special to the entire family. The center offers preconception counseling, pregnancy tests, complete holistic prenatal care, nutrition assessment and counseling, prenatal lab work and testing, childbirth classes, pregnancy and infant massages, water births, continuous support during labor, postpartum care, and family planning education/referral. Many women today have discovered the positive aspects of midwifery. If you have questions or would like additional information, the staff encourages you to call.

Spiritual Guidance

With a population that includes people of every faith, ethnic origin, and culture, northeastern Arizona offers a place of worship for just about everyone. There is no dominant religion here, and residents are as apt to gather in parks and homes to worship as they are to gather in a more traditional church setting. The Unitarian Universalist Fellowship is a liberal religion born of the Christian and Jewish traditions, without adhering to any particular belief or creed. These Unitarian Universalists celebrate Christmas and Hanukkah, as well as other holidays held sacred by several other religious sects. The Jewish community meets twice a month for services and many churches serve congregations of interdenominational or non-denominational preferences.

For a compete listing of places of worship in the Flagstaff area, log onto www.flagstaff.about.com/flagstaffreligious/index.htm

Whatever your spiritual needs, you'll find a congregation in northeastern Arizona that will meet those needs and embrace you as a friend.

Retirement

If you're looking for a place to retire, you might want to consider Flagstaff. *Modern Maturity* magazine named this beautiful northeastern Arizona community one of the 50 "Most Alive" places to live in retirement. Flagstaff was listed in the magazine's "green and clean" category. The city has much to offer retirees, including volunteer opportunities, exercise classes, and continuing education.

Seniors who want to volunteer have countless choices through Northern Arizona University's Senior Volunteers Program. If you'd like to be a foster grandparent, tutor a student, mentor a child, help other retirees with shopping and errands, or participate in the Senior Olympics, NAU's Senior Volunteer Program will help you find a volunteer opportunity you'll enjoy. Log on to www.nau.edu/~nargi-p/rsvp.htm to check out all you can do to help others.

NAU also offers an Elderhostel program for seniors. One of the largest in the United States, the university's 31 programs range from on-campus classes to seminars in the Grand Canyon, Lake Powell, Monument Valley, Chaco Canyon, Sedona, the Hopi and Navajo reservations, Petrified Forest/Painted Desert, and Canyon de Chelly. The opportunities are endless, the challenges exciting, and the results are fun. Call the university at (520) 523-2359 between 8 A.M. and 5 P.M. Monday through Friday for more information.

How about an education vacation? The University of Northern Arizona offers a unique opportunity to engage in a variety of educational programs, ranging from two to ten weeks. Classes are designed for seniors and aid in their growth and knowledge. Courses include political science, current topics, literature, music, art appreciation, and philosophy. Special lecture series featuring national speakers, authors, traveling professors, local celebrities, and historians are also offered. Senior Summer School provides seniors a taste of today's college life. If you never attended college, or simply want to recapture some of that college magic, log on to www.seniorsummerschool.com/universityinfo.html.

For seniors who want to stay—or get—fit, Flagstaff gives you several options. The city of Flagstaff has an ice skating rink, a therapeutic recreation center, and an adult and community center, all of which offer opportunities to exercise. For information, contact the city at (520) 774-5281.

This Arizona portion of the Four Corners has attracted many retirees who enjoy the climate, the scenery, the great mountain air, and all the area has to offer. While Flagstaff may be a university community, almost 23 percent of its population is in the 40-64 age bracket, and almost 6 percent is 65 years and older. With the senior generation sharing a lifestyle with college students, the best of both worlds can be found, and you've found it in Flagstaff.

For those who need a little help with daily living, The Peaks provides a senior living community.

The Peaks
3150 N. Winding Brook Rd., Flagstaff
(520) 774–7106

The Peaks is a senior living, learning, and wellness community that is part of an intergenerational campus that includes the Museum of Northern Arizona. The Peaks offers independent living, assisted living, skilled nursing, and the Memory Center, which has apartments with specialized care for seniors who have dementia, Alzheimer's disease, or a memory loss. A lovely campus that offers more than just healthcare, the Peaks offers the opportunity to live each day to its fullest. The staff that is committed to the seniors and their families.

Joe Haughey
Elk View Realty, Inc.
323 South River Run Rd. Flagstaff
(520) 556–0009

For those who want to purchase a home or land in Flagstaff, there are many real estate agents who are knowledgeable and professional and happy to serve you. I spotlight one because of his special interest in working with seniors.

Haughey has lived in Flagstaff for more than 21 years and earned the nationally recognized real estate designation SRES (Seniors Real Estate Specialist). Seniors Real Estate Specialists help seniors with their real estate needs, whether it's selling the family home, buying rental property, estate tax implications of owning real estate, obtaining a reverse mortgage, or moving to a senior community.

Media

New Mexico
Colorado
Utah
Arizona

Wherever you're from in the grand ole USA, you'll be able to keep in touch with what's happening in your home state while you visit the Four Corners. The members of the media who live in the Four Corners are here because they love what they do and where they live, and you'll discover that in the work they do. Enjoy our local newspapers, watch our local television affiliates, and sing along with our local radio stations. We enjoy your company.

New Mexico

Newspapers

The Daily Times
P.O. Box 450, Farmington
(505) 325–4545

The Daily Times is the only daily newspaper that covers San Juan County. For many years, *The Daily Times* was a family-owned newspaper, but was purchased several years ago by the MediaNews Group. A yearly subscription to the newspaper is $88, and cost of a single copy is $.50 during the week and $1 on Sundays. *The Daily Times* is a progressive newspaper, which strives to cover a rather large area with a rather limited number of reporters. The newspaper covers local news in all of San Juan County and on the Navajo Reservation. It offers special sections regularly, with a special emphasis on the oil and gas industry, which has a huge economic impact on the county. It also publishes special issues, which cover the Connie Mack World Series and the San Juan County Fair, both of which are August events. The newspaper puts a strong emphasis on sports and recreation, which are important to local residents, and on investigative reporting. *The Daily Times* is an award winning newspaper, and owners and staff are proud of the product they publish.

The Four Corners Business Journal
205 W. Arrington, Farmington
(505) 564–4671

The Four Corners Business Journal is published every Monday and covers businesses primarily in San Juan County and in Durango, Colorado. Subscriptions are $30 for 26 issues and $45 for 52 issues. *The Business Journal* was also purchased by the MediaNews Group several years ago, after being established in the area for many years. *The Business Journal* puts its emphasis on economic development, the oil and gas industry, and retail trade, while including news of most professional businesses. It is an interesting, and well-written and edited publication that is offered free to those who pick it up in many businesses in San Juan County and Durango. Its readership is primarily the professional and the business executive, who strive to keep up with the goings-on in the business community.

The Gallup Independent
500 N. 9th St., Gallup
(800) 545–3817

The Gallup Independent is a family-owned newspaper that has been part of Gallup for many years. It's the only daily (except

Sunday) newspaper in Gallup and has a reputation for hard news reporting. *The Independent* strives to cover the Navajo Reservation, as well as Gallup and the surrounding area, and usually does an admirable job. Subscription rates are $57 for six months and $114 for a year.

Television Stations

KOBF-TV 12
825 W. Broadway, Farmington
(505) 326–1141

While northwestern New Mexico receives all major television networks, it does have one local affiliate, KOBF-TV 12, part of the KOB network out of Albuquerque. KOBF offers news at 6 A.M., 5 P.M., 6 P.M., and 10 P.M., as well as spot news throughout the day. It covers all of San Juan County and strives to present news from Gallup, Shiprock, and southwestern Colorado as well. KOBF puts an emphasis on sports, and every Friday night while school is in session, it presents Game Day, which focuses on local sports.

TCI Cablevision
1911 N. Butler, Farmington
(505) 327–6143

TCI is San Juan County's cable provider. While it does provide cable programming, it doesn't do any local news or general interest programs. The company is active in the community, however, and supports many local charities.

Radio Stations

There are several radio stations in northwestern New Mexico, with an emphasis on country music. There are also classic rock stations and easy listening stations. All of the stations offer quality programming and many of them offer local talent on-air. You're bound to find something you like to listen to when you turn your radio on in northwestern New Mexico.

KDAG Big Dog - 96.9 FM

Big Dog offers classic rock.

KENN - 1390 AM

Roberts Radio owns KENN, along with KISS Country, 97.9, and KRWN, 92.9. KENN offers talk radio and spotlights Paul Harvey, Rush Limbaugh and Don Imus. It is also proud of the fact that for 50 years, it has provided sports coverage for Farmington High School. KISS Country plays 50 minutes of country music every hour, and KRWN offers rock music.

KFROG - 104.5 FM

Country music at its best, that's what you'll hear on KFROG.

KTRA - 102.1 FM

KTRA is a long-standing radio station in Farmington and offers country music favorites.

KWYK - 94.9 FM

The local talent on KWYK has been with the station for many years, and the station has a large and loyal following. It offers contemporary adult music, CNN news, and jazz every Sunday morning.

KNDN - 960 AM

KNDN is a nationally recognized radio station because it provides information to the Navajo Reservation in Navajo. For more than 40 years, KNDN has been serving the Navajo people, and offers them an open microphone to use. The Navajo have used KNDN to locate missing relatives, to talk about chapter meetings, and for many other public needs.

KSJE - 90.9 FM

KSJE is a public radio station from San Juan College in Farmington and offers wonderful classical music. This station, too, has a large listening audience who enjoy the masters.

KPCL is a Christian station and offers programs and music for those of the Christian faith.

Colorado

Newspapers

Durango Herald
1275 Main Ave., Durango
(970) 247–3504

The *Durango Herald* is a family-owned newspaper that has served the Durango area for many years. It is a daily paper, with subscription rates at $52 per year. The *Herald's* priority is local news, and the staff does an excellent job of covering local issues and events. While definitely not a small-town newspaper, the *Durango Herald* manages to maintain that great small town feeling while incorporating big city reporting and coverage. The *Herald* publishes several special issues each year, with its annual holiday shopping issue one of its great accomplishments. The *Herald* also publishes *Inside/Outside Southwest Magazine*, a monthly publication that covers recreation, health, fitness, entertainment, and culture. In addition, the company also owns the *Cortez Journal* in nearby Cortez, Colorado, which is a small weekly newspaper devoted to local news.

Radio Stations

Southwestern Colorado doesn't have a local television affiliate, but it does have plenty of radio stations. You won't have to push the select button many times before you're certain to find a radio station that will keep you humming along.

KISS Country - 97.9 FM

This is the same country music station that serves Farmington, so you'll find the same great music.

KDGO - 1240 AM

Oldies—lots and lots of wonderful oldies. This station is for when you want to recapture your youth, when you want to be able to sing along and know all the words, or when you want to just drive your kids crazy.

KRWN - 92.9 FM

This station, too, covers Farmington and offers great rock.

KCQL - 1340 AM

All sports, all the time—that's what this station offers. For those die-hard sports fans who just can't get enough baseball, football, golf, basketball, or any other sport, you'll find what you're looking for on KCQL.

KDAG Big Dog - 96.9 and 106.7 FM

Classic rock keeps rockin' in Durango.

KDUR - 91.9 and 93.9 FM

KDUR comes from Fort Lewis College in Durango. This is great college-student type music that even Mom and Dad can enjoy.

KFROG - 104.5 FM

Today's country music at its best. If you're a Garth fan, a Faith fan, an Alan fan—if it's country and its great, it's on KFROG.

KIQX - 101.3 FM

Local, regional, and national news highlight this radio station, which also gives up-to-the-minute sports news.

KTRZ - 98.7 FM

More country music for the Four Corners.

KVFC - 740 AM

Music from the '50s, '60s, and '70s—all the great songs from those incredible years.

KSUT - 90.1 and 89.5 FM

A public radio station, KSUT offers news, music, multicultural programming, and public affairs. Good listening and great information.

Utah

Newspapers

Canyon County Zephyr
P.O. Box 327, Moab
435) 259–7773

Canyon County Zephyr isn't your ordinary newspaper. Published bi-monthly, the paper is irreverent, thought provoking, and fun. Editor and publisher, Jim Stiles, offers opinions about everything, and people either love him and his newspaper or can't stand the sight or thought of either. Whether you agree with Stiles or not, the newspaper is worth reading and will definitely make you think. The paper is offered free.

Blue Mountain Panorama
329 W. 400 North, Blanding
(800) 910–NEWS

The *Panorama* is published weekly and covers issues of importance to areas of San Juan County, Utah. The paper hits the newsstands on Wednesday and subscription rates are $14 for a year. A good, local newspaper.

The San Juan Record
49 S. Main St., Monticello
(801) 587–2277

The *Record* is published weekly in Monticello and hits newsstands on Wednesdays. This is another quality local newspaper that strives to bring issues of importance to its readers while providing small town color. Subscriptions are $15 each year.

The Salt Lake Tribune/Deseret News
143 S. Main St., Salt Lake City
(801) 237–2900

Jointly operated by the Newspaper Agency Corporation, they provide readers two perspectives on the news and give advertisers the most bang for their buck. The papers are circulated statewide and offer news of communities throughout the state as best they can. Since southeastern Utah is sparsely populated, the *Tribune* and *News* are primary sources of information. Subscriptions are about $10 per week and papers may be purchased at major retailers throughout southeastern Utah.

Television and Radio Stations

Southeastern Utah receives major networks from a Salt Lake City translator. Two public broadcasting stations from the University of Utah and Brigham Young University are also received. Cable television is available in Blanding and Monticello. Most of the radio stations available in this part of the Four Corners come from Durango, Cortez, and Grand Junction, Colorado, and from Farmington, New Mexico.

KZMU - 89.7 FM

An excellent radio station, KZMU is public radio and offers entertainment and information with the help of volunteers. There is always something lively and fun going on at KZMU.

KCYN - 97.1 FM

This is another good station, which offers country music at its best.

Arizona

Newspapers

Arizona Daily Sun
1751 S. Thompson St., Flagstaff
(520) 774–4545

The *Arizona Daily Sun* covers Flagstaff and the surrounding area. A top-notch staff reports on local issues, and national news is given equal space. The *Sun* publishes several special sections each year. Recent special tabs include information on building a new home, health and beauty, women in business, and the "Best of Flagstaff," all quality publications that are well done and interesting reads. You can subscribe to the *Sun* for $110 each year.

The Navajo Hopi Observer
417 W. Santa Fe Ave., Flagstaff
(877) 627–3787

The *Navajo Hopi Observer* is a weekly newspaper dedicated to providing news to the Navajo and Hopi reservations. With a professional staff, the *Observer* covers tribal politics and does in-depth articles on major issues facing the Navajo and Hopi people.

The Navajo Times
AZ Hwy. 264 at C.R. 12, Window Rock
(520) 871–6632

The *Navajo Times* is privately owned and is published weekly. Subscription rates are $55 for one year. The *Navajo Times* is a newspaper for the Navajo people and includes information about tribal politics, news, sports, and business. It has an accomplished team of editors and reporters who do an excellent job of covering the Navajo Nation.

Radio Stations

KAFF - 83 AM/FM

Country music at its best. KAFF also offers Rush Limbaugh, the American Country Countdown, and Paul Harvey.

KFLX - 105.1 FM

If you're a blues fan, you'll enjoy KFLX. The station offers new blues releases as well as great, classic blues. The 4 O'clock Funnies program offers stand up comedy routines and the Acoustic Café is a great program that provides acoustic music and rare recordings. This is the perfect radio station for true-blue blues fans.

KMGN - 93.9 FM

Rock 'n roll—lots of it, is provided by KMGN. Every Sunday afternoon, it offers Flashback, which mixes great rock 'n roll favorites with actual newscasts, classic television and movie clips, and classic commercial and comedy bits. A fun radio station, KMGN declares that "no one should have to live without rock 'n roll."

KNAU - 88.7 FM

The public radio station of Northern Arizona University, KNAU offers university news, classical music, and lots of local programming. This is public radio at its best.

Index

About the Author

Dorothy Nobis grew up in a small town in Colorado, just north of Denver, and has a fierce loyalty to the state and to its Denver Broncos. When she and her husband, Phil, moved their family to northwestern New Mexico, however, she discovered a beautiful area that captured her heart and became part of her soul.

The Four Corners is rich in history, alive with color, and spirited with the cultures that combine to make it one of the most unique parts of our country. Her love of the area has manifested itself in her writing, which has been a creative outlet for more than 20 years. As a reporter, assistant managing editor, and managing editor of several papers in northwestern New Mexico, Dorothy has had the opportunity to share with others the personalities of the Four Corners and the determination and dedication that was displayed in the early days of the Southwest. Dorothy has received numerous awards for her journalism efforts.

A humorous column she wrote made its way onto the New York Times News Service, and was published in newspapers throughout the country. With five children, a cat that has lived a dozen lives, and a home in which chaos reins, Dorothy has shared the vagaries of life as a mother, caretaker, homemaker, and wild woman with readers who empathize with her!

Always willing to take on a new challenge, Dorothy has been a marketing coordinator for a large regional hospital and a major fast food chain, as well as the owner of an upscale resale shop and, with her husband, owner of an environmental company. She enjoyed a year as the news director at a prominent radio station, where she also hosted a daily talk show.

As the public relations director for the San Juan County Fair in San Juan County, New Mexico, Dorothy has relished the opportunity to help promote the largest county fair in the state. Working with hundreds of young people each year, Dorothy has enjoyed learning how to groom animals for show (use lots of hair gel and hair spray, and shampoo with built-in conditioners!) and watching goats exercise on a treadmill.

Her marketing, public relations and journalism skills, combined with her extensive background in management, have proven useful as the executive director of the Bloomfield Chamber of Commerce.

When not working at her many career opportunities, Dorothy and her husband enjoy fishing, football (she has a "Wall of Fame" for her Denver Broncos), stock car racing, traveling, and riding their Harley Davidson. With her five children now adults and living away from home, the only "child" she has is Bob, the cat, who believes he is royalty, but is actually, Dorothy says, simply a royal pain in her backside!